Margaret Pole, Countess of Salisbury, 1473 1541

Margaret Pole, Countess of Salisbury, 1473–1541

LOYALTY, LINEAGE AND LEADERSHIP

Hazel Pierce

UNIVERSITY OF WALES PRESS
CARDIFF
2003

British Library Cataloguing-in-Publication Data
A catalogue record for this book is available from the British Library.

ISBN 0–7083–1783–9

Jacket illustration:
Unknown woman, formerly known as Margaret Pole, Countess of Salisbury, by unknown artist.
By courtesy of the National Portrait Gallery, London.

Jacket design: Olwen Fowler, The Beacon Studio.

Typeset by Bryan Turnbull
Printed in Great Britain by Dinefwr Press, Llandybïe

Contents

༄

List of Illustrations

Between pages 84 and 85

Preface

~

The origins of this book can be found in my Ph.D. thesis completed in 1997. At that time my external examiner, Dr George Bernard, kindly suggested that the fall of the Pole family would make a very good article. However, I am grateful that the University of Wales Press has published Margaret as a biography. Although I hope that the fall of the family in 1538 will prove helpful towards an understanding of Henry VIII's relationship with his nobility, the rest of Margaret's life is equally worthy of attention. In fact, she has proved to be one of the most fascinating, yet elusive of individuals. Her elusiveness is a result of the dearth of personal letters – only a few survive – and the fact that neither her will nor that of her husband are extant. Nevertheless, a considerable amount of other material does exist including a full inventory of her household at Warblington and a complete set of ministers' accounts for her lands in 1538. The survival of earlier ministers' accounts, along with various estate papers, has made it feasible to investigate the administration of Margaret's lands and thus evaluate her success as a 'good lord' and her status as a female magnate. The fascination lies in the vicissitudes of her life which were extreme: from royal princess, to knight's wife, to impecunious widow, to wealthy and independent peeress and finally to igno-minious death at the age of sixty-seven, butchered at the hands of an inexperienced executioner. The challenge of this work has been in trying to discern and understand how Margaret dealt with each of these different stages of her life and what that reveals about the world in which she lived and operated.

I have incurred many debts of gratitude during the writing of this book and it is a pleasure for me to thank all those individuals whose help and assistance have been instrumental in the preparation of this work. Gratitude is due to the staff of the School of History and Welsh History at the University of Wales, Bangor, Dr Anthony Claydon, Dr Alan Dyer and, most especially, Professor Anthony Carr for all his help over the years. I should also like to thank Duncan Campbell at the University of Wales Press, Dr David Starkey, Peter and Carolyn Hammond and the late Dr Jennifer Loach. I am very grateful to Dr David Joyner for his diligent proof-reading and enlightening suggestions, Professor Michael Hicks for his helpful advice regarding the duke of Clarence, Dr Bev Murphy for all the thought-provoking conversations we have enjoyed and Professor Colin Richmond for his invaluable encouragement.

I am grateful to the archivists at the various record offices I have approached, to Mr James Collett-White of Bedfordshire Record Office concerning Edith St John, Mr C. D. Webster and Ms Sue Oatley at the Isle of Wight Record Office, Kenneth Tullett, archivist at Christchurch Priory, Father Ian Dickie, archivist at the Westminster Diocesan Archives and in particular to Mrs Helen Poole, director of the Sussex Archaeological Society, for her tireless provision of information regarding the Lewknor and Pakenham families. Thanks are also due to the staff of the Public Record Office, especially Mrs Karen Grannum, to the staff of the manuscripts room in the British Library and to the staff of Havant Museum, Hampshire for their advice concerning Warblington Castle. I should like to thank all those who have provided help regarding the illustrations for this book, in particular Mr Geoffrey Wheeler for his photographs of the duke of Clarence and the Salisbury Chantry, Mrs Gill Steedman for helpfully arranging our visit to photograph the Hastings Tomb in St Helen's Church, Ashby de la Zouch, Mrs Diana Bishop for kindly allowing me to photograph Warblington Castle, Miss Karen Lawson at The Royal Collection and the staff of the National Portrait Gallery.

I should like to pay tribute to my late friend and fellow historian, Andy Downham, whose love of history and encouragement of my work remains a compelling stimulus, and to his parents, Peter and Jean Downham, for their continuing friendship and support. Also to friends and family whose help has been valued: Julie Bowker, Gillian Galston, Robert Lewis, Terry Jones, Terry Williams and my late aunt, Mrs Rosemary Williams. I owe a debt of gratitude to my mother Shirley and son Jacob for the sacrifices that enabled me to undertake the initial research for this project. In particular, I wish to thank my Ph.D. supervisor, Professor David Loades, whose lectures and tutorials fostered my fascination with this period while I was an undergraduate student. I am indebted to him for the advice and unstinting help he has continued to give me over the years, which have been intrinsic to the development of this work, and for the constructive comments he made on an earlier version of this manuscript. Most especially I wish to thank my husband, Brian, for his invaluable help with formatting, for his preparation of the family tree and map and for providing one of the photographs for this book. Without his constant support, and tolerance of this other woman who has, by now, become as much a part of his life as mine, this project would never have come to fruition.

List of Abbreviations

❧

Add. MS	Additional Manuscripts
APC	J. Dasent (ed.), *Acts of the Privy Council of England, 1550–1552*, vol. 3 (London, 1891)
BL	British Library
CAD	*Catalogue of Ancient Deeds*
CCR	*Calendar of the Close Rolls*
CPR	*Calendar of the Patent Rolls*
CSP, Domestic	*Calendar of State Papers*, Domestic Series
CSP, Spain	*Calendar of State Papers*, Spanish
CSP, Venetian	*Calendar of State Papers*, Venetian
DKR	*Deputy Keepers Report*
DNB	*Dictionary of National Biography*
EHR	*English Historical Review*
Excerpta Historica	S. Bentley (ed.), *Excerpta Historica or, Illustrations of English History* (London, 1831)
HMC	*Historical Manuscripts Commission*
L&P	J. S. Brewer, J. Gairdner and R. H. Brodie (eds), *Letters and Papers, Foreign and Domestic, of the Reign of Henry VIII, 1509–47* (21 vols, London, 1862–1910)
LL	M. S. C. Byrne (ed.), *The Lisle Letters* (6 vols, London, 1981)
PRO	Public Record Office
SAC	*Sussex Archaeological Collections*
TRHS	*Transactions of the Royal Historical Society*
VCH	*Victoria County History*
WHR	*Welsh History Review*

1
Ancestry and Marriage, 1473–1504

❧

'my Lady Margaret Pole Doughter to the Duc of Claraunce'[1]

Margaret Plantagenet was born on 14 August 1473 at Farleigh Castle near Bath.[2] She was a royal princess of the House of York whose father, George, duke of Clarence, stood third in line to the throne of England. Her mother, Isabel Neville, was the daughter of Richard Neville, earl of Warwick (the kingmaker) and co-heiress to one of the greatest landed estates in England. Tewkesbury Abbey was in the patronage of the duke and duchess of Clarence, and Margaret's birth was proudly recorded in the abbey's chronicle.[3] This is hardly surprising, for the arrival of a new member of the royal house, especially a royal house that had taken possession of the crown by force a mere twelve years earlier, was a significant event. Margaret's uncle, Edward IV, had ascended the throne in 1461 during the dynastic struggle known to history as the Wars of the Roses. Having deposed the Lancastrian king, Henry VI, Edward ruled for eight years before a rebellion placed his adversary once again upon the throne. By this time Henry VI's fragile mental condition had deteriorated further and the prime movers behind his readeption were none other than Richard, earl of Warwick, Edward's erstwhile supporter and Margaret's grandfather, and George, duke of Clarence, Edward's own brother and Margaret's father. Both Warwick and Clarence felt that their ambitions had been thwarted by Edward, and this had prompted them into joining forces with the Lancastrians, although Clarence's initial motives may have been to obtain the crown for himself, as the Lincolnshire rebellion of 1470 suggests. However, Clarence soon realized that being the brother of a deposed monarch would yield far less than being the brother of the king of England and he changed sides once more, a decision that was instrumental in re-establishing Edward on the throne in 1471. It was this that allowed Clarence's reconciliation with the Edwardian regime despite his previous disloyalty and marriage to Isabel Neville in 1469 against Edward's express wishes. The shock of his deposition in 1469 prompted Edward to take action that would ensure such a thing could never happen again. Henry VI's only son and heir had conveniently been killed at the Battle of Tewkesbury on 4 May 1471, while Henry himself was quietly put to death at the Tower, probably from a blow to the head, on Edward's orders three weeks later. In the absence of a strong dynastic opposition, Edward now felt secure upon the throne and could not have known that he represented the last successful rearguard of the Plantagenet dynasty which had ruled England, and at times parts of France, since 1154. In just fourteen years the House of York would fall and the House of Tudor would take its place on the throne of England for the next 118 years.

In 1473 such events could not have been imagined and, consequently, Margaret Plantagenet's future looked entirely promising. Her father was one of the wealthiest magnates in England and she was his sole heir. From the moment of her birth she would have been treated with extreme deference and her education would have ensured that she was fully aware of the role and responsibilities of her royal position. An easy familiarity with all aspects of court etiquette was one important element. The court of Edward IV's queen, Elizabeth Woodvyll, was replete with formality and ritual. For instance, at her coronation banquet in 1465 the duke of Suffolk and earl of Essex knelt on either side of her at the table holding the sceptres of St Edward and of England, while the countesses of Shrewsbury and Kent also knelt throughout.[4] The duke of Clarence took equal pride in how his household was presented, and in 1468 drew up an ordinance that dictated its management.[5] This reveals the immense size of the household in which Margaret spent part of her childhood. The duke maintained a staff of 188 persons and kept 93 horses in his stables, remarkable considering that many other magnates had felt the need to close their stables and rely on hired transport. Margaret's mother was no less well served, in her household 125 servants awaited her command while 16 grooms attended the 43 horses in her stable. Other regulations included the strict observation of holy days, the prohibition of gambling except during the twelve days of Christmas, and the attendance during mealtimes of 'the kervers, ameners, cup-bearers, and sewers, and all other officers assigned to serve the seid Duke, the chambre, and the halle; to the intent, that the seid Duke be welle and honorablye served'.[6]

Margaret's education also equipped her with other abilities required of a well-born lady. She was taught to play musical instruments and in later life kept three pairs of virginals, a harpsichord-type instrument without legs, at Warblington Castle, her seat in Hampshire. She could also sew, skills she later taught her grand-daughters and the other young ladies she educated in her household as countess of Salisbury, keeping 'silke for to set the yong a worke'.[7] Although she was not the son her father desired, she still had an important role to play. As a member of the royal house she was a valuable commodity on the marriage market and the object of her union would be to strengthen not only her father's position and influence but her family's through a strategic and important alliance. Her status and dowry would ensure there would be no shortage of suitors for her hand. Although no extant evidence indicates that Clarence had initiated any negotiations for her marriage, a high-ranking peer of England or Europe, or even a member of a foreign royal house, would have been the ultimate choice. Certainly, in 1484 discussions were under way for the marriage of Margaret's cousin, Anne de la Pole, daughter of Edward IV's eldest sister, to the future King James IV of Scotland. However, in 1475 Margaret's prospects as the duke's heir were eclipsed by the birth of her brother, Edward, at Warwick Castle on 25 February. The baby's status was immediately recognized, and at his christening the king himself stood as his godfather and created him earl of Warwick, a title held by Clarence but relinquished in his son's favour.[8] Although Warwick superseded Margaret in relation to their hereditary expectations, her position was not seriously affected. She was still the king's niece and, after Clarence's death if both she and her brother reached maturity, would be sister to one of the most powerful magnates in England. Certainly, Warwick's birth had not diminished the duke's interest in his daughter's welfare, for on 1 May 1475 it appears that he temporarily enfeoffed several manors to her use. As he was about to cross the sea to France on military campaign, he wished to ensure that his daughter had a regular income of her own in the event of his death.[9]

The following year the duchess of Clarence was pregnant once more and on 6 October gave birth to a son in the new infirmary of Tewkesbury Abbey. Named Richard, the baby was baptized amidst solemn ceremony at which several members of the ecclesiastical hierarchy officiated. Unfortunately, the duchess became ill following the birth and on 12 November Clarence returned to Warwick Castle taking his wife with him, with hindsight an unwise decision considering her condition. After her arrival at Warwick Castle Isabel failed to recover and died aged twenty-five on 12 December 1476.[10] There is every reason to believe that Clarence genuinely mourned his wife's death.[11] They had been married for seven years and although Clarence was 'semly of person and right witty and wel visagid'[12] no evidence suggests that he had ever been unfaithful to her. In some respects Isabel's life as the duchess of Clarence was blessed, for her husband was a man capable of great loyalty, if only to selected individuals, and of forming deep emotional bonds.[13] However, she was also required to bear the consequences of his often erratic behaviour, which she did with fortitude. For instance, in April 1470, eight months pregnant and in no condition even to travel within England, Isabel had accompanied her husband to France where he fled with her parents and sister following the failure of the Lincolnshire rebellion. Refused entry to Calais, Isabel went into a difficult labour aboard ship and did not even have the benefit of herbs or wine to help dull the pain. Although Lord Wenlock, who was in charge of Calais, took pity on the duchess's suffering and sent two casks of wine, Isabel gave birth to a dead child which was buried at sea.[14] Obviously, Clarence would feel the loss of such a loyal and steadfast partner keenly and her elaborate obsequies at Tewkesbury Abbey, while calculated to do her great honour, also appear to reflect the duke's grieving. In addition to the vigils held and the masses said, Isabel's body lay in state for over a month before being interred in a specially constructed vault behind the high altar.[15] Compounding this tragedy was the death, on 1 January 1477, of their baby son, Richard. Michael Hicks has revealed the significance of the duchess's death in relation to events leading up to Clarence's execution in 1478.[16] As his attempts to secure a second marriage, first with Mary of Burgundy and secondly with Margaret, sister of the king of

Scotland, were thwarted by Edward IV, Clarence's bitterness grew. As relations deteriorated 'flatterers' carried tales between them of insults secretly spoken which exacerbated their mutual resentment and suspicion. Two of these flatterers may have been Ankarette Twynho and John Thursby, former servants of the duke and duchess, who were summarily executed by Clarence in April 1477. The charge put forward to ensure their conviction was their alleged poisoning of the Duchess Isabel and her baby son, but in reality it was more likely to have been Clarence's revenge for their damaging indiscretions. The execution of Thomas Burdet for treason the following month, a man closely associated with Clarence, added fuel to the fire. At Clarence's behest, Burdet's recorded protestation of innocence was recited by Dr William Goddard, a Franciscan friar, before a shocked council and in the duke's presence. Clarence's action threw doubt upon the validity of the king's courts, it also associated him with a man who had been convicted of 'seeking the death and destruction of the King and Prince'. Although his behaviour was wholly unacceptable, under normal circumstances Clarence might have received only a strong reprimand from his brother accompanied by a possible term of imprisonment. However, recent events combined with his previous activities dictated his now inevitable fate. Not only had he been disloyal to Edward IV between 1469 and 1471, he had also quarrelled furiously with his younger brother, Richard, duke of Gloucester. Gloucester had married Isabel Neville's younger sister Anne in 1472, and both brothers wished to influence the partition of the Warwick inheritance to their advantage. Although Gloucester was as avaricious as Clarence in the matter, he was at least prepared to acquiesce in Edward's decisions and act in good faith, as opposed to Clarence who remained inflexible until he absolutely had to capitulate under the threat of total forfeiture in 1474. This lack of fraternal affection between Clarence and his brothers, compounded by his difficult relations with Edward's queen and her family, left him exposed and without the support of those that mattered when he most needed it. He was arrested in June 1477 and privately executed at the Tower of London on 18 February 1478.

In just over a year Margaret's parents had both died, and from the security and honour of being the daughter of 'the right noble Prince my Lord of Clarence',[17] she was now the daughter of an executed traitor. We cannot know how this shocking change in circumstances might have affected Margaret who, in February 1478, was not yet five years old. In a practical sense she and her brother were now orphans, but as niece and nephew of the king of England they immediately became royal wards and Edward IV assumed full responsibility for their care. Unlike her brother, Margaret had no prospects of inheritance and, as far as evidence suggests, no lands had been set aside for her maintenance. She was, therefore, wholly dependent upon the generosity of the king. On 11 January 1482 Edward IV sent an order to the Exchequer to pay 40 marks for 'such clothing and other neccessaries as belongen unto our dear and well beloved niece Margaret daughter unto our brother late Duke of Clarence as for contentation of wages unto such persons as we have commanded to attend upon her'.[18] Again, on 16 November 1482, Edward paid 50 marks for her 'arrayment as for the wages of her servants'.[19] Although the lands held by Clarence in his own right had been forfeit to the crown due to his attainder for treason, the lands he had held in right of his wife were exempt. Consequently, Margaret's brother was still heir to valuable estates in the South and Midlands, in addition to retaining the title earl of Warwick which he had held in his own right from birth. As such, Warwick's wardship was a very valuable asset, and on 16 September 1480 the custody and marriage of the young earl was granted to Thomas Grey, marquess of Dorset, son of Elizabeth Woodvyll by her first husband, for the substantial sum of £2,000.[20] Because of the large amount Dorset had paid he was also granted permission to take possession of the custody and marriage of Margaret in the event of her brother's death. Not only did this grant benefit Dorset, but it also helped to safeguard Warwick's lands from the dubious intentions of his uncle, the duke of Gloucester. The arrangements of 1474 relating to the Warwick inheritance had pleased neither duke, and each had looked with covetous eyes upon the other's gains. Immediately following Clarence's death Gloucester had appropriated two manors, Essendine and Shillingthorpe in Rutland that he had always objected to Clarence receiving, and held on to them despite commands from the royal Exchequer which ordered their surrender.[21] However, the grant of Warwick's wardship to Dorset provided the earl with the protection of the powerful Woodvyll clan, a suitable match for the king's younger brother, while furthering Dorset's plan to consolidate his land-based power centred on the Devon and Somerset estates acquired through his marriage to the heiress, Cecily Bonville. It was therefore in Dorset's interest to ensure that Warwick's lands remained intact and safe from the ambitions of the duke of Gloucester.

For five years Margaret's care had been the responsibility of the king of England, and in 1483 that situation prevailed, but with one important difference, the king was now Richard, Duke of Gloucester. The unexpected death of Edward IV on 9 April 1483 had set in motion a train of events leading to the usurpation of the crown by Gloucester who was crowned Richard III on 6 July 1483. It is not necessary to plot the course of Richard's usurpation, which has been more than adequately covered elsewhere, but it is necessary to look at these circumstances in relation to the dynastic profile of Clarence's children. During the course of events running from Edward's death in April and culminating in Richard's coronation in July, he secured the persons of Edward IV's sons, Prince Edward and his younger brother Richard, duke of York, which was imperative if his usurpation was to be successful. At some point in June Richard also commanded that Edward, earl of Warwick should be conveyed to London and placed in the household of his maternal aunt Anne, duchess of Gloucester, Richard's wife, who by June had arrived in the capital. This is not surprising, for Warwick's significance was widely recognized. Indeed, Dominic Mancini, the Italian ecclesiastic writing as the usurpation unfolded, believed that Richard 'feared that if the entire progeny of King Edward [IV] became extinct, yet this child, who was also of royal blood, would still embarrass him'.[22] Richard's subsequent actions would seem to prove Mancini right. In order to justify his usurpation of the throne Richard strove to demonstrate the illegitimacy of Edward IV's children by declaring that Edward's marriage to Elizabeth Woodvyll had serious flaws. It had, he insisted, been carried out without the knowledge or assent of the peerage; his bride and her mother had used witchcraft to secure it; it was conducted in secret and when Edward was already contracted to marry Lady Eleanor Butler. The validity of Richard's claims have been discussed by historians at length and there is no need to launch into a detailed investigation here. However, despite what many contemporaries might have felt in their hearts about Richard's assertions, the fact that he ascended the throne, an anointed monarch, meant that during his reign the illegitimization of Edward IV's children was, in practice, accepted. Obviously, this act of bastardization which had removed Edward's children from the succession, greatly enhanced the position of Margaret and her brother in relation to the throne. As the son of Richard's elder brother, Warwick, it could be argued, was now the rightful heir to the throne while Margaret, if not quite second in line due to her sex, would be able to transmit a very strong claim to any male child she might bear. Richard was not slow to realize the dynastic threat posed by Clarence's children, whose claims, as well as those of Edward IV's children, would have to be explained away. He did this by announcing that Clarence's children were 'barred by his attainder for high treason from any claim to the crown'.[23] Many historians agree that this was a weak barrier to the earl of Warwick's rights. To begin with, Clarence's attainder specifically stated 'that the same Duke, by the said auctorite, forfett from hym and his heyres for ever, the Honoure, Estate, Dignite and name of Duke', no mention was made of his children's right to the throne.[24] Even if the attainder had mentioned his children's claims, later events suggest that this would not have affected Warwick's ability to succeed anyway. When Henry Tudor assumed the title of king the judges stated that 'the King was responsible and discharged of any attainder by the fact that he took on himself the reign and was King'. They continued: 'he that was King was himself able to invest himself, and there was no need of any act for the reversal of his attainder.'[25] No direct evidence reveals Margaret's whereabouts at this time, but they are probably a reflection of Warwick's movements which clearly demonstrate Richard's determination to maintain control over anyone whose claims posed a threat to him.

The two young sons of Edward IV were immediately incarcerated in the Tower while Margaret and her brother took up residence in the secure, but far more salubrious, confines of Sheriff Hutton Castle in Yorkshire under the watchful eye of their cousin, John de la Pole, earl of Lincoln.[26] Sheriff Hutton Castle had, ironically, had been in the hands of Margaret's family, the Nevilles, for 300 years before being granted to Richard, duke of Gloucester in 1471. Indeed, four shields displaying the arms of the Neville family can still be seen over the remains of the gateway. Protected by a double moat and primarily a military construction, Sheriff Hutton was nevertheless an extremely commodious and grand residence. Following a visit to the castle in 1534 John Leland remarked in his *Itinerary*: 'I saw no house in the North so like a Princely Logginges.' Vaulted chambers and the intricate ceilings of the passageways revealed medieval craftsmanship at its best, while a magnificent stairway led up to the great hall. Enjoying an extremely pleasant vista on one of the first rises off the Plain of York, on a clear day residents of Sheriff Hutton could see the city of York and its cathedral, York Minster, some ten miles away. It was here in this comfortable fortress that Margaret and her brother Edward would spend the next two years of their lives.[27] However, Warwick's residence at Sheriff Hutton also served another purpose. The Council of the North established by Richard was nominally associated with Richard's only son, Prince Edward, in order to bolster the authority and status of the king's councillors there, but in March/April 1484 Prince Edward died, which deprived the king of an heir and titular head of the Northern Council. Consequently, the actual headship was granted to Richard's nephew, the earl of Lincoln, while it appears that the earl of Warwick became nominally associated with it, presumably to maintain and promote its royal status.[28] Certainly, on 13 May 1485 in a letter from the mayor of York to the Council of the North at Sheriff Hutton, Warwick's name preceded that of the earl of Lincoln.[29] Although Richard might have utilized Warwick's royal status for the purpose of the Council of the North, it appears that the king's sensitivity regarding the young earl's proximity to the throne precluded his formal designation as heir following the death of the king's son. Although John Rous reported that 'the young Earl of Warwick, Edward, eldest son of George Duke of Clarence, was proclaimed heir apparent in the royal court, and in ceremonies at table and chamber he was served first after the king and queen',[30] Rosemary Horrox notes that Rous is the only source for this claim and that Warwick was never formally recognized as heir. In truth, Richard could not have afforded to acknowledge him as heir, for if he accepted that Warwick could ascend the throne despite his father's attainder, then there was no reason why he should not already be king.[31] His tacit approval was therefore given to the safer heir designate, the earl of Lincoln who, as the son of Richard's sister, had an obviously weaker claim than Richard.[32] Richard had every reason to fear the claims of Clarence's children and took determined steps to minimize the danger of their falling into the wrong hands. These steps would continue to be taken by the man who defeated Richard III at Bosworth and who had even more cause for concern: Henry VII.

During this period there was no fixed law of succession to the crown; only custom offered a guideline. If that guideline had been strictly adhered to, on 22 August 1485, Margaret's brother Edward, earl of Warwick, would have ascended the throne as King Edward VI. He was the only direct male descendant of Edward III via Edward III's fourth son, he was descended in the female line from Edward III's second son, he was the strongest male claimant of the House of York and could also argue that he represented the House of Lancaster. This latter claim was the result of a possible Act of Parliament passed during the readeption of Henry VI which vested the succession in the duke of Clarence should the male line of Henry VI fail. J. R. Lander has argued that such an act was never passed and casts doubt upon the veracity of Clarence's attainder which charged the duke with possessing an exemplification under the great seal of Henry VI of appointments made between himself and Queen Margaret.[33] Among these was one which vested the succession in Clarence and his heirs and did not restrict it to heirs male,[34] theoretically making Margaret herself a Lancastrian claimant and, after her brother, the lawful successor of Henry VI. Whether this act existed or not, the knowledge that it might have could provide useful propaganda against Henry VII and further enhance the earl of Warwick's position. In comparison to Warwick, Henry VII's claim came solely through the illegitimate Beaufort line of his mother, who was the great-granddaughter of John of Gaunt, Edward III's third son.[35] Clearly, Henry VII was king for only two reasons: firstly, the lack of a fixed law of succession had enabled him, with force of arms, to maintain that he was king; secondly, so unpopular had Richard III made himself that even a man with Henry's dubious dynastic claims, who had spent most of his life abroad and was supported at Bosworth by England's traditional enemy, France, was preferable. The fact that Henry was an adult and Warwick a child also strengthened his position but, as K. Pickthorn noted, 'such a tenure does not amount to a legal or constitutional title.'[36] Henry, even at the moment of his triumph at Bosworth, was well aware that his position was not unassailable, and the fate of Margaret and her brother at his hands bears witness to this.

Immediately after Bosworth the new king moved to secure the persons of the little group at Sheriff Hutton, and before leaving Leicester sent Robert Willoughby to take possession of Warwick. Henry was, the Tudor chronicler Polydore Vergil tells us, 'fearful lest, if the boy should escape and given any alteration in circumstances, he might stir up civil discord'.[37] It is important to remember that Warwick was not only the son of the duke of Clarence, he was also the son of Isabel Neville and thus might enjoy the advantage of northern loyalty to the house of Neville. Certainly, his dynastic profile was high. On 1 March 1486, Mosen Diego de Valera, retired servant of Ferdinand and Isabella of Spain, wrote to them reporting events surrounding Henry VII's accession. He claimed that a Lord Tamorlant, possibly identifiable as Henry Percy, fourth earl of Northumberland, was imprisoned because he had intended Edward, earl of Warwick to be king and planned to marry him to one of his daughters. Northumberland may have viewed Richard III's replacement with the earl of Warwick as an opportunity to gain the northern hegemony previously monopolized by the king.[38] We cannot be sure of this story but, as it is certain that Northumberland assisted neither Henry nor Richard at Bosworth, it would not be too unrealistic to accept that such an idea had crossed his ambitious mind. In October 1485, only two months after Bosworth, John Morton was shocked upon his arrival at the Calais garrison first to be to be told that Henry had died of the plague and secondly that many of the garrison assumed Edward, earl of Warwick would be his successor.[39] Back in England in 1486, two minor risings broke out in March and April. The second of these, organized by Humphrey Stafford, a former member of Richard III's household, was partially prompted by rumours of Warwick's escape to the Channel Islands. At Birmingham the cry 'A Warwick, A Warwick' was raised by Stafford's supporters.[40] It must have been patently obvious to Henry VII that it was not going to be easy to erase the young earl from public memory, either at home or abroad.

With this in mind, Henry ordered that Warwick and his sister should be conducted to the household of his mother, Margaret Beaufort. Fellow 'guests' of the king's mother included Elizabeth of York and her sisters, the earl of Westmoreland and the duke of Buckingham, the latter who, as a descendant of Edward III through his youngest and fifth son Thomas, duke of Gloucester, was another child possessing a plausible claim to the throne.[41] Henry VII recognized that just as his mother had transmitted her claim to him, so could the daughters of Edward IV and the duke of Clarence to their future sons. Furthermore, in Margaret's case, although she was preceded by Edward IV's daughters in relation to the succession, her legitimacy was assured, whereas the illegitimacy of Edward's children had been proclaimed and accepted to the extent that Richard, duke of Gloucester was able to ascend the throne.[42] Henry's sensitivity on this point is revealed in his attempts to eradicate that very slur of bastardy on his future wife, Elizabeth of York. On the day of Bosworth he ordered the arrest of Robert Stillington, bishop of Bath and Wells, the supposed originator of the story that claimed Edward IV's children were illegitimate due to his pre-contract to Lady Eleanor Butler. In addition, he had the act confirming Richard III's title, in which was contained the details of Elizabeth's illegitimacy, repealed without its rehearsal as was usual and ordered that it, and all other copies, were to be destroyed so that everything stated in the act 'may be forever out of remembrance, and also forgot'.[43] Margaret Plantagenet's dynastic importance should not, therefore, be underestimated. A possible heir designate of the House of Lancaster and an indisputable heiress of the House of York, whose unchallenged legitimacy theoretically enhanced her claims over those of Henry's own queen, Margaret was a liability he could ill afford to ignore. She therefore remained under the close watch of the king as she began to play an active role in the life of the court.

Contrary to his parsimonious image, Henry's court was a lively and lavish affair fulfilling all that was expected of a royal court. Banquets, dancing, music and elaborate pageantry were the settings for courtiers to shine in sumptuous clothes against a backdrop of massive and expensive wall hangings of every kind. Despite its grandeur, this magnificent environment would not have overwhelmed the twelve-year-old Margaret, to whom such an arena was by now second nature. In September 1486 'my lady Margaret of Clarence' headed the list of ladies attending the christening of the king's first-born son, Prince Arthur,[44] and in November 1487 she viewed the coronation of Elizabeth of York on a specially erected stage between the pulpit and the high altar of Westminster Abbey in the company of Henry VII and his mother. Significantly she is referred to as 'my Lady Margaret Pole Doughter to the Duc of Claraunce',[45] indicating that sometime between September 1486 and November 1487 her marriage to Sir Richard Pole had taken place. It has previously been accepted that Margaret married around 1491–4,[46] although 1494 is certainly incorrect, as Margaret's eldest son, Henry, the future Lord Montague, was born in June 1492.[47] Nevertheless, if a claim for an earlier marriage is to be based upon one document, then that document needs close examination.[48] Unfortunately, this description of Elizabeth's coronation is not contemporary but a later copy written around the latter part of the sixteenth century. Therefore, the writer could have inserted Margaret's then surname rather than the surname she bore in 1487. However, if we take into account the events of 1487 coupled with other relevant facts a strong case does emerge for her marriage taking place in late 1487.

Henry VII's fears concerning Edward, earl of Warwick have already been mentioned. In 1486 he ordered the eleven-year-old earl's confinement in the Tower, and in November of the same year he moved against his estates. Perhaps it is significant that the name Lambert Simnel was already being whispered by the end of November[49] when Henry issued a warrant, on 30 November, regarding Warwick's lands. It provided for 500 marks annually to be paid to Anne, countess of Warwick, the earl's maternal grandmother, out of the Warwick and Spencer lands which formed part of his inheritance.[50] In 1490 Henry took more extreme action to undermine his opponent by restoring these lands to the countess, who, in return, made the king her heir and thus disinherited her grandson. Warwick did, however, remain heir to the Montague estates until his attainder and execution in 1499. In 1487 Henry's concern about the threat Edward posed proved to be valid. According to the government's version, a young boy named Lambert Simnel had been trained by a priest to impersonate Warwick and, although the attempt was ridiculed later, at the time Henry was not laughing. One problem was that he could not be sure who was involved in the conspiracy and was shocked at the defection of John de la Pole, earl of Lincoln, whose support immediately enhanced the credibility of the cause. Furthermore, Warwick's paternal aunt, Margaret the dowager duchess of Burgundy, was another prime mover in the affair, raising and dispatching troops to assist. The gravity of the situation should not be underestimated, for Simnel had a larger number of troops than Henry had commanded at Bosworth.[51] Although the rebels were defeated at the battle of Stoke and had attracted little support in England, the fact that Henry had been constrained to defend his crown on the field of battle barely two years after Bosworth understandably unnerved him. Although Warwick remained in custody in the Tower, Henry still had the problem of Margaret and her cousins, Edward IV's daughters, to deal with, and his immediate solution appears to have been marriage as the safest and most appropriate way of disposing of two of the most dynastically threatening of them. Marriage to men upon whose loyalty Henry could count would neutralize the possibility of their abduction and a marriage detrimental to his interests. Evidence suggests, therefore, that in November 1487 the two eldest females of the House of York were married: Margaret Plantagenet to Sir Richard Pole and Princess Cecily, to John, Viscount Welles.[52] Margaret's marriage has earned Henry VII some criticism due to her union with a man perceived to be so far beneath her in station. In 1497 Perkin Warbeck, who was challenging Henry's throne in the guise of Edward IV's youngest son, Richard, duke of York, declared in disgust that the king had 'married upon compulsion certain of our sisters and also the sister of our foresaid cousin the Earl of Warwick, and divers other ladies of the blood Royal unto certain of his kinsmen and friends of simple and low degree'.[53] Shakespeare also felt it was a matter for censure, but prudently laid the blame at the door of Richard III, having Richard declare in the play bearing his name that Clarence's daughter 'meanly have I matched in marriage'.[54] It is true that Richard Pole was not a member of the aristocracy, nor did his personal wealth amount to much, his two Buckinghamshire manors of Medmenham and Ellesborough providing him with an income of only £50 per year.[55] Comparing this with the duke of Clarence's wealth, which at the time of Margaret's birth was estimated at an immense £6,000 a year, puts the marriage very much into perspective.[56] Juxtaposed to this, however, is the fact that Richard Pole was Henry VII's half-cousin and, as such, a member of the royal family. He was also a man on whom, by 1487, Henry was beginning to rely more and more.

Born in Buckinghamshire in 1458 or 1459, Richard was the eldest child of Geoffrey Pole esquire and Edith St John of Bletsoe.[57] Originally from Wales, Geoffrey was a staunch supporter of Henry VI and enjoyed a successful career in his service.[58] An esquire of the body from 1440, most of his offices were concentrated in south Wales, suggesting his knowledge of the area was being utilized. As he was also one of the councillors of Jasper Tudor, earl of Pembroke, it seems likely that the earl played a significant role in arranging Geoffrey's marriage. Edith St John was the half-sister of Margaret Beaufort, countess of Richmond, the widowed sister-in-law of Jasper Tudor, and the match was clearly a prestigious one for Geoffrey. However, Jasper no doubt recognized the benefits of introducing this faithful supporter of the House of Lancaster into the Lancastrian family orbit, and his trust in Geoffrey's loyalty was not ill placed. Following the overthrow of Henry VI, Geoffrey withdrew from royal service and, although not actively disloyal to Edward IV, remained stubbornly aloof from the Yorkist regime. Living quietly in Buckinghamshire, he concentrated on accumulating property there, culminating in the manors of Medmenham, Ellesborough and Stoke Mandeville.[59] After Geoffrey's death in 1479 this way of life was continued by his son, and it was not until the accession of Henry VII in 1485 that Richard emerged from obscurity to begin a successful career in the service of his royal cousin. Having fled to Brittany at the age of fourteen, where he remained for thirteen years before moving on to France, Henry VII was a stranger to England. Apart from those supporters who had shared his exile in Brittany, Henry had not had the opportunity to become personally familiar with any of the important and influential men of the realm. Consequently, he immediately brought into his service, at a high level, those whom he did know, the individuals who had served him in exile. Some of these were his relatives, for instance his uncle, Jasper Tudor, and half-uncle, John, Viscount Welles. However, Henry also had a family in England to whom he could turn and, although its members were personally unknown to him, he would have become familiar with them through his mother. Michael Jones and Malcolm Underwood have revealed the closeness that existed between Margaret Beaufort and her St John half-siblings, in whose company she spent her childhood,[60] and this closeness would naturally help to ensure their introduction into the Henrician regime. As he lacked the support of a large, immediate family, these relatives were valuable commodities. Furthermore, Henry's willingness to employ the services of the St John family was also related to their status. A middling gentry family, they would naturally depend upon Henry's continuing success to ensure their own prosperity. Thus, on 22 October 1485, Richard Pole was appointed an esquire of the body for life and in the following year received the constableship of Harlech Castle and shrievalty of Merioneth, again offices for life.[61] These appointments are an immediate indication of Henry's faith in Richard. The office of esquire of the body entailed close personal contact with the king, whilst Merioneth was a notorious trouble spot.[62] At the battle of Stoke in 1487 Richard continued to prove his worth and was knighted immediately afterwards.[63] As a loyal member of the king's family who had fought valiantly against the forces representing Edward, earl of Warwick, Richard was clearly a sensible choice upon whom to bestow the hand of Warwick's dynastically dangerous fourteen-year-old sister.

The marriage of Princess Cecily to John, Viscount Welles should be viewed in a similar light. Like Richard Pole, Welles was a member of Henry's half-blood family, his half-uncle, and a man Henry could trust. In 1483 he had been involved in the rising against Richard III and, following its failure, had joined Henry in exile. Accompanying Henry to England in 1485, he was knighted at Milford Haven and restored to the barony of Welles in the first Parliament of the reign. Shortly after the battle of Stoke in September 1487, Welles was elevated to the rank of viscount[64] and by Christmas 1487 had married Princess Cecily.[65] Clearly, the Pole and Welles marriages followed a similar pattern: both husbands were the king's relatives, both were elevated in status shortly after the battle of Stoke and both married female representatives of the House of York soon after that, possibly at the same time. It was to be early November before Henry returned to London where Parliament was to meet on 9 November, and it is likely that both marriages took place around this time. With most nobles in London for Parliament, it would provide the perfect opportunity to give the marriages a high profile. Moreover, the queen's coronation was scheduled for 25 November, an event at which the two couples could be, and were, displayed. The marriages took place before the king and queen and 'sume officers of armes',[66] and afterwards both couples were given prominent roles to play at Elizabeth's coronation. Lady Margaret attended the king's mother while Sir Richard Pole was one of twelve knights of the body chosen to bear the canopy over the queen throughout her journey from the Tower to Westminster Abbey. Cecily travelled in the coronation procession, borne in a litter behind the queen, and at Westminster carried her train. Her husband, Viscount Welles, was also present through-out.[67] At the end of such a divisive year these two marriages would provide, as the king's own marriage to Elizabeth of York had done, a successful and much-needed illustration of the union between York and Lancaster.

On a personal level, the union between Margaret and Richard had the potential to be much less successful. Richard's relationship to the king of England gave him an unexpected prominence which might have enabled him to obtain the hand of an heiress in marriage, but Margaret was heiress only to a noble ancestry and possessed no lands or property at all. Equally, it is not unreason-able to suppose that Margaret, a proud Plantagenet princess who had expected to marry at the least a high-ranking member of the aristocracy, might have been offended by the husband chosen for her. However, despite these possible problems, the marriage appears to have been a happy one. At the time of their marriage Margaret was only fourteen, but Richard was twenty-eight or twenty-nine years old. Intelligent, prudent and reliable, he provided his wife with the safe haven not only which Henry VII required, but which she herself must have desired after a somewhat tumultuous childhood. With Richard, Margaret enjoyed a rare period of peace and stability, and evidence suggests she respected and trusted her husband, and may even have loved him. After 1488 when Richard's royal duties in Wales increased, Margaret eschewed her place at court in order to remain close to him, and Henry VII granted them the use of Stourton Castle in Staffordshire. Originally built as a royal hunting lodge, by the time of Margaret's and Richard's occupation it had become a fortified manor house. Located on the bank of the river Stour about half a mile north-east of the village of Kinver, it was not more than a day's ride away from the prince of Wales's council at Ludlow, and it was here in 1500 that their son Reginald was born.[68] In 1536 a letter she wrote to Reginald up-braiding him over his criticism of Henry VIII provides further evidence of her feelings: 'there went never the death of thy father or of any child so nigh my heart.'[69] As countess of Salisbury she had two receptacles prepared in her chantry at Christchurch Priory to which she probably intended the body of her husband to be transferred at her death.[70] Richard's influence is also seen in the associations with several of his friends and colleagues which

Margaret made every effort to continue after his death. In 1538 the countess of Salisbury still possessed mementoes of her husband: a celure and tester embroidered with garters, a cushion displaying his arms and, a clear indication that she did not view his status with disdain, silver and gilt bowls proudly boasting his device next to that of her father, the duke of Clarence.[71] Margaret began her married life at Bockmer, a house restored by her father-in-law and situated in her husband's manor of Medmenham, Buckinghamshire.[72] Richard's annual income from his two manors was deemed insufficient to support himself and his wife honourably and, consequently, Henry VII granted him the manors of Fifield and Long Wittenham in Oxford, most probably as part of Margaret's dowry. These manors were among those confiscated from John de la Pole, earl of Lincoln, after the battle of Stoke and were worth £120 a year, thus increasing Richard's land-based income to a theoretical £170 a year.[73] With the salary Richard earned from his steady accumulation of appointments, his basic income between 1490 and 1499 was probably around £300–400 a year.[74] This is not an inconsiderable sum and would have provided a comfortable lifestyle for himself and his wife. Nevertheless, life at court was expensive and, like most courtiers, Richard was constrained to live beyond his means. He sold off large amounts of land at Medmenham for the sum of £452 16s 8d to Reginald Bray, was apparently forced to mortgage his manor of Ellesborough to raise money and, by 1491, had sold the entire manor of Stoke Mandeville.[75]

Henry utilized Richard's services mostly in north Wales and, as a result, we have few glimpses of Margaret during this period. At the feast of St George in 1488 'the Lady Margaret of Clarens, Wife of Sir Ric Poole' waited upon the queen and the king's mother, as she was to do again during the Christmas festivities of 1488 which were held at Sheen.[76] As usual, Margaret headed the list of ladies, preceded only by peeresses and the queen's sisters, clearly illustrating that her high status continued to be recognized. Margaret's attendance at these Christmas celebrations of 1488 is the last reference to her at court, but on 30 September 1493 Henry VII made a gift to 'my Lady Pole in corons, £20',[77] most probably in recognition of the office bestowed upon her husband a few months earlier, that of lord chamberlain to Prince Arthur.[78] The office of lord chamberlain to the king's son and heir was an extremely honourable and important one, entailing the oversight of the prince's private and public service and the staging of ceremony.[79] As the office required Richard's personal attendance on the young prince, Arthur's whereabouts at this time are significant. There has been considerable discussion over when the prince's council was set up and when Arthur actually went to Ludlow himself. Caroline Skeel claims that Arthur went to the marches soon after his marriage in 1501, but evidence suggests otherwise.[80] David Powel states in his 1584 edition of a *History of Wales* that 'about the seventeenth year of king Henries reigne, Prince Arthur went againe to Wales', 'again' being the crucial word.[81] Furthermore, the accounts of the bailiffs of Shrewsbury indicate that long before 1501 Arthur and his council were at Ludlow, from where they made frequent trips to Shrewsbury. For the year beginning Michaelmas 1494, there is an entry for 'Expenses of the Bailiffs, and others, riding to Ludlowe by command of the Lord Prince, 21s 2d', and in the same year Arthur, accompanied by Richard Pole and several other members of his council, visited Shrewsbury, where a miracle play was performed for them.[82] Moreover, in 1493 Arthur was seven years old, an age when it would be appropriate for him to preside over his own household and begin to learn the art of kingship, while his participation in the affairs of the march would increase as he grew older. In the same year he was appointed the king's justice in the marches of Wales and, not quite two months after his seventh birthday, was granted a substantial number of lordships and manors in Wales and the marches, including the entire earldom of March.[83] Consequently, it was to Stourton Castle that Margaret most likely travelled in 1493 in order to be close to her husband while he attended upon his young master. Indeed, we have a charming glimpse of Richard gently assisting Arthur through the solemn and convoluted ceremonies of a chapter of the Garter in 1500:

> Having with him his Chamberlain Sir Richard Poole a most deserving knight of the same Order, he omitted nothing at the Mass, the first or second vespers, which solemn usage required to be done. In walking, in incensing in making Procession, in offering, as well he, as his Knight Companion performed and did all Things exceeding properly.[84]

In addition to this prestigious appointment and his membership of the Council of the Marches, Richard was also involved in the administration and security of north Wales. He was appointed constable of several north Wales castles including Harlech, Conwy, Caernarfon and Beaumaris, and the importance of maintaining these castles should not be underestimated. Wales was an area open to invasion and this would not have slipped Henry's mind as he had launched his own invasion, from Milford Haven in south Wales, while Beaumaris was the port where the duke of York had chosen to land in 1450 on his way from Ireland to London. Indeed, Beaumaris 'was one of the ports of access into north Wales for shipping from Ireland'.[85] With the threat of Perkin Warbeck's invasion hanging over the king's head, and bearing in mind the support Ireland was in the habit of giving to Yorkist pretenders, the importance of holding these castles securely must have been dramatically increased. It is significant, therefore, that they were entrusted to Richard, who discharged his duties efficiently. At some point during Richard's tenure Harlech Castle was actually taken, but Richard ensured that the disturbance was quickly and effect-ively contained, Henry acknowledging that Richard had 'sustained costs beyond the duties which he had as custodian in the work of reducing and taking into his hands and possession the aforesaid King's castle'.[86] In 1490 Richard became more firmly entrenched in Welsh administration, reflecting the important changes that were initiated regarding north Wales. William Griffith, a member of a leading Gwynedd family which had enjoyed ascendancy in the administration of Gwynedd during the fifteenth century, was appointed chamberlain of north Wales by Richard III, and this appointment was confirmed by Henry VII in the first year of his reign.[87] However, by 1490 Henry felt secure enough to remove Griffith, marking 'the beginning of intensified administration in the Principality under the control of men higher in the king's confidence'.[88] Significantly, the man replacing Griffith was Richard Pole who, considering his 'faithfulness and circumspection', was appointed chamberlain of north Wales for life on 6 March 1490.[89] The chamberlain of north Wales was the most important financial officer in the Principality and Richard must have discharged his duties competently for more offices were to come his way with the fall of Sir William Stanley. The perceived treason of Sir William Stanley, who was the king's step-uncle and lord chamberlain, shocked and disconcerted Henry, who began to turn to those men upon whose loyalty he felt more able to depend and who were more stringently under his control. Therefore, on 31 March 1495, Richard Pole replaced Sir William Stanley in the responsible position of justice of north Wales, relinquishing at the same time the chamberlainship of north Wales which was subsequently granted to Samson Norton.[90] On 21 April in the same year, Richard was also appointed constable of Caernarfon Castle and captain of the town, again offices once held by Stanley.[91] It was not until 1500, however, that he became 'the most important financial officer in the county palatine of Chester', when he was appointed chamberlain of Chester. The office naturally brought with it considerable duties, as had the chamberlainship of north Wales. In addition to accounting to the king or the prince for the revenues and expenditure of Chester and Flintshire, the great seal of Chester was also entrusted to his care. With this he produced and sealed writs at the Chester Exchequer, where he was also responsible for holding sessions, and where individuals would enter into recognizances.[92]

Although Richard's offices were concentrated in north Wales and the marches, he also operated elsewhere, especially in times of national emergency. In 1493, the year in which Perkin Warbeck gained the support of the Emperor Maximilian and Margaret, dowager duchess of Burgundy, Richard's appointments to the commissions of the peace increased dramatically. These commissions took him to Yorkshire, Gloucestershire and Lincolnshire, although the chances that Richard personally sat on all of them are slim. On 15 February 1495, the day before Sir William Stanley's execution, Richard was named to a commission of oyer and terminer for the counties of Bedford, Buckingham, Cambridge, Huntingdon, Norfolk and Suffolk and, three days later, to four commissions of the peace.[93] Of course, the royal demands upon Richard were not solely concerned with judicial and administrative services, but also military duties. On 21 February 1489 'our trusty and wellbeloved knight for our body Sir Richard Pole is amongs other appointed to be one of the captains of our armee into Bretaine for which cause we have given unto him by way of Reward the sum of fyfty Marks sterling.'[94] Although the Breton mission was abortive, in 1492 Richard was once again given the chance to test his martial skills. In April he entered into an indenture with the king to serve overseas with a retinue containing men of arms, demi lances and archers mounted and on foot.[95] The campaign was launched from

Sandwich on 2 October 1492 and on 18 October Henry's troops
left Calais under his command to lay siege to Boulogne; but by 3
November it was all over and the treaty of Étaples was concluded.
On 30 July 1495 Richard took part in a more pressing campaign
when he was appointed one of eleven captains sent with an
emergency army from Chester to augment the defences of the Irish
Pale. This was suffering attack from the combined forces of the
earl of Desmond and Perkin Warbeck, and Richard was granted
substantial sums of money to cover the costs of the wages,
victualling and conveyance of 200 men and 100 horses over the
sea.[96] On 3 August the relief force marched behind the lord deputy
of Ireland, Sir Edward Poynings, and Desmond and Warbeck were
forced to withdraw. As reward, Henry gratefully presented his
cousin with £33 6s 8d.[97] One year later Richard was again chosen,
this time to help contain the Scottish threat, and on 23 April 1496
was sent with several others, including two members of his family,
John, Viscount Welles and Oliver St John, 'to muster and array the
men of Lincoln (Kesteven) in view of the warlike preparations of
the king of Scots, which threaten the town of Berwick'.[98] The
esteem in which Henry held his cousin and his affection for him
were given clear expression in April 1499 when Richard was
appointed a Knight of the Garter which, according to S. B.
Chrimes, was 'the ultimate mark of honour favoured by Henry
VII'.[99] Sponsored by Prince Arthur, eight peers and three knights,[100]
Richard successfully triumphed over such illustrious competitors
as Sir Rhys ap Thomas and Sir David Owen. Richard took his
duties as a Knight of the Garter very seriously, obviously proud of
his position and of the honour associated with it. At the wedding
of Princess Margaret to the king of Scotland in 1503, Richard
attended 'rychly arayd in his Coller'[101] and, although the accounts
of the sixteenth and seventeenth years are missing, Richard
assiduously attended every chapter until his death. During these
years when Richard's career in royal service prospered, his wife
chose a more anonymous lifestyle. Living alternately at Bockmer
and Stourton Castle, Margaret seemed content to concentrate
upon her wifely duties. She bore her husband five children, possibly
six. Henry was born in 1492, with Arthur, Ursula and Reginald
following by 1500 and Geoffrey entering the world around 1504.
Lodovico Beccatelli, Reginald Pole's secretary, claimed that
Margaret bore Sir Richard six children, four sons and two

daughters, and as Beccatelli must have gained this information from Reginald it should not be too readily dismissed. A second daughter may have been born to the Poles and then died in her infancy.[102] However, this life of peaceful anonymity was brought to an abrupt end in 1499 when Margaret's dynastic inheritance intruded upon her life once more. On 28 November she learned that her brother, Edward, earl of Warwick, had been executed for treason.

The earl of Warwick had been incarcerated in the Tower in 1486, where he remained until his execution, but evidence suggests that he did not enjoy an honourable confinement. This evidence is gleaned partly from a long-held misconception concerning the earl's mental state. Many historians, especially those writing towards the end of the nineteenth and the beginning of the twentieth century, have casually accepted as truth Warwick's mental retardation. Agnes Strickland described him as an 'imbecile' and 'very stupid, not knowing the difference between the commonest objects', while Garrett Mattingly chooses 'half-daft' for his appraisal of Warwick. James Gairdner goes further, maintaining that this 'mental incapacity' was the reason why Edward was set aside as heir to the throne after the death of Richard III's son. Later scholars have sensibly been more circumspect, Michael Bennett attributing merely 'a suspicion of simple-mindedness' to him while James Williamson, who gets a little closer to the truth, feels his long incarceration was to blame for his weakened wits.[103] In reality, no contemporary evidence indicated that Warwick was anything but normal, and this suggestion of mental incapacity is based entirely upon a statement made by Edward Hall in his chronicle of 1548. According to him, Warwick was kept in the Tower from his tender age 'out of al company of men, and sight of beastes, in so much that he coulde not descerne a Goose from a Capon'.[104] It is obvious that this statement alone is insufficient to claim mental retardation. If there had been any question of mental incapacity, then Margaret, who of all people should have been aware of such a condition, would have mentioned it in her petition for restoration in order to strengthen her case. Her success depended on Henry VIII accepting that her brother did not know what he was doing when he became embroiled in Warbeck's attempt to escape from the Tower in 1499, and therefore was not guilty of treason. Margaret, however, did not say any such thing:

her justification for Warwick's behaviour rested upon his unworld-liness. Due to his long incarceration, she stated, he had 'none experience nor knowledge of the worldly policies nor of the laws of this realm, so that if any offence were by him done concerning such matters specified in the said act of attainder it was rather by innocence than of any malicious purpose'.[105] Moreover, a mentally retarded Yorkist claimant would have been far more desirable from Henry Tudor's point of view, but Henry did not mention such a condition either. Indeed, when Warwick was led through London to St Paul's as a means of proving Lambert Simnel's imposture, he 'fell to prayer and took part in worship, and then spoke with many important people and especially with those of whom the king was suspicious'.[106] Surely, if the twelve-year-old earl had been mentally retarded, someone amongst those 'important people' would have noticed and remarked upon it. Warwick's 'condition' lay only in his lack of worldliness as his sister maintained, and this fact must cast dark shadows upon Henry VII, for it indicates that the boy was never properly educated and that his mental welfare and develop-ment were ignored. While seemingly accepting Warwick's rights to his remaining lands,[107] Henry probably never intended him to enjoy them, despite the suggestion that his rehabilitation fleetingly crossed the king's mind in 1488.[108] This is not the place to launch into a detailed account of Warbeck's and Warwick's escape attempt of 1499; suffice it to say that the earl's innocence is generally accepted. Although Ian Arthurson does not accept unequivocally that the whole plot was an invention of Henry VII's to secure the executions of Warwick and Warbeck, he nevertheless admits that Warwick 'was an innocent bystander'.[109] Even Polydore Vergil felt strongly enough about the affair to lodge a guarded protest:

> Why indeed the unhappy boy should have been committed to prison not for any fault of his own but only because of his family's offences, why he was retained so long in prison, and what, lastly, the worthy youth could have done in prison which could merit his death all these things could obviously not be comprehended by many.

A little further on, however, Vergil makes a less veiled statement: 'Earl Edward had to perish in this fashion in order that there should be no surviving male heir to his family.'[110] According to

Edward Hall, Henry was under pressure from Ferdinand and Isabella of Spain to neutralize, once and for all, the earl's threat before they would conclude the marriage between their daughter Catherine and Henry's son Arthur. Ferdinand, Hall believed, feared 'as longe as any erle of Warwicke lyved, that England should never be clensed or purged of Cyvyle warre and prevy sedicion, so muche was the neme of Warwyke in other regions had in feare and gealousy'.[111] Certainly, no one can doubt the excitement of the Spanish ambassador, Dr Rodrigo de Puebla, following the executions, nor his eagerness to reassure his masters:

> there being divers heirs of the kingdom and of such a quality that the matter could be disputed between the two sides. Now it has pleased God that all should be thoroughly and duly purged and cleansed, so that not a doubtful drop of royal blood remains in this kingdom, except the true blood of the king and queen, and above all, that of the lord prince Arthur. And since of this fact and of the executions which was done on Perkin Warbeck and on the son of the duke of Clarence, I have written to your highnesses by various ways.[112]

With tragic irony, it was Sir Richard Pole who had held the hands of Prince Arthur and the Spanish ambassador, de Puebla, in his when he officiated at the proxy wedding of Arthur to Catherine of Aragon in May 1499, even commemorating the event by commissioning a carved screen at Aberconwy church, north Wales.[113] Six months later, on 28 November, the twenty-four-year-old earl of Warwick was beheaded at three o'clock in the afternoon. The following day his remains were conveyed up the Thames to Bisham Priory for interment with his ancestors, the king covering the costs of the burial and transportation which amounted to £12 18s 2d.[114] It is significant that the king bore the expenses for Warwick's burial and that he was not interred at the Tower as was the custom for traitors executed there. Although no evidence exists recording her reaction to his execution, this was a particularly unpleasant time for Margaret who, to compound matters, was three months pregnant with Reginald. Her feelings must have been a mixture of grief and fear. Grief for a brother who should have been one of the greatest magnates in England but who lost his liberty at the age of eleven and his life at the age of twenty-four simply because he was Clarence's son, and fear for the fate of Clarence's grandsons, her own children. The execution must also have put a strain, if only temporarily, upon the Poles' marriage as the unfortunate Richard was torn between loyalty to his king and consideration for his pregnant wife's feelings. If this was not bad enough, Richard also suffered in a material sense as the earl's attainder for treason meant that all hope of inheriting his remaining lands, should he have died naturally, was now lost. We can only wonder whether Richard considered his election to the Garter in that same year adequate compensation for the unhappy consequences of Warwick's death.

On 2 October 1501, after a stormy crossing, Catherine of Aragon finally arrived in England and her long-awaited marriage to Prince Arthur took place on 14 November amid lavish celebrations and elaborate pageantry. In December Richard set off to Wales once more, in the company of the prince and his new bride, and it is almost certain that Margaret was amongst the entourage. Although no direct evidence places Margaret in Catherine's household at this time, Catherine was certainly attended by both Spanish and English ladies. This is indicated at the funeral of Prince Arthur when thirty yards of material were allocated 'for the ladies of Spain attending upon the princess' and thirty-three yards for 'the Lady Darcy and other attending upon the princess'.[115] This Lady Darcy is probably the same lady appointed to run Arthur's nursery in 1486 who presumably headed a contingent of English ladies attending upon the new princess of Wales. This contingent of ladies most likely included Margaret Pole, whose noble lineage and position as wife to the lord chamberlain made her a most appropriate choice. Despite Catherine's indirect role in Warwick's death, Margaret held no grudge against the innocent young woman, and an enduring friendship was formed between them in these few months spent at Ludlow Castle. Unfortunately, a mere five months after his wedding Prince Arthur died and Richard, probably reeling from the shock himself, had the unpleasant task of informing the king and council at Greenwich of the tragedy.[116] Richard had served the young prince for the past eight years and had watched him grow up; his death therefore was a personal as well as a professional loss. Margaret concentrated on consoling the newly widowed Catherine, but, with the termination of her husband's appointment as the prince's lord chamberlain and Catherine's now uncertain role, Margaret was forced to give up her position as one of the princess's ladies. Nevertheless, they maintained a correspondence and continued to support each other throughout the difficulties they both subsequently suffered until the accession of Henry VIII in 1509.

Over the two years following Arthur's death, life for Margaret and Richard continued much as before. Richard's services were still required in Wales, and Margaret continued to reside at Stourton Castle and Bockmer in the company of her husband. In 1504 Richard was reappointed, for the third time, to the chamberlainship of Chester[117] and Margaret was pregnant with their fifth child. Unfortunately, we do not know if he ever saw his son, for by the end of October 1504 Richard was dead[118] and Margaret had lost the man who, over the past seventeen years, had cared for her and given her a much-needed sense of security. Although their life together had not been characterized by the great affluence and luxury Margaret had been brought up to expect, she appears to have been happy and contented with this 'very worthy gentleman',[119] and his death was a huge loss to her, not only on an emotional level, but on a practical level too. If Margaret was to ensure that her children received the best start in life through their connections at court, there was only one man to whom she could look, but he was the one man who still considered her to be the inconvenient liability she had been in 1485: Henry VII.

2
Widowhood and Restoration, 1504–1519

'Avarice slinks away far from the people; generosity scatters wealth with lavish hand.'[1]

In October 1504 Margaret Pole was thirty-one years of age, a widow with several children to care for and possibly still pregnant with her fifth child, Geoffrey. Once again another pregnancy had been marked by tragedy in her personal life, whilst the risk of her own death was now dramatically increased due to the impending birth of her child. One of the chief causes of death among women during this period was childbirth; medical texts and household books contained instructions to aid the expectant mother, but many did nothing but make matters worse. For instance, one instructed that the unfortunate woman's nostrils should be stopped once labour had started 'so that the vital spirits can go down to the uterus, and encourage her with her burden', whilst another suggested making her sneeze by throwing pepper powder and castory powder up her nose. We can only hope that Margaret's attendants did not use these particular handbooks for reference, nor the Hippocratic treatise which stated that running up and down steps, being fastened to a ladder which was shaken violently or lying in bed with the foot end raised high before being dropped, would help bring forth a reluctant foetus.[2] Certainly, the worry of what would become of her children in the eventuality of her death would have been at the forefront of Margaret's mind and this period must have been one of the most traumatic for her. Apart from the grief she must have felt for the loss of her husband, she had no close family to whom she could turn for help, and her financial future was now precarious. Margaret's jointure in her husband's modest manors would not have provided a great deal of revenue, while Richard's considerable salary as a royal servant ceased with his death. Richard Morisyne, not the most reliable of sources admittedly, claimed that during this period Margaret had been reduced to living with the nuns of Syon.[3] Indeed, between January 1505 and September 1516 John Evans, the bailiff of Medmenham and Ellesborough, spent £20 11s 1d of his own money on certain necessaries for Margaret, which she eventually repaid after her restoration to the earldom of Salisbury.[4] In fact, Margaret's straitened circumstances might have been one of the reasons behind Reginald's ecclesiastical career and do appear to have been a source of resentment on his part. Writing to his mother in 1536 he reminded her:

> you had given me utterly unto God. And though you had done so with all your children, yet in me you had so given all right from you and possession utterly of me that you never took any care to provide for my living nor otherwise, as you did for other, but committed all to God, to whom you had given me.[5]

Despite the worries of meeting day-to-day expenses and supporting her family with a much-reduced income, there were other bills to be paid, including her husband's funeral costs. Richard was to have every honour appropriate to his position as the king's cousin and a prominent royal officer, and thus on 20 October 1504 Margaret borrowed £40 'for the burial of Sir Richard Pole'.[6] The scale of the loan is put very much into perspective when we consider that Richard's annual income from Ellesborough and Medmenham was £50. However, Margaret was not left totally alone to cope with this, for taking out the loan with her was Sir Charles Somerset, the illegitimate son of Henry, duke of Somerset. Henry, duke of Somerset was the first cousin of Margaret Beaufort, and therefore Charles was Henry VII's third cousin. Sir Charles had been a friend and colleague of Richard Pole, and both men had worked together in Henry VII's service. Although Richard's will does not survive, it is probable that Somerset was named as one of his executors or as an overseer of the will with the request to be good lord to his wife and children, and was acting in that capacity. Further help came, unexpectedly, from the coffers of

Henry VII. The king's consideration for Richard's long and loyal service is demonstrated by a grudging generosity towards Margaret in the immediate aftermath of his cousin's death, a generosity that, as far as evidence suggests, was never repeated. Firstly, he stipulated that the loan of £40 was to be repaid 'of the first money that shall be received of the profits of his [Richard's] lands'.[7] As the king was in possession of these lands due to Henry Pole's minority, it seems that Margaret would be repaying him with his own money. Secondly, on 8 December 1504 Margaret received £52 6s 8d from the king for her 'finding and rayment'.[8] These two marks of 'kindness' were enough to discharge the king's conscience and persuade him that he had done enough for Margaret and her family. Although Richard's eldest son, the twelve-year-old Henry, was the king's ward and kinsman, it appears that he never attended court, did not receive any gifts and never served in the royal household. Of course, the real reason which probably kept Henry Pole from the court was the fact that he was Margaret's son and the duke of Clarence's grandson. As such, the young Henry possessed an arguably superior claim to the throne than Henry VII who, from 1502 had only one male heir to succeed him, the future Henry VIII. Indeed, in 1506 John Flamank reported to the king remarks heard by Sir Hugh Conway, the treasurer of Calais, made by 'many great personages' while Henry lay sick at his manor of Wanstead.[9] Speculating upon the succession,

> some of them spake of my lorde of Buckingham, saying that he was a noble man and would be a royal ruler. Other there were that spake, he said, in likewise of your traitor Edmond de la Pole, but none of them, he said, that spake of my lord prince.[10]

The precariousness of the succession, compounded by Henry VII's unpopularity, meant that he did not wish to make too much of Henry Pole; he did not want him to come to court, where he might make strategic alliances and possibly offer an alternative to those disenchanted with the Tudor regime. Consequently the Poles were not helped out of their financial difficulties, and the boy was kept very much on the periphery along with his mother.

Whilst Margaret struggled to make ends meet and coped with the unpleasant reality of being *persona non grata* at court, her friend Catherine of Aragon was experiencing troubles of her own.

Catherine had been betrothed to Arthur's brother, Prince Henry, on 23 June 1503 but in November 1504, just after the death of Margaret's husband, Catherine's mother, Isabella, died. The political repercussions of Isabella's death rendered Catherine a less valuable match for the heir to the throne, and in June 1505, at his father's behest, the young prince made a formal protest to his betrothal thus allowing Henry VII to look for more suitable brides. To add insult to injury, the king also stopped Catherine's monthly allowance of £100, forcing her to give up her separate establishment and live at court. Her position was far from enviable; her status as Prince Henry's intended bride was unclear, she was stranded in a foreign land with only a few attendants, and her financial situation was desperate. Often lodged in the most unsalubrious of quarters above the royal stables and forced to endure the contempt and insolence of the royal servants, Catherine faced her situation with stoical determination. Darning her clothes in the absence of new ones and eating rotten fish that her ambassador 'would not give his horse boy'[11] because it was cheap, Catherine maintained her dignity and continued to treat Henry VII with the greatest respect and obedience. Her father-in-law, meanwhile, busily evaluated the merits of Eleanor, daughter of Philip, duke of Burgundy, and Marguerite d'Alençon, sister of the future Francis I, as potential brides for his son. Throughout this period Margaret and Catherine were widows in financial distress, and the trials suffered simultaneously by both of them probably strengthened their friendship further. Catherine's wedding to Prince Henry should have taken place on 29 June 1506, his fifteenth birthday, but nothing happened and it was now considered most unlikely that Catherine would ever become queen of England. Margaret's support for Catherine, which continued throughout this period, reveals that her friendship was genuine and not opportunistic. That Margaret's friendship was fully reciprocated by Catherine is clearly demonstrated by the events following Henry VII's death on 22 April 1509. Within two months Catherine, to everyone's astonishment, was married to the new King Henry VIII. Although Henry explained that he was obeying his father's dying wish, the most likely reason is that he married Catherine simply because he wanted to. Although five years older than Henry, at twenty-three Catherine was an extremely pretty and striking young woman with auburn hair and blue eyes. Unlike most other monarchs of his day,

Henry was not a man who could bring himself to marry solely for political reasons. There had to be a real attraction, and it seems that Henry was genuinely attracted to Catherine. They were married on 11 June 1509 and three weeks later, on 1 July, the new king paid £26 13s 4d to a Lady Williams for the board of 'Dame Margaret Pole' after her arrival in London for the coronation.[12] Although Catherine's influence is clearly at work here, Henry would not have been averse to welcoming members of his family to court, even though he probably hardly knew Margaret. Indeed, this pattern was to be repeated with other family members and individuals who, like Margaret, had been marginalized by Henry VII. The new king was determined that his reign should be a contrast to that of his father's, and the heady atmosphere of the time was one of celebration, joy and generosity, a welcome escape from the misery, fear and suspicion which had latterly characterized the court of Henry VII.

For Margaret, and especially her seventeen-year-old son Henry, who had never before had a proper opportunity to experience the magnificence of a royal court, it must have been an exciting period in their lives. Rescued from the obscurity and poverty of the past five years, Margaret was appointed one of Catherine's principal attendants,[13] whilst Henry was immediately employed as one of the king's servants. Placed high on the list of ladies attending Catherine at the coronation under the heading of the queen's chamber, Margaret received the maximum allowance of material usually accorded to a countess, superseding the baronesses, an especial mark of favour indicative of the queen's deep affection for her.[14] This new-found favour continued, and on 31 July the king granted 'our right dere and wellbiloved the Lady Margaret Pole' a £100 annuity during pleasure, a definite improvement on the one-off payment of £52 6s 8d which was all she had received from Henry VII.[15] Meanwhile, Henry Pole began to receive regular gifts of clothing, including gowns of French tawny, tawny velvet, black velvet, black damask, and by 1512 had been appointed one of the king's sewers.[16] At the same time Henry VIII began to support the education of Margaret's third son, the twelve-year-old Reginald who, with unfortunate irony, would use his learning against the king during the 1530s. In March 1511 Reginald received £12 for 'his exhibition at school' and a year later, assisted financially by Henry, he left the Carthusian monastery at Sheen for Magdalen College,

Oxford. In April 1513 he received a pension which the prior of St Frideswide 'is bound to give to a clerk of the King's nomination until he be promoted to a competent benefice by the said prior'.[17] For the first three years of Henry VIII's reign Margaret and her children certainly enjoyed an enhanced lifestyle as a result of the king's generosity. This benevolence could quite easily have continued in the same vein with Henry eventually negotiating an advantageous second marriage for Margaret in order to give her financial security. Henry, however, went much further, and in 1512 Margaret's life changed dramatically when Henry granted her petition for restoration to the earldom of Salisbury which, at a stroke, made her countess of Salisbury in her own right and potentially one of the most influential and powerful women in England.

Although Henry had his own motives for restoring Margaret, this should not detract from the fact that the terms of her restoration were very advantageous. When we compare the 6,500 marks that John Tuchet, Lord Audely was constrained to pay in 1512 for the restoration of lands worth £545 17s 7d[18] with Margaret's 5,000 marks for lands worth over £2,000, it becomes clear just how generously she was treated. For Henry, the restoration of Margaret Pole would garner him further popularity, not least because contemporary opinion had not, in general, approved of the earl of Warwick's execution. Just as he enhanced his reputation by the cancellation of his father's hated recognizances, Henry VIII would play the merciful prince to his father's hard-hearted king by the restoration of Warwick's sister. Reginald Pole, however, offers another, more unlikely, explanation by apportioning a significant role in his mother's restoration to Henry VII himself. Apparently racked with guilt on his deathbed and 'repenting of the acts of injustice committed by him during his reign' Henry VII, Reginald declared, instructed his son to restore Margaret. This Henry VIII did, but only on the condition that Margaret forgave Henry VII 'the injuries received from him'.[19] Reginald also claimed that Catherine's guilt over the earl of Warwick's execution prompted her to help the family because she felt 'very much bound to recompense and requite us for the detriment we had received on her account'.[20] Catherine would certainly have promoted her friend's suit and, whilst she might have regretted the execution of Margaret's brother, her prime motive would have been her friendship with Margaret. Catherine's support of Margaret's petition would have significantly strengthened its potential for success. In the first years of their marriage, the king genuinely loved his wife and relied upon her advice. Furthermore, over the past three years Henry had had the opportunity to become acquainted with Margaret, and there is reason to believe that relations were extremely cordial. According to Reginald, Henry had looked upon Margaret as a parent,[21] while Margaret had cause to respect and admire the young king who had not only been generous to her, but who had married Catherine and rescued her from her predicament.

Helen Miller believes that Margaret's restoration was not unusual but part of the king's plan to rehabilitate all those who had fallen out of favour with Henry VII.[22] Miller's sentiments are shared by David Loades and David Starkey, the latter feeling that Henry's attempts to 'woo' the aristocracy were prompted by his desire for war, which obviously necessitated the support of his nobles.[23] The early years of Henry's reign were times of conciliation and it must be remembered that the Pole family were not the only relatives Henry restored to favour. First Sir William Courtenay in 1511, then his son Henry in 1512 were restored as earls of Devon while Katherine, Henry Courtenay's mother and Henry VIII's aunt, was granted an annuity of 200 marks on the same day as Margaret Pole received her £100 annuity in 1509.[24] Contemporary with Margaret's restoration was the elevation of her kinsman and friend, Charles Somerset, now Lord Herbert, to the earldom of Worcester. This was not a restoration but a reward of war, for Somerset had been captain of the rear-ward in the French campaign of 1513. Nevertheless, Somerset's blood relationship to Henry probably helped to facilitate his rise to fortune in much the same way as Margaret's. Appointed lord chamberlain in 1508, he was reappointed to this office by Henry VIII.[25] Moreover, Henry built up Somerset's power in Wales and the marches, finally making him sheriff of Glamorgan for life, an appointment he had long coveted during Henry VII's reign.[26] In 1523 Arthur Plantagenet, the illegitimate son of Edward IV, was created Viscount Lisle, while in 1525, Thomas Manners, Edward IV's great-nephew, became earl of Rutland. Manners's creation was certainly a reflection of his royal lineage, for this title had been extinct since 1460, when its last holder, Edmund Plantagenet, Edward IV's younger brother, was killed. To emphasize further his descent Henry allowed Manners to quarter two fleurs-de-lis gold and two lions passant guardant gold, with his arms.[27]

The petition for restoration presented by Margaret[28] was a very carefully worded document; it had to be, for it sought to exonerate Margaret's brother of treason, the crime for which he was executed, whilst at the same time avoiding the condemnation of Henry VII for judicial murder. After stressing her descent from Alice Montague, countess of Salisbury, Margaret turned to the act of attainder passed against her brother in the Parliament of 1503. Referring to Henry VII in the most respectful of terms, she detailed the effects of the attainder on her brother's property, before proceeding to disclose why the attainder should be repealed. Tactfully dating his strict incarceration from 1483, she went on to explain that Warwick, due to his confinement, had no knowledge of the laws of the realm, so that if he had committed an offence, it was the result of ignorance rather than malicious motives. Margaret then reminded Henry that she was his 'poor kinswoman and hath no living but by help of your highness', and appealed to Henry's 'benign goodness, abundant grace, pity and charity' to revoke the attainder completely as though it had never been passed, and allow her to be restored to 'the estate, name, degree, style and title of Countess of Salisbury' and her heirs as earls of Salisbury. The act then went on to specify the lands to which Margaret and her heirs were to be restored. She was to possess all the lands that her brother had held at the time of his said treason, and to inherit them as if the attainder had never been passed. By making clear that they were the lands held at the time of his treason, the lands of his grandmother Anne, countess of Warwick, were excluded from the restoration and a proviso specifically stated that the restoration was not to extend to any lands that were part of her inheritance. The act then stipulated that Margaret was to take the issues only after 25 March 1513, and made clear that the restoration was to Margaret and her heirs. Two saving clauses ended the act: one protected Henry VIII's rights as the heir of Margaret Beaufort, and the other protected any right he might have to the Salisbury lands other than by Warwick's forfeiture. These two clauses would prove significant later on during Margaret's dispute with the king over her title to several manors initially restored to her. In order to enter the earldom, Margaret paid 5,000 marks towards the king's wars, 'for his high and great goodness showed unto her, as restoring her to the inheritance of her said brother'.[29] In May 1513, Wolsey acknowledged receipt of £1,000 as the first instalment leaving £2,333 6s 8d outstanding, and on 1 May 1513 both Margaret and her eldest son were bound in a recognizance to pay this debt for 'the redeeming of Salisbury lands'.[30] She must have obtained the initial £1,000 in loan, borrowed on the strength of her restoration, for she would not have been able to raise such an amount from her widow's jointure. Restored on 4 February 1512 in the second Parliament of Henry VIII's reign, the new countess of Salisbury formally entered her manors in January 1514.[31]

The restoration ostensibly granted Margaret the Montague lands of her great-grandmother, Alice, to hold in fee simple along with her title countess of Salisbury. Her estates fell within seventeen English counties, in addition to manors in Wales, the Isle of Wight and Calais.[32] Although predominantly in the South and the Midlands, with the greatest concentration in the counties of Hampshire, Somerset, Devon and Buckinghamshire, her lands also extended up into Lincolnshire and Yorkshire. In addition to the forty-four manors she received as a result of her restoration, she also eventually held a further four manors in Kent, two manors in Wales, properties in Lincoln whose origins are obscure,[33] and in 1534 augmented her estates with the purchase of Aston Chevery in Buckinghamshire and Chalton in Hampshire. By the time of her arrest in 1538, Margaret held fifty-six manors in England and Wales, the large mansion and tenements in London known as Le Herber and her widow's jointure in Ellesborough and Medmenham. Of these fifty-six manors, six were valued at over £100 a year between September 1538 and September 1539. The wealthiest manor appears to have been Stokenham in Devon worth £155 a year, followed by Cottingham in Yorkshire with annual issues of £127, and Christchurch in Hampshire worth £124 a year. The other three manors, Clavering in Essex, Ware in Hertford and Yealmpton in Devon, were valued at £113, £105 and £103 a year respectively.[34] In 1527 ten 'noblemen of the degree of baron and above' were assessed for the subsidy intended for the French campaign and originally granted in 1523. Out of a total of ten nobles Margaret came a respectable fifth, assessed on lands worth £1,220. She actually preceded Thomas Howard, duke of Norfolk and the duke of Suffolk with lands valued at £1,000 each.[35] Obviously, it would be unwise to take at face value a source such as this as nobles were never too forthcoming about their actual incomes when being assessed for a subsidy. Indeed, Margaret herself appears to have been guilty of just this, for the 1538 minister's accounts for her estates reveal that she actually enjoyed a gross income of £2,311.[36] Nevertheless, what this source does reveal is that the countess of Salisbury featured prominently in the financial pecking order and was probably the fifth or sixth wealthiest noble in early sixteenth-century England. Margaret's sudden rise in status and affluence was nothing short of spectacular, and the effects of this good fortune upon her, in a material and emotional sense, should not be underestimated. To put it into current context, it is akin to winning the lottery or inheriting a million-pound corporation with all the benefits and responsibilities which that entails. Although she was the duke of Clarence's daughter, his early death had deprived her of the opportunity to enjoy the lavish lifestyle that he would have provided. Between the ages of four and twelve she had been dependent for her care upon her two uncles, Edward IV and Richard III, and, until her marriage in 1487, on the cautious generosity of Henry VII. For the next seventeen years she enjoyed a secure but not lavish lifestyle as the wife of Sir Richard Pole, but from his death in 1504 she struggled to maintain her family on a much-reduced income. Hence, the restoration of 1512 gave Margaret Pole her first real experience of wealth and affluence, while her position as countess of Salisbury promised more independence than she could ever have expected.

In accordance with her new rank and status, the countess of Salisbury maintained four principal residences: Clavering in Essex, Bisham in Berkshire, Le Herber in London and her seat at Warblington in Hampshire. Unfortunately, little is known about Margaret's household at Clavering except that it was a castle, covered an 'extensive area' and possessed a moat.[37] Between 1523 and 1524 she initiated a number of repairs and renovations at considerable expense, paying particular attention to the chapel where St Edward and St John were to be painted on its walls at a cost of 40s. A chamber was also freshly painted at a cost of 13s 4d 'for my lady's councill to ly in when they come thither'.[38] Clavering was geographically well placed, lying approximately thirty-five miles from London. Likewise was Margaret's next residence, Bisham. Conveniently on the banks of the Thames, it lay only three miles from Lord Montague's seat at Bockmer in Medmenham. She probably took up residence there soon after her restoration although the earliest known references to her occupancy are made in September 1517 and April 1518.[39] Mostly demolished later in the sixteenth century, the building, which had originally belonged to the Knights Templars, had been used as a residence by the earls of Salisbury following the suppression of that order.[40] By her occupation of the house, Margaret was continuing the tradition of her ancestors, for her family's links to Bisham began in the fourteenth century, when her forebear, William, first Montague earl of Salisbury, founded a monastery of Austin canons in 1337. Bisham was also the resting place of many of Margaret's ancestors and immediate family, including her grandfather Richard Neville (the kingmaker), her brother Edward, earl of Warwick and her son Arthur, who died in the late 1520s. According to Sir Thomas Hoby, whose brother, Sir Philip Hoby, was granted the manor in 1553, the house adjoined the monastery founded by William Montague and was of considerable size. Built partly of stone and partly of timber with a tiled roof, it possessed a great chamber over which was situated another great chamber and an inner chamber. Six other chambers and more lodgings were also provided for, whilst a cloister led into two gardens, one 60 feet by 78 feet and the other 84 feet by 133 feet. In 1902 Margaret's coat of arms impaled with her husband's was still visible in the window of the then council chamber.[41] Obviously a very pleasant residence, it must have been an impressive one, for immediately following her attainder it was reserved for Henry VIII's own use.[42]

Only the most wealthy nobles possessed residences in London, and Margaret's residence, known as Le Herber, was a building of great size and grandeur. Variously described as a 'great tenement', a 'great old house' and a 'vast house or palace', in the reign of Richard III it was known as the King's Palace.[43] In 1584 Sir Thomas Pullison, the mayor, rebuilt it and afterwards it became the residence of Sir Francis Drake. Not far from Baynard's Castle, it was probably similar in size, for in 1458 the earl of Salisbury, with 500 men, was housed at Le Herber, while Baynard's Castle accommodated 400 men under the command of Richard, duke of York.[44] By 1790 Le Herber was no longer standing, but it had been situated in Dowgate, less than a mile from the Tower of London and on the site where Cannon Street Station now stands.[45] It comprised not only the great house but several tenements and dwellings lying close by, which Margaret rented out. Among these was a large building called the Chekker, described as an inn or hospice, a fuller's shop in Bush Lane, stables in Carter Lane, a timber house rented to William Mabson, a carpenter in Margaret's employ, and a tenement rented to William Okeley, Margaret's receiver for her London properties.[46] Margaret's concern to maintain her residences is again evident from the various repairs carried out at Le Herber in January and February 1521. Among these, weather boarding was bought for the back of the great chamber while a dauber and his labourer spent three days working on two sides of the same chamber. As at Clavering, Margaret's devoutness is revealed when on 3 July 1520, preceding more necessary repairs, she paid 13s 4d for a new tabernacle 'wherein of our lady was enclosed the which was painted in the Erbor'. She presented the old tabernacle to the man who had originally made it with 3s 4d in money 'of her piety'.[47]

The residence which most clearly illustrates Margaret's tastes and preferences is the residence she herself commissioned, Warblington Castle in Hampshire.[48] On the borders of Hampshire and Sussex, Warblington occupied a pleasant aspect on the coast, barely a mile from the sea. Built of brick, the fashionable building material at that time, the dressings around the doors, windows and angles of the building were faced with high-quality stone from Caen, France and the Isle of Wight.[49] Basic stone seems to have come from Hambledon quarry, while blue stone and slate were also used.[50] Laid out on simple lines, the castle formed a quadrangle covering an area 200 feet long by 200 feet wide and was surrounded on every side by a substantial moat, the remains of which are still visible today. The gatehouse was flanked by two crenellated turrets roofed with lead, and the one surviving turret clearly reveals arrow slits and gun holes.[51] Buildings extended around the inside of the court 'With a fare gallery and Diveres Chambers of great romthe'. In addition, it boasted 'a very great and spacious halle parlor and great Chamber And all othere housses of offices What soever Necessary for such a house With a very fare Chapell Within the said house'.[52] The inventory taken at Warblington following Margaret's arrest in 1538 goes further, revealing the extensive and complex suites of rooms at the castle. In addition to the great hall, there was a waiting chamber, a dining chamber, a great parlour and a lower parlour, with a chapel chamber and chapel closet adjoining the chapel. Margaret's servants occupied a total of nineteen chambers while Margaret's own apartments comprised two rooms. Several other chambers were empty and unallocated, presumably available for guests.[53] Before the gatehouse was 'a fare grene court' stretching to two acres, and adjoining the castle 'a very spacious garden With plasent Walkes', again extending to two acres. Close by was a grove of trees amounting to two acres and '2 orchards and 2 little meadows plates contayning 3 acres'. There was 'a fare fishe ponde neare the said place . . . And 2 Barnes . . . with stables and other out houses'.[54] Indeed, the cost of the building work that was carried out between 21 November 1517 and 8 November 1518 amounted to the very substantial sum of £469 2s 3d.[55]

The grand scale of Warblington is a direct result of Margaret's determination to proclaim her status and affluence, and we can imagine that she cut an impressive figure as she presided over her luxuriously furnished and elaborately staffed household. Although considered middle-aged by contemporary standards, there is every reason to believe that at forty-five years of age Margaret was still a very handsome woman. Tall, slim and elegant, she still boasted the auburn hair of the Plantagenets and the pale skin which accompanied such colouring. Her preference for dark-coloured clothes would have offset her complexion to striking effect. Progressing gracefully but purposefully through the halls and chambers of her household flanked by her lady attendants, Margaret could have been observed wearing a black velvet gown bordered with raised work, or a black satin gown trimmed with marten fur and large sable-lined sleeves dramatically folded back to the elbow. Another black velvet gown in her possession had satin-lined sleeves, while tawny damask and tawny velvet kirtles could also be found among the garments in her wardrobe.[56] In the portrait believed to be of Margaret which currently hangs in the National Portrait Gallery, she again wears a dark gown, but the sleeves are lined, this time with ermine, and her gable hood trimmed with the same fur to proclaim her royal status.[57] In 1538 Margaret employed seventy-three servants at Warblington and the offices held by certain of these servants reveal the grandiose and intricate organization of her household.[58] Her marshal of the hall along with his deputy, the usher of the hall, maintained discipline and order whilst Margaret was entertaining. He made sure that her guests were seated

correctly by rank and coordinated the activities of her six gentlemen waiters to ensure that guests wanted for nothing at table. As
large amounts of alcohol were usually consumed at such banquets,
he was also required to prevent the outbreak of fighting and
drunken brawls. Her comptroller maintained accounts for the
entire household, while her clerk of the kitchen also kept accounts
for all foodstuffs bought. In overall charge of the smooth running
of the household was her steward, who was responsible for the
enforcement of household policy and whom we might describe as a
'general manager'.[59] Revealing that life with this middle-aged
widow was not to be dull is the presence of a fool, who was kept to
entertain the household and guests.[60] The scale of Margaret's
household is understood when we consider that, at a rough
estimate, the cost of its maintenance, including servants' wages,
amounted to between £700 and £900 a year![61]

Margaret's pride in her rank and lineage is clearly revealed in the
items with which she furnished her residences. No female modesty
prevented her arms from being emblazoned on the windows of her
properties and on various items within her household; celures and
testers to hang above the beds, sumpter cloths to drape over her
pack horses, the hanging above the fireplace in the dining chamber
at Warblington all bore the countess of Salisbury's arms. Other
hangings of verdure and arras also decorated the walls, some
telling stories such as the discovery of Newfoundland and Ulysses'
journey. As in her other residences, Margaret ensured that her
chapel at Warblington was well attired. The two altar cloths of
blue and yellow silk damask had a matching vestment and also
vestments of tawny velvet and bawdkin, while 'ij great Imaiges of
the Trinitie and our Lady' looked down from the walls. Her
tableware was mostly silver and silver and gilt interspersed with
items of gold, Venetian glass and those decorated with mother of
pearl.[62] No visitor to Warblington could fail to be impressed by its
imposing façade and sumptuous furnishings. Indeed, it was
another of Margaret's residences that was fit enough for a king. In
the summer of 1526 Henry VIII stayed at Warblington whilst trying
to avoid the plague.[63] However, Henry and Catherine were no
doubt entertained by Margaret at Warblington before this, for
among her possessions in 1538 were a number of items decorated
with the Tudor rose, the portcullis and the pomegranate, probably
relics of such occasions.[64] Furthermore, according to Geoffrey

Pole's evidence in 1538, Lord Montague had considered it a slight when the king failed to visit his mother while in Sussex in that year, suggesting that he had once been in the habit of doing so.[65] The countess of Salisbury intended her resting place to be equally impressive, and in Christchurch Priory, further along the coast from Warblington, she commissioned a magnificent chantry. Again, high-quality Caen stone was used in the construction, which is English Gothic in design with Italian ornamental carving. The fan vault of the roof reveals three bosses, two boasting the countess's coat of arms and the middle showing her kneeling before the Trinity. Unfortunately, these were defaced by the royal commissioners in December 1539.[66]

Margaret's increased affluence and status, combined with the friendship she enjoyed with the king and queen, also helped to promote her court career further. In 1516 she was accorded a great distinction when she was chosen to be one of the godmothers to Henry's and Catherine's daughter, the Princess Mary. Mary was born on Monday, 18 February, and her christening took place two days later at Greenwich. Conducted with elaborate ritual and pageantry, it was well attended by the aristocracy. However, the prevalence of the king's blood kin is noticeable, turning the event into something of a family affair. Henry VIII's first cousin, Henry Courtenay, earl of Devon, carried the basin supported by Lord Herbert, Charles Somerset's son. Thomas Grey, marquess of Dorset, son of Henry's half-uncle, carried the salt and his wife, Lady Dorset, the chrism. Charles Somerset, earl of Worcester was present in his capacity as lord chamberlain, while Henry's great-half-uncle, Sir David Owen, was among those who bore the canopy over the princess. Lady Katherine Courtenay, the king's aunt, was one of the godmothers at the font, while Margaret was godmother at the concurrent confirmation.[67] This early association with the princess was to mark the beginning of a long and affectionate relationship between them although, ultimately, it was to have mixed blessings for Margaret. Throughout this period Margaret remained in Catherine's household, and her continuing place in the king's and queen's affection is illustrated in the New Year's gifts of 1519. Out of fourteen ladies, with the exception of Mary, the king's sister, and his aunt, Katherine Courtenay, Margaret was presented with the largest payment, 40s, the same amount as the dukes of Buckingham and Norfolk each received.[68] In the following year, however, Margaret received the ultimate honour when she was appointed governess to Princess Mary, the king's only legitimate heir. According to Reginald, so desirous was Catherine for Margaret to accept the appointment that

> she did not content herself with ordering her to take up the burden as the king had written to her and commanded her, but her majesty wanted to leave all the commands aside and go to my mother's house together with the king and implore her to take up the burden willingly.[69]

It is not possible to be sure exactly when Margaret's appointment took place, but she was certainly in office by 1 May 1520, having succeeded Elizabeth Denton and Margaret Brian to the post.[70] The selection of Margaret for this highly responsible position is understandable and a clear indication of the regard that both Henry and his queen had for her. 'Only a person of the highest rank and dignity was suitable to have the custody of a child who might one day be queen of both England and France.'[71] In addition to this, she was a mature woman of forty-seven years of age who had five children of her own, including a daughter. Furthermore, she was intelligent, unquestionably virtuous, traditionally pious, and possessed an easy familiarity with the convoluted etiquette of a royal court. Having been treated with deference herself as a young princess of the House of York, she was able to identify with Mary and help her cope with her position. In 1525, when the nine-year-old Mary was sent to Ludlow, Margaret was apprised of the duties the king expected of her. She was to ensure that Mary received an 'honourable education and training in virtuous demeanour; that is to say, to serve God, from whom all grace and goodness proceedeth'. She was to make sure that Mary enjoyed 'moderate exercise', became accomplished at dancing and was to 'pass her time, most seasons, at her virginals or other musical instruments'. Her study of Latin and French was to be undertaken moderately as Henry did not wish his daughter to become overtired. Henry also laid down stipulations concerning her diet which was not only to be well and cleanly prepared, but served with 'joyous, and merry communication'. Her garments were to be clean and her chamber spotless, 'so that everything about her be pure, sweet, clean, and wholesome, as to so great a princess doth apertain: all corruption, evil airs, and things noisome and unpleasant, to be eschewed'.[72] These instructions reveal that the duties of Mary's governess would be somewhat demanding especially as the princess was not the easiest of charges. She was rather pernickety regarding her diet and also suffered, in later years, from chronic menstrual problems and the associated bouts of mood swings often associated with this type of problem.[73] Thus, in addition to her other qualities, Margaret would have needed compassion, understanding and patience, which Mary's affection for her suggests she possessed.

As supporters of the 'new learning' Henry and Catherine would have been keen to ensure that someone like-minded was appointed to oversee the upbringing of their daughter. Again, as a patroness of humanist scholars Margaret had the right credentials. Gentian Hervet of Orleans had studied with Erasmus and was a pupil of Thomas Lupset for two years at Corpus Christi College, Oxford. In 1526, as a 'layman in the Countess of Salisbury's household', he was commanded by her to translate Erasmus' *De Immensa Misericordia Dei* (Concerning the infinite pity of God) into English. He was also appointed tutor to Margaret's grandson Arthur, and commissioned by Arthur's father, Geoffrey, to translate Xenophon's *Oeconomicus* (Treatise of the household) from Greek to English. Indeed, his association with the Pole family was to last for nine years.[74] Margaret's association with humanist scholars is not surprising, considering the circles in which her son Reginald moved. His tutors at Oxford included the renowned humanist Thomas Linacre and the classical scholar William Latimer. Among his friends he could count Thomas More, with whom he was 'on terms of familiarity and friendship', once asking Margaret to prepare a medicine for More, while More's scholarly daughter Margaret considered Reginald to be 'noble as he is learned in all branches of letters'.[75] John Helyar, who matriculated at Corpus Christi College in 1522 and also enjoyed the patronage of Wolsey, was appointed Margaret's domestic chaplain in 1532 and rector of Warblington in 1533,[76] while Thomas Starkey, who had also studied at Oxford and was Reginald's chaplain by 1530, was genuinely fond of Margaret and her sons, staying at Margaret's London residence after his return to England in 1534.[77] Margaret also enjoyed a friendship with Thomas Lupset's mother Alice, obviously acquainted through their sons, whose close friendship is well known.[78] By 1538 Alice had lent Margaret the considerable sum of £100, and the president of Corpus Christi College had lent £33 6s 8d.[79] There is no doubt that Reginald provided a channel of introduction between his humanist friends and his mother which helped to create Margaret's links with Oxford University.[80] Although Margaret's appointment as Mary's governess promised to be a successful arrangement, her association with the princess was not constant. Although she was to play an important and significant role in Mary's life, this did not really begin until much later, as her first appointment as governess was of limited duration. In post by May 1520, she had lost the office by 24 July 1521 and did not regain her position until 1525, but this second appointment would last for eight years until she was dismissed once again in 1533.

The standard of living Margaret enjoyed after her restoration was naturally shared by her children, whose prospects were dramatically enhanced. In 1513 her eldest son, Henry, entered his twenty-first year and the two Buckinghamshire manors inherited from his father: Medmenham and Ellesborough.[81] The administration of these two modest manors would allow him to 'cut his teeth' and help prepare him for the extensive estates he would one day administer as earl of Salisbury. Henry appears to have been a responsible landowner, immediately initiating various repairs within his manors. He spent 36s on a copyhold called Barnetts and £7 on the manor of Bockmer in Medmenham, which he made his seat. Here he indulged in all the pastimes expected of a young nobleman such as hunting and hawking. The keeping of his hawks cost £6 8s 2d over two years, but as the son and heir of the countess of Salisbury these were pastimes he could now afford. He also became involved in that other pre-requisite of the aristocracy: litigation. John More of the king's Exchequer was paid 66s for 'certain business of my Lord Montague', while expenditure of 20s was incurred through several suits brought against Henry by the abbot of Medmenham.[82] The year 1513 was indeed significant for Henry, who not only assumed control of his manors, but also took part in his first military campaign. More fortunate than his father, whose first military experience had been to try to keep the crown on Henry VII's head at the battle of Stoke, Henry's initiation was to be a glamorous war of conquest conducted with all the pomp and pageantry Henry VIII's court could muster. On 30 June 1513 Henry VIII, having been invested with the kingdom of France by Pope Julius II, set off to claim his prize. Although the campaign resulted in no more than English possession of Tournai, at least Henry Pole had the honour of being included in the army that won the first territorial gains from France in seventy-five years.[83] Appointed a captain of the middle-ward, which was under the king's direct command,[84] Henry's duties also included responsibility for 'the good rule and guiding of his people at his parcel and charge, as he will answer for them to the King'.[85] On 25 September, following the fall of Tournai, Henry VIII ceremonially entered the city and attended Mass in the cathedral before knighting forty-nine men 'who had distinguished themselves in the campaign'.[86] Henry Pole must have discharged his duties successfully for he was among these forty-nine men and, like his father, knighted following his first military campaign.[87] The entire event must have been an overwhelming experience for Henry, an exciting initiation into the art of warfare for any young man. Between 35,000 and 40,000 men marched under the king of England's banner, no expense was spared on artillery, armour and display, while the young nobles had the opportunity of sitting in the presence of the Holy Roman emperor himself.

Although Henry was knighted in 1513, by 1514 he enjoyed the superior title of Lord Montague. There has been some discussion over whether this was a courtesy title or whether Henry had actually been created a baron by word of mouth. He was not summoned to sit in the House of Lords until December 1529, and as his mother continued, from time to time, to be referred to as Lady Montague, we must deduce that it was probably a courtesy title.[88] It was not unusual for the sons of earls to be known by baronial titles and be summoned to the House of Lords by that title as Henry was in 1529.[89] His entitlement to the barony of Montague was as the descendant of Simon de Montague, created Lord Montague in 1299, the grandfather of William de Montague, first earl of Salisbury.[90] The first surviving reference which alludes to Henry as Lord Montague was made in 1514, possibly October, in a document which describes Arthur Pole as the brother of Lord Montague.[91] This is also the first record of Arthur's arrival at court, upon which he was to make quite an impression. Of all Margaret's sons, it was Arthur, her second son, who proved to be the supreme courtier, and his career suggests that, like his maternal grandfather, the duke of Clarence, he was an attractive and charming young man.

Arthur's entrance onto the court stage appears to have occurred in 1514 when he was included among those who accompanied Mary Tudor, the king's younger sister, to France for her marriage to King Louis XII. His inclusion may indicate one of those rare instances of patronage exercised on behalf of the Pole family by Margaret's in-laws, the Verneys. Mary's chamberlain was Sir Ralph Verney, who, by 1496, had married Eleanor Pole, Richard Pole's sister. As a result of his royal connections Sir Ralph had enjoyed an enhanced royal career, becoming chamberlain first to Princess Margaret then to Princess Mary following Margaret's marriage to the king of Scotland. Eleanor had been one of Queen Elizabeth's favourite ladies-in-waiting and had also enjoyed the good will of Margaret Beaufort, the king's mother. Although relations between Margaret and her in-laws appear never to have been close, the benefits of a connection with the new countess of Salisbury probably prompted this belated act of patronage in 1514. As Princess Mary's chamberlain Sir Ralph would be responsible for appointments to her household, and his influence was probably needed to obtain Arthur a place. These positions were highly prized due to the French court's reputation for elegance and sophistication, and Arthur's command of French must therefore have been, at the least, competent. Margaret probably felt that a spell at the French court would polish Arthur's skills as a courtier, imperative if he was to establish a successful career at court. Also summoned to join Mary's entourage was Anne Boleyn, whose French sophistication, mastered over a period of eight years, certainly helped her to make an impact upon the English court when she returned in 1521. Unfortunately, the valuable experience that Margaret hoped her son would gain in France ended prematurely. Mary's marriage had taken place on 9 October 1514, but, not quite three months later, Louis died on 31 December. It is impossible to be sure when Mary's attendants began to return home, especially as events were complicated by her marriage to Charles Brandon, but presumably all were back in England by 2 May when the two penitent newly-weds landed at Dover. Although Arthur could not have spent longer than seven months at the French court, the experience he did gain, combined with his own natural talents, was enough to guarantee him a successful career at Henry's court during the early part of the reign.

By 1516 Arthur Pole was a squire of the body with an annuity of £33 6s 8d for life, while his debut on the jousting field also took place that year.[92] Jousting should not be dismissed as merely a frivolous sport; those chosen to take part had an important responsibility. Much as the pressure is on an international football team today to play well, members of the jousting team were also expected to give reputable performances, especially if foreign royalty or dignitaries were being entertained. A joust could attract large crowds of spectators, the atmosphere was one of carnival with successful jousters becoming the heroes of the day and enjoying all the attendant adulation. Nevertheless, it was a very dangerous sport. The horses used were of a substantial height and weight in order to bear a rider in full armour and a bard (horse armour), while 'the power and weight involved as two riders approached each other at a combined speed of about 50 mph with that force directed at each other through the extended length of their lances'[93] reveals the extensive risks involved. Clearly, those chosen to joust would have to be strong and athletic with courage and boldness. It was important for Arthur, lacking the inheritance to which his elder brother looked forward, to shine at such activities, and on 7 July 1517 he was led onto the field as a member of the king's own team to joust before the Flemish ambassadors at Greenwich Palace.[94] The opposing team was led by the experienced Charles Brandon, duke of Suffolk, and the tournament was a huge success, fulfilling Henry's intention thoroughly to impress the ambassadors. First to enter was Sir Edward Guildford, acting as marshal of the jousts, attended by twenty-four trumpeters who heralded the start of proceedings. Following them came forty Spears[95] who proved a spectacular sight in their crimson uniforms riding horses bearing silver trappers. Last to enter was the king himself, who led his fourteen challengers, including Arthur Pole, and the duke of Suffolk leading his fourteen answerers. Each knight ran six courses, and that it was a nail-biting event is indicated by a supposed report that 506 spears were broken in total. Following the jousts the king gave a magnificent banquet at which twenty different sorts of jellies were served sculpted in the form of animals and castles. After seven hours at the banqueting table, the revellers danced until the early hours of the morning.[96]

Arthur's debut on the jousting field had been a heady experience and one that he was keen to repeat. Therefore, three years later his jousting skills were sufficiently practised to earn him a prize at the Field of the Cloth of Gold.[97] Margaret must have looked on with great satisfaction as the careers of both her eldest sons appeared to flourish, and in September 1518 they were involved in the reception of the French embassy in London. This event is significant, for it clearly illustrates the extent of royal favour enjoyed by Arthur Pole. While Lord Montague entered London in procession as one of the young gentlemen of honour, his brother followed him as one of six recently created gentlemen of the privy chamber.[98] It is important to remember that those invited into the inner sanctum of the privy chamber were invited by the king himself; they were the men he considered to be his friends and with whom he wished to spend time. In addition to entertaining and amusing the king, the gentlemen of the privy chamber were also expected to carry out various other duties such as conveying sensitive messages or acting in an ambassadorial capacity. Arthur must have carried out such tasks, for on 12 September 1518 he was given the considerable sum of £66 13s 4d 'to be by hym employd aboute certain of the king's busignes'.[99] Described by Sebastian Guistinian as 'the very soul of the King',[100] the gentlemen of the privy chamber were in a powerful position, and membership of such an elite and privileged group promised to boost Arthur's burgeoning career still further.

Of Margaret's remaining three children, Reginald, Ursula and Geoffrey, Reginald had taken his BA at Oxford in 1515, and in 1518 the king presented him as dean to the collegiate church of Wimborne Minster. A little later two prebends in Salisbury Cathedral were bestowed upon him. Finally, in 1521, he left England for the University of Padua, having been presented with £100 from the king for his first year of study, and probably to be received annually.[101] Margaret's youngest son, Geoffrey, might have been a little too young to make any great impression at court as yet, and this might have been the reason for his sister's equally low profile. No evidence indicates that Ursula ever served in the queen's household or in the household of Henry VIII's sister, Mary, as we would expect. Nonetheless, on 22 November 1513 the king commanded that several gowns and kirtles with various costly materials for edging and lining 'be delyvred unto our dear and wellbeloved cousin Ursula Poulle'.[102] The sumptuousness of the gowns and materials, combined with the style of her address, reveals the king's generosity and her status as a member of the royal family. This is not surprising when even abroad the Poles were recognized as members of Henry VIII's family. On 16 February 1515, Sir Robert Wingfield wrote to Henry VIII from Innsbruck concerning the duke of Milan: 'if my lady of Devonshire your aunt have [a daughter] of age that is to marry, or my lady of Saly[sbery] think verily the said duke would be more [ready to] be joined with your blood than with any other.'[103] Indeed, Ursula's greatest claim to fame was to be her spectacular marriage. Margaret's elevation had greatly improved her children's prospects on the marriage market, and she must have breathed a sigh of relief that no marriage had been arranged for her eldest son prior to 1512!

As Margaret's heir and the future earl of Salisbury, Lord Montague was a valuable commodity on the marriage market. No doubt numerous approaches were made to the countess regarding the marriage of her son, but the young lady who eventually became Lady Montague and the future countess of Salisbury was Jane Neville. The daughter of George Neville, Lord Bergavenny, Jane was a distant kinswoman of Montague's, both being descended from the Beauchamp earls of Worcester and Joan Beaufort. The date of Montague's marriage is not recorded, and the surviving documents, which concern negotiations for the marriage, are not dated. It is certain, however, that they were man and wife by March 1519, when the duke of Buckingham presented Lady Montague with £6 6s 8d, but they were no doubt married earlier than this, probably by 1517.[104] Although marriage to the future earl of Salisbury was an advantageous match for a baron's daughter, Jane herself was quite a catch. In 1517 Bergavenny was at least forty-eight years old and it was quite unlikely that he would father any more children.[105] Therefore, at the time of her marriage Jane was co-heiress[106] to his considerable lands, assessed in 1527 at £500, which made him one of the leading noblemen in Kent.[107] Furthermore, he held manors in the county of Monmouth, and in Berkshire, Essex, Hampshire, Norfolk, Shropshire, Staffordshire, Suffolk, Surrey, Sussex, Warwickshire, Wiltshire and Worcester-shire.[108] Although it is impossible to be sure what exactly was agreed to, as these documents are only drafts of articles made during the negotiations, they do reveal that Margaret and Bergavenny were tough negotiators. Bergavenny requested an immediate jointure worth £200 a year, to which Margaret agreed, providing Bergavenny made a reciprocal estate upon his daughter and Lord Montague. Moreover, if Bergavenny failed to have male issue he wished to be paid 1,000 marks by the countess, but also agreed to pay 1,000 marks should he have male issue, a sum Margaret tried to raise to £2,000.[109] In addition, Bergavenny wished it to be made clear that Montague would inherit all Margaret's estates, only allowing the countess freedom to dispose of issues amounting to £666 13s 4d.[110] In another article Bergavenny went further, requesting that Margaret place her whole estate in the hands of feoffees, leaving £1,000 a year to her use for life, and Bergavenny would reciprocate with his estate, saving those lands in tail male and others to the value of £300 for his wife. Of course, should he have male issue then such an agreement would not apply. Fortunately, the arrangements for the actual wedding celebrations were more straightforward. Margaret was to pay for her son's apparel and Bergavenny for his daughter's, while the cost of meat and drink on the day of the marriage, and of the licence, were to be equally borne by the countess and Bergavenny.

At some point between 1519 and 1522 Arthur Pole's marriage took place.[111] Jane Pickering, née Lewknor, was a young widow and mother probably aged sixteen or seventeen in 1519.[112] Margaret must have been particularly pleased with this marriage as Jane was the daughter of Sir Roger Lewknor of Trotton, Sussex, by his first wife Eleanor Tuchet. In 1519 Jane was his only child, her mother having died sometime after 1503, and as his second wife Sir Roger had married Constance Hussey. Constance was born in 1458, and therefore by 1519 she was sixty-one years old having borne her husband no children.[113] Sir Roger himself was fifty years old, elderly by sixteenth-century standards, and hence it was most likely that Jane would remain her father's only child and a considerable heiress.[114] The Lewknors were an old and prominent Sussex family, and among his manors Sir Roger held Bodiam in Sussex along with its impressive moated castle dating back to the fourteenth century. In addition, he held lands in Northampton-shire, Middlesex, Oxfordshire, Leicestershire, Huntingdonshire and Bedfordshire.[115] Sir Roger's lands, providing an annual income of approximately £480,[116] were worth almost as much as Lord Bergavenny's and, as Jane was his only daughter, she might have stood to inherit much more than her sister-in-law, Jane Neville. In fact, Sir Roger's income exceeded even that of Sir David Owen of Cowdray, Henry VII's illegitimate half-uncle, who was still honoured at the Tudor court.[117] For a second son lacking the brilliant prospects of his elder brother, this was an extremely lucrative match.

Obviously, the prospects of Margaret's youngest son, Geoffrey, were even less promising, but nevertheless he too contracted marriage to an heiress. By July 1525 Geoffrey had married Constance Pakenham, one of the two daughters of Sir Edmund Pakenham of Sussex.[118] Sir Edmund died in 1528 and his inheritance was divided between his two daughters, Constance and Katherine.[119] As a result, Geoffrey enjoyed the possession of manors in Sussex and the Isle of Wight, where his mother held the manor of Swainstone, the largest manor on the island.[120] In addition to ensuring that her sons concluded advantageous matches, these marriages also illustrate Margaret's attempts to augment her lands in the south, concentrating especially upon Sussex. This ambition is not surprising, for Margaret held manors in all the southern counties except for Sussex and Surrey, resulting in a lacuna among her holdings along the southern coast. Her sons' marriages were therefore intended to remedy that and generally reinforce her power and influence in the south. Over and above this, Lord Bergavenny's Welsh lands in the county of Monmouth would, should Jane inherit them, complement perfectly the three manors held by Margaret in the same county.

While her sons had been found the most suitable of brides, Margaret's daughter, Ursula, was no less well served in the provision of a husband. Of all her children's marriages, Ursula's is the most outstanding. Consequently it is the one for which most evidence survives and the only one that can be definitely dated. On 20 October 1518 Ursula was married to Henry Stafford, only son and heir of Edward Stafford, third duke of Buckingham.[121] The duke of Buckingham was the greatest peer in the realm, an honour his son one day expected to enjoy. Ursula, as duchess of Buckingham, would be one of the highest-ranking ladies in England, outranking her own mother in status. Moreover, her husband stood to inherit 124 manors, 12 castles, 9 hundreds, 11 boroughs, 9 forests, 24 parks, the advowson of 58 churches and 65 other properties![122] Henry Stafford's ancestry was equally impressive. A kinsman of the Poles, he was descended from Thomas of Woodstock, Edward III's youngest son. His father, a man of great pride who considered that 'women of the Stafford family were no game for Comptons or Tudors', had no qualms about an alliance with the Pole family, nor should he. Ursula's father was Henry VII's cousin, while her mother's lineage was as impeccable as the duke's. Nevertheless, Ursula was not Buckingham's first choice. Initially he had approached the earl of Shrewsbury, first in 1509 and again in 1516, but on both occasions Shrewsbury had declined due to the exorbitant terms he considered Buckingham was demanding. Buckingham's approach in 1516 is evident from a letter written by Sir Richard Sacheverell to Shrewsbury. Apparently Wolsey, having initially suggested Ursula as a suitable bride ('My Lady Salisbury has a good young lady to her daughter'), proceeded to promote Shrewsbury's daughter when Buckingham refused the match with Ursula.[123] Two years later, however, Buckingham accepted Ursula as his son's bride. Although an annuitant of Margaret, Wolsey would not have suggested a marriage of which the king disapproved; hence Henry VIII's support of the match suggests that he was not overly concerned about the succession at this time. The marriage of Henry Stafford and Ursula Pole united two very respectable claims to the throne, a fact of which neither Henry nor Wolsey would have been unaware.

By 1518 Buckingham was ready to negotiate the terms for his son's marriage. Having spent considerable sums of money obtaining suitable marriages for his daughters, the duke was determined to drive a hard bargain for the marriage of his son in order to recoup some of those expenses.[124] Margaret's keenness for the marriage is evident from her acceptance of all Buckingham's demands. In 1512 Buckingham had paid Thomas Howard, son of the earl of Surrey, 2,000 marks as dowry for his daughter Elizabeth and, in 1519, another 2,000 marks on the marriage of his daughter Mary to Lord Bergavenny.[125] As Ursula's dowry, Buckingham required 3,000 marks from Margaret with a further 1,000 marks if she should obtain certain lands from the king.[126] Although marriage with the son of a duke was more advantageous than marriage with the son of an earl, as Thomas Howard was in 1512, 4,000 marks was still a very large sum for a dowry. Not surprisingly, Buckingham had to accept that such an amount could not be paid all at once and agreed to receive regular instalments over the next six years with completion by Christmas 1524. However, Buckingham was obliged to settle lands worth £500 upon Ursula after his death and, should her husband predecease her, she was to enter the lands immediately in the duke's lifetime.[127] Both Carol Rawcliffe and Barbara Harris have mistakenly claimed that Margaret settled lands worth 700 marks upon the couple.[128] The mistake appears to have originated from Sir William Dugdale, to whom Harris refers.[129] In reality, Margaret enfeoffed to use lands worth 700 marks only to ensure the payment of Ursula's dowry.[130] As with Lord Montague's marriage, Margaret was to cover the expense of her daughter's wedding apparel, although all other costs would be borne by Buckingham.[131] Upon the marriage, Margaret's maintenance of her daughter ceased, and Ursula entered the duke's household, where she enjoyed a luxurious and cosseted lifestyle in the company of her scholarly young husband. An inventory of the young couple's apparel and wardrobe, taken in 1521 after Buckingham's arrest, provides a fascinating insight into the splendour and magnificence which characterized their lives. Garments of velvet, satin and damask are interspersed with those of cloth of gold and cloth of silver, not to mention other items such as elaborate horse harnesses, tapestries and carpets. For instance:

> A hole hors harness of crymsyn velvet, fringed with damaske cloth of gold, and a pilyon of crymsyn velvet for my Lady, embroidered with damaske cloth of gold . . . A dublet of cloth of sylver, lyned through and underlayd with damaske cloth of gold, and lined with white sarcenet through, with a placard . . . A gowne of damaske cloth of gold, lined with crymsyn saten . . . A gowne of crymsyn velvet, perled, and lined with damaske cloth of gold, A christening gown of blewe velvet, furred and powdered with armins.[132]

During this period the fortunes of the Pole family were at their zenith. Margaret, as countess of Salisbury, was not only one of the wealthiest peers in England but also enjoyed the favour of the king and a warm friendship with Queen Catherine. Her eldest son had discharged himself honourably in battle and occupied a respectable position at court. Despite being a younger son, Arthur's attributes had earned him the king's good opinion and a coveted and privileged place as one of the gentlemen of the privy chamber. Even though Margaret had paid dearly for her childrens' marriages, she had achieved her aims and each son had married an heiress while their sister was the future duchess of Buckingham. In addition, her scholarly son Reginald looked forward to a successful career in the Church, encouraged and supported by the king himself. Margaret had certainly worked hard to consolidate her good fortune for the benefit of herself and her family. However, 'fortune' is the crucial word, for as the wheel revolves, those who reach the top must inevitably fall and, with hindsight, it was indeed at the very moment of Margaret's greatest success that the wheel began the inexorable revolution downwards.

3

The Countess of Salisbury:
A Female Magnate

❧

'I am become the most perfect Empress of my own Will.'[1]

'To take away the empire from a man, and to give it to a woman, seemeth to be an evident token of thine anger toward us Englishmen',[2] lamented Thomas Becon to God at the accession of Mary I. For Becon, the divinely ordained structure had been turned upside down. In consequence of the Fall and Eve's transgression, women were not only to suffer the pains of childbirth, but they were also to be subject to the authority of their husbands: 'the head of every man is Christ; and the head of woman is the man; and the head of Christ is God.'[3] The received opinions regarding the position and role of women were clear. Considered physically, socially and intellectually inferior to men, it was only right and proper that they should be ruled by men; a wife 'sholde be subget to hire housbonde' for if 'the womman hath the maistrie, she maketh to muche desray'.[4] Within such a context Margaret Pole can be described, without any exaggeration, as a rare phenomenon, and that rarity sprang from a combination of two things. Firstly, she was restored to the earldom of Salisbury in her own right, one of only two women so honoured throughout the whole of the sixteenth century.[5] This meant that, unlike a dowager, she would not have to retire into the background upon the majority of her son. Secondly, she was a widow, which gave her the legal status of *femme sole*, in other words, she was an independent figure able to make her own decisions and was not constrained to submit to the authority of a husband.[6] If Margaret had held the Salisbury lands because she was the widow of the earl of Salisbury, one of the king's tenants-in-chief, the king's feudal rights would have meant that he would have been in control of her marriage. Although the king and his ministers were not known to force widows to marry against their will, they did exert considerable pressure on them at times.[7] However, Margaret as countess in her own right was the tenant-in-chief herself, and therefore the king's authority over her marriage extended merely to an expression of his desire should he wish her to remarry, and to the granting of his permission should Margaret wish to marry a chosen individual. Consequently, she refused an offer of marriage from Sir William Compton, one of Henry's favourite courtiers, and did so without incurring the king's displeasure. As head of her family with responsibility for the rule and administration of extensive estates, it is clear that the requirements of Margaret's position were in direct contradiction to the role advocated for women. As landlord, Margaret wielded authority over her officers, servants and tenants, the majority of whom were men. As countess, accountable for negotiating the marriages of her children and augmenting her estates, she would have to deal with her peers, all of whom were male, on an equal footing. As peeress, she would provide advice to, and look after the interests of, her affinity, the majority of whom were men. Margaret's position was indeed incongruous, but such situations were not unknown.

Historians now accept that there was a definite breach between what was advised for women and what, in practice, occurred. Although women were not permitted to hold any public office, this restriction did not apply to any offices that were inherited as part of a fief. As Pollock and Maitland explain, although women had no public functions, regarding private law they enjoyed equality to men.[8] As a result those women, especially widows, who inherited fiefs could find themselves wielding considerable authority over men, for instance when they presided over their manor courts, ensured the king received the required military service and maintained good order among the tenants on their estates. For example, Elizabeth de Burgh, the youngest daughter of Gilbert de Clare, lived as a widow for forty years and administered an estate worth approximately £3,000 in the late 1320s, while in the fifteenth century Joan, Lady Abergavenny, widow of William Beauchamp, administered an estate worth in the region of £2,000 a year.[9] Furthermore, some women found themselves holding offices which were traditionally male, like Joan, Lady Abergavenny, who in 1431 was one woman amongst 156 commissioners appointed to raise a royal loan in Warwickshire. In 1236 Ela, countess of Salisbury, found herself sheriff of Wiltshire and chose to exercise the office herself, while Ranulf Glanville's wife, Bertha, held the shrievalty of Yorkshire.[10] Furthermore, Margaret Beaufort, Henry VII's mother, was declared *femme sole* in the first Parliament of her son's reign despite that fact that she had a living husband, Lord Stanley. She was not only responsible for running her own estates, but also presided over a regional court which dealt with royal business. Her position was such that it provoked a debate in the Inner Temple concerning the eligibility of a woman who was *femme sole* to be appointed a justice of the peace.[11] Margaret Pole, as countess of Salisbury, was a similarly independent woman but the important question is: how did she cope with her position? Did she wield the powers she theoretically possessed? Did she attempt to operate as a 'male' member of the aristocracy or accept the conventions of her sex? How far did the restrictions of her gender limit her ability to fulfil her role as an independent member of the nobility? Attempting to provide answers to these questions will hopefully reveal something of the essence of Margaret, as a woman and as a peeress, and shed more light upon the attitudes towards women and authority during the reign of Henry VIII.

It has already been shown in chapter 2 that Margaret fully subscribed to the idea of conspicuous consumption and maintained four impressive and luxuriously furnished households. This is understandable, for in a hierarchical society unsupported by a standing army, conspicuous consumption served to overawe those under a noble's authority by revealing the massive resources that could be brought to bear should they attempt to flout that authority. One method of advertising wealth and power was through an impressive household, something which Margaret did to dazzling effect. Therefore, her lifestyle, thus far, does not appear to have differed greatly from that of her male counterparts. However, there were other responsibilities incumbent upon an aristocrat favoured with the kind of status that the countess of Salisbury enjoyed. Barbara Harris has revealed that aristocratic women were very active in petitioning those 'about' the king for favours, and that many of these women consequently maintained relationships with some of the most powerful men at court.[12] However, Margaret's position differed in that she herself was one of these powerful figures. With lands and offices at her disposal, influence with the royal family through friendship and kinship and, after 1525, an important court office, it is not surprising to discover that her favour and assistance was solicited. Her response was in full accordance with the expectations of the nobility, and she utilized her position to advance her relatives and associates and strengthen her family's relationship with other noble and gentry families. By being a 'good lord' and promoting the members of her affinity she advertised her power and standing and encouraged others to look to herself and her family as prospective patrons.

Few court offices were available for well-born ladies; hence Margaret was in a very enviable position. As governess to the king's daughter she had the potential to influence appointments to Princess Mary's household. Just as her brother-in-law, Sir Ralph Verney, had used his position as chamberlain to Mary Tudor to obtain a place in her household for Margaret's son Arthur, Margaret did the same with her position as Princess Mary's governess. Therefore, we find among the ladies on the princess's household list of July 1525 Catherine Pole, Margaret's grand-daughter who was a similar age to the princess; Constance Pole, Margaret's daughter-in-law; and Mary Dannet, one of Margaret's annuitants whose family had enjoyed a long association with the Pole family.[13] Furthermore, Sir Thomas Denys, who replaced Sir Giles Greville as Princess Mary's comptroller in 1526, was steward of Margaret's manor of Pyworthy in Devon and probably owed his position to the countess.[14] Although the princess's household was disbanded in December 1533, Margaret continued to use her influence on behalf of Mary's servants. In March 1534 she wrote to her cousin Arthur Plantagenet, Viscount Lisle, on behalf of Richard Baker who, by 1533, had risen to the position of gentle-man usher.[15] It was Sir Brian Tuke, in whose household Baker's wife Alice had served as governess, who first approached Lisle on Baker's behalf in January 1534, writing that 'both my said Lady Mary, the King's daughter, and also the Lord Hussey, late chamberlain there, sent to me desiring me to be good unto the said Mr Baker'.[16] By March Margaret's help had also been enlisted. Although by now Lisle had agreed to find a place for Baker, to ensure that he would do his utmost Margaret wrote 'that where my friend Richard Baker is by your favour appointed to the king's service in Calais, it may please you to be good lord unto him', and, employing her friendly relationship with Lisle and their bonds of kinship, she continued, 'and the rather for my sake, in all such things as ye may do him favour therein'.[17] As Lisle's cousin and a high-ranking member of the aristocracy, Margaret's intervention encouraged Tuke to write once more to Lisle explaining that 'the recommendation of him unto me from my said lady, hath moved me to be bolder upon your lordship than I have deserved'.[18] Obviously, Tuke felt Margaret's involvement was significant enough to move Lisle and that her recommendation of Baker justified his approach to him. In addition to her position at court, Margaret was a substantial landowner, which also gave her regional influence, influence which she was again able to use to benefit family and friends. Thus, in 1529 she nominated her son Geoffrey to Parliament as MP for Wilton, a borough in her possession, and Geoffrey Lee, a member of her affinity and an annuitant, as MP for Portsmouth.[19]

The education of young ladies in the households of noble women was an accepted way for women to become involved in creating and maintaining the patronage networks of their family.[20] Margaret's household, while obviously functioning in this way, also provided a suitable place for her various grandchildren. Included among her eleven ladies in 1538 were five of her granddaughters: Lady Margaret Stafford, Ursula's daughter; Winifred, Lord Montague's youngest daughter; Katherine, one of Geoffrey's daughters; and Mary and Margaret Pole, the daughters of Margaret's late son, Arthur.[21] Of the six other ladies, three were married to members of Margaret's affinity. Johanne Frankelyn was married to Margaret's receiver-general and comptroller, Johanne Cholmeley was the wife of one of Margaret's annuitants, and Anne Ragland was married to one of the Pole family's dependants. The identities of the three remaining ladies, Dorothy Erneley, Alice Denstill and Elizabeth Cheyney, have proved more difficult to establish. It is unclear whether they were children sent to be educated alongside the countess's granddaughters or whether they were adults. Whatever their exact position in Margaret's house-hold, a preliminary investigation suggests that they were members of prominent local families. Dorothy Erneley could have been connected to Sir John Erneley, chief justice of the common pleas who died in 1521. A man who had lands in Surrey and Sussex, he had been an associate of Lord Lisle, which makes the presence of a

relative in Margaret's household likely.[22] Equally, Dorothy might
have been a member of the family of William Erneley, an established Sussex gentleman who was a fellow justice of the peace and
colleague of Sir Geoffrey Pole.[23] Alice Denstill was possibly related
to John Densell of Cornwall who died in 1536. He was in the
service of Lord Lisle, retained for his legal counsel along with
Edmond Mervyn, Geoffrey Pole's brother-in-law.[24] Elizabeth
Cheyney may very well have been connected to Sir Thomas
Cheyney, who became treasurer of Henry VIII's household and
lord warden of the Cinque Ports.[25] In 1535 a marriage was
arranged between Thomas's son and heir, John, and Margaret
Neville, daughter of Lord Bergavenny.[26] Thus Elizabeth Cheyney's
introduction to Margaret's household would have been made
possible through John Cheyney's marriage to Lord Montague's
sister-in-law. Although by 1538 Margaret's importance at court
had waned, her former position as governess to a princess would
still make her household an attractive proposition to the daughters
of the local gentry. Under her tutelage the young ladies would
receive all necessary instruction regarding the required social skills,
while her domestic chaplain, John Helyar, might also have been
employed as tutor to her young charges.[27]

The exchange of gifts and granting of annuities was another
method of strengthening kinship networks for it gave 'donors and
recipients a specific claim on each other's resources and assistance'.[28] Again, this was an area in which women could play an
active role. Margaret's known annuitants included dependants,
associates and servants but her most illustrious annuitants were
Thomas Wolsey, Thomas Cromwell and Charles Brandon, duke of
Suffolk. Receiving £20 a year, Cromwell's services were apparently
not valued quite as highly as Wolsey's, who had been granted 100
marks a year![29] However, Charles Brandon received the ultimate
annuity when he was granted the extremely generous sum of £40 in
1514, an amount he was still receiving in 1538.[30] The giving of gifts
and tokens was an area in which Honour Lisle was particularly
busy as the *Lisle Letters* reveal, and Margaret also employed such
means. On 9 July 1525 she sent the marquis of Exeter three female
falcons,[31] and in June 1536 she herself received the more intimate
gift of a token from Honour Lisle who was trying to obtain a
position for her daughter with the queen and wished to enlist
Margaret's help. On this occasion Margaret had to apologize to

Honour for not having a token with which to reciprocate.[32] Proof of Margaret's generosity to religious institutions is, surprisingly, rather scant. She presented a taper of 3 lb in weight to St Mary Bothaw, a church close to Le Herber whose priest she employed at her London residence, and one to the church of All Hallows Staining, London.[33] Furthermore, she founded a hospital near Warblington and was a patron of Christchurch Priory, Hampshire, where she commissioned her impressive tomb chapel.[34] However, any more evidence of this kind is lacking, as is proof of marked socializing within her peer group. Although it is most likely that she did play a more active role than surviving evidence indicates, it was possibly not as pronounced a role as we might expect.

From 1525 until 1533 Margaret held the position of governess to Princess Mary, and although there were short periods of leave, the majority of her time was spent with Mary. The princess's household did entertain, and was entertained by, local notables, which gave Margaret the opportunity for wider socializing. Nevertheless, her attendance on the princess meant that she was often absent from her own households and the court. As a result, when Lord Montague visited Mary in 1533, Richard Lister, Margaret's chief steward, accompanied him in order to discuss estate business with his mistress.[35] Indeed, in 1528 a letter written by a member of her council concerning the dispute over Canford and her debt to the king, stated in her defence that 'her charge of attendaunce apon the prynces grace and so far frome the Kyngs grace as they be so that she canne nott sue unto his grace after suche facyon in her one persone as showld be her helpe and remedy in that behalfe'.[36] Clearly, the countess did not have a great deal of time for the type of socializing necessary to maintain her family's links with other aristocratic and local gentry families. The problem of Margaret's distance from court was compounded by her gender. The countess of Salisbury's counterparts, titled heads of families, were all men and therefore her relationship with them would be one of decorum, distance and formality. She could not indulge in such backslapping activities as gambling and carousing into the night, yet it was those very activities which often created deeper and more effective friendships. As a woman, Margaret was clearly at a disadvantage, and it is here that the importance and significance of her sons becomes clear. Evidence suggests that good relations with other noble families were facilitated for the most part by

Margaret's sons, and especially by her eldest son, Henry, Lord Montague, who proved to be the driving force. A loyal friend, an affable companion and a man of intelligence, he was described by Martin de Cornoça in 1534 as 'a very virtuous, prudent and magnanimous gentleman, very much loved and respected by all classes'.[37] With such attributes it is not surprising that he was successful in this sphere. Moreover, as Margaret's son and heir, any alliances made would be mutually beneficial upon his succession to the earldom. The Pole family sat within the centre of an extensive network of connections which it is important to understand. Examining the family's relationships with those to whom they were linked by marriage, by blood and by friendship will help to reveal the roles of Margaret and her sons more clearly and the position of the family within contemporary society.

To obtain a strategic marriage was important, but it was only the beginning. To ensure that the maximum benefits resulted from it depended on an ensuing good relationship between the spouses and their families. Obviously, Margaret's most important in-laws were the Staffords, and fortunately relations between the duke of Buckingham and the Pole family were extremely warm. Barbara Harris has claimed that this was because the head of the family was a woman and therefore not the duke's rival at court.[38] There might be some truth in this, as Margaret would not be as politically active as her male counterpart. Although she enjoyed the king's favour, she would never sit on the council and wield influence in that way. Another element which contributed to the success of the relationship was the fruitful marriage of Ursula and Lord Stafford. Within two years of marriage Ursula had fulfilled her most important duty by providing a son and heir, and Buckingham was fond of her. Addressing her as daughter, in 1519 he gave 'to my daughters Ursula and Mary £3 6s 8d'.[39] Ursula and her husband remained in the duke's household after their marriage, where her brothers visited her frequently and took the opportunity to maintain and develop their friendship with the duke. In 1519 Buckingham granted 'to my cousin Arthur Pole, 20s', and in March of that year he gambled and lost £15 to Lord Montague and his son-in-law, Lord Bergavenny. He lost a further £40 when he gambled with his brother, the earl of Wiltshire, and Lord Montague, while in June he lost the phenomenal sum of £65 2s 9d dicing with Lord Montague yet again.[40] Indeed, so close were Buckingham and Margaret's two eldest sons that the Venetian ambassador, Antonio Surian, actually thought they were the duke's nephews.[41] After Buckingham's fall the Pole family endeavoured to continue the friendship with Ursula's husband, Lord Stafford. Margaret took one of their daughters into her household and paid 22s 6¾d towards her board during her stay in London in 1538, while Lord Montague and his brother Geoffrey continued to visit their brother-in-law.[42]

Cordial relations also existed between Lord Montague and his father-in-law, Lord Bergavenny. Barbara Harris has shown that this was not the case between Bergavenny and his father-in-law, Buckingham, and she has charted their reported quarrels up to 1519.[43] It is a testament to Montague's affability and diplomacy that he was able to maintain a friendship with both of them, and he may even have attempted to facilitate better relations between them. When the duke fell, Margaret, Montague and Arthur all fell under suspicion due to the closeness between the two families. However, it may be significant that Lord Bergavenny was also arrested for his connection to the duke, indicating that by 1521 Bergavenny was no longer considered the duke's enemy by contemporaries. Bergavenny's friendship with Lord Montague lasted until the former's death in 1535, despite an age gap of twenty years and the birth of Bergavenny's son, Henry, which disinherited Montague's wife. According to Jerome Ragland, one of Lord Montague's most trusted gentleman servants, Montague often lamented Bergavenny's death and described him as 'a nobyll man and assuryd a ffreend as any was lyvyng'.[44] He lent Bergavenny considerable sums of money which amounted to £1,000 and 600 marks at his death, and in 1532 Montague and others, including his son-in-law Lord Hastings, brother-in-law Lord Stafford and third cousin the marquess of Exeter, were enfeoffed to the use of Bergavenny and his heirs with the ultimate goal of fulfilling Bergavenny's will.[45] Montague was also appointed one of the executors of Bergavenny's will, which made the sons of Montague and his wife, Jane, heirs to use of manors in several counties in default of male issue to Bergavenny and his two brothers, Thomas and Edward.[46] Unfortunately, little evidence survives concerning the relationship between Montague and his wife, but, if we can believe Geoffrey Pole, the death of Jane affected her husband badly, causing him to lose interest in the state of the realm and the religious changes which before had concerned him.[47]

The marriage of Montague's eldest daughter, Catherine, to Francis, Lord Hastings, son of the earl of Huntingdon and Anne Stafford, sister of the duke of Buckingham, was of equal importance. The Hastings family had a respectable lineage, and a somewhat heroic one, for Francis was the great grandson of William, Lord Hastings, who was executed by Richard III in 1483. The family's main area of influence lay in Leicestershire and Yorkshire, but they also held manors in Buckingham, Wiltshire, Somerset, Devon and Cornwall through Francis's grandmother Mary, Lady Hungerford.[48] In 1532 the earl's revenues were worth just under £1,000.[49] Naturally, such a connection would further help to consolidate the Pole family's influence in the south, a policy consistently followed with regard to their various marriages. Indeed Winifred, Montague's youngest daughter, went on to marry Lord Hastings's younger brother, Thomas. Another benefit of this marriage was the royal favour enjoyed by the earl of Huntingdon: 'Throughout his life he seems to have been a favourite of the king.'[50] Moreover, he was also an ally of Anne Boleyn's father, the earl of Wiltshire, a man even Margaret was prepared to patronize.[51] Obviously, the connections Huntingdon enjoyed meant his influence and support was worth having, and, although evidence is slight, it seems relations between the two families were amicable. Geoffrey Pole informed his friend George Croftes that in the summer of 1538 'he hadd byn att the lord of Huntington's with his brother and byn a fortnight and made merry there'.[52] Of course, Huntingdon's seat at Stoke Poges in Buckinghamshire was only between twelve and fifteen miles away from Montague's seat at Medmenham and Margaret's residence at Bisham. Indeed, Montague and Huntingdon were on relaxed enough terms to complain to each other about the apparent submission of Parliament to the king's will in the 1530s.[53] Moreover, both Margaret and Lord Montague were greatly concerned for Lord Hastings's welfare. In 1534 Lord Montague, who was then at court, received the news that his son-in-law had fallen ill. It was the eve of St George, and immediately after he had discharged his ceremonial duty of bearing the sword before the king 'he rode straight unbeware to anybody into Leicestershire to my said Lord of Hastings, where he remaineth yet, though the said young lord be past danger'.[54] Although there might have been a mercenary element here as Francis's death would have deprived Catherine of her position as countess of Huntingdon and the Poles of an enduring connection with a wealthy and important family, two years later Margaret herself rushed to the young lord's bedside after he fell sick with a fever. Fevers were often contagious, but this did not prevent Margaret from risking her own health by staying with Francis while her household remained at Warblington.[55]

Relationships with those in-laws primarily linked to Montague were far more successful than with those in-laws connected to his brothers, Arthur and Geoffrey. Sir Edmund Pakenham's disenchantment with his son-in-law is clear from his will of 1528. Geoffrey was accorded only one mention when his wife, Constance, received 'the tenne pounds which I paide to hir husbonde Geffrey Poole for his interest that I had by him in the ferme of Gatcombe'.[56] Sir Edmund referred to Geoffrey as his daughter's husband, whereas he referred to his other son-in-law, Edmond Mervyn, as 'my sonne'. In addition, Mervyn received a number of bequests and was designated heir, with his wife, to the jointure of Pakenham's widow even though his wife was the younger daughter. Despite having attended an Inn of Court, Geoffrey was not appointed an executor of the will either; this fell to Pakenham's cousin Henry White and Edmond Mervyn.[57] The most likely explanation, considering Geoffrey's likeable and jovial personality, is that the debts he would run up in the 1530s had already begun to accrue and it was this that had earned Sir Edmund's disapproval.[58] Nevertheless, despite his lack of financial prudence Geoffrey fully understood the expectations engendered by kinship and marriage, and endeavoured to meet them. Both he and Edmund Mervyn became embroiled in a case brought before the court of requests in support of their mother-in-law, Katherine Pakenham. The dispute did not directly concern either Geoffrey or Mervyn as it involved the forcible expulsion in December 1529 of a William Downer from certain lands in Bosham which Katherine Pakenham claimed belonged to her. Nevertheless, Geoffrey and Mervyn backed their mother-in-law to the extent that all three were threatened with a £100 fine by order of the king himself for deliberately prolonging the proceedings. Although the outcome is not known, it seems that this dispute was still ongoing in 1539.[59] Despite the anxiety his behaviour over the years must have caused her, relations between Geoffrey and his wife, Constance, do appear to have been affectionate. She pleaded for his release from the Fleet prison in

September 1540, and in December 1552, during his exile, he sent a letter to her 'whom he pined to see after 4 years'.[60] In her will Constance stipulated that 'my bodye to be buryed in the Churche of Stoughton nere unto my deere and welbeloved husbande Syr Jeffrey Poole knighte deceased',[61] Although relations with his father-in-law could have been better, Geoffrey's marriage at least was a success, whilst Margaret also played a part in fostering links with the family, resulting in a mutually advantageous arrangement with Mervyn. A talented lawyer who was made sergeant-at-law in 1531 and who was also retained by Lord Lisle, he became an annuitant of the countess in receipt of 40s and was among those who acted upon her behalf in a legal capacity.[62]

Relations with the Lewknor family were far less successful than those with the Pakenhams due, in most part, to the clash of personalities between Arthur Pole and his irascible father-in-law, Sir Roger Lewknor. Arthur Pole's eagerness to obtain his father-in-law's lands to farm and the heavy-handed way he tried to achieve this led to a dispute which eventually involved Christopher More, the earl of Arundel, Sir Thomas More, Viscount Lisle and, ultimately, the king. From a letter written by Arthur most probably to Christopher More, an annuitant of Lewknor, Arthur proposed to pay Lewknor 300 marks a year for the lands, making the questionable claim that this was more than they were worth, whilst offering to allow him to retain the manor of Trotton.[63] Lewknor had no intention of relinquishing his lands and, full of indignation, turned to the earl of Arundel, who gave him his full support and made his feelings known in no uncertain terms. It appears that Arundel resented the Poles' emergence upon the Sussex scene, which stood to threaten his pre-eminence, and in 1531 his son also clashed with Geoffrey Pole over the latter's enclosure of Lysley Wood.[64] Arundel was aware that Margaret had been purchasing lands and arranging marriages for her sons which would increase her family's presence in Sussex, and was therefore keen to prevent Arthur taking possession of his father-in-law's lands. As a counterpoise to Arundel, Arthur went straight to the king, whose favour he obtained for his suit, the king being 'gretly miscontent' with Arundel. At this juncture Sir Thomas More became involved, required by the king 'to devyse a sharp letter' to the earl. However, More, always the diplomat, advised Arthur to send first 'a lovyng letter' followed by a sharper one should the first fail. Having obtained two letters from the king, one to Arundel and one to Lewknor which he required Christopher More to deliver, Arthur was more optimistic of Arundel's support. It would seem that the king felt Lewknor could not discharge competently the military requirements of his lands, and Arthur, exuding unconvincing self-sacrifice, explained to Christopher More that he did not desire the lands 'so much for my profit . . . but only for to do the kyngs graces servyce whych thyng the kyngs grace thynkyth my father-in-law as far onmet consyderyng both hys age and also the smale expeyence that he has had in the wars'. He apologized to Christopher More for getting him involved in such a difficult situation, adding: 'I know very well that it shall be a gret troble unto you to medell with such a man.' As the dispute gathered momentum it was reported to Arthur that Viscount Lisle did not support him. Lisle was under the unhappy impression that Margaret had informed her son of this, and wrote to Christopher More, who reassured him that 'it was a mere mistake, and did not grow by my lady'. He added that if Lewknor 'would not be good to his own child, and that shall become of her, it were pity he lived'.[65] He concluded by advising Lisle not to allow his friendship with the Pole family to be adversely affected by 'one unkindness and default', and offered to be a mediator between Lisle and Margaret. Clearly, the altercation had taken on unpleasant proportions, threatening as it did the good relations between Lisle and the Poles. We cannot be definite about the outcome of this struggle, but as Arthur was assessed for the 1524 subsidy at only £63, it suggests that his father-in-law had remained implacable despite the intervention of the king.[66] Margaret, again recognizing ability, and possibly as a reward for his mediation between Lisle and her family, added Christopher More to her list of annuitants, granting him the substantial sum of £10 a year for life.[67] He was also appointed one of Lord Lisle's attorneys and in 1532 was described as a 'gentleman which my Lord (Lisle) knoweth well'.[68]

The situation between Sir Roger Lewknor and the Pole family appears to have temporarily improved by 1526, possibly as a result of Lord Montague's intervention. In that year, on 10 April, Montague presented his brother, Reginald, to the rectory of Harting. Montague had been granted the right to present by Sir Roger and his wife, Constance, but it is significant that it was Montague who received this favour rather than Arthur, Sir Roger's own son-in-law.[69]

Certainly, problems with the Lewknor family were not at an end. If we accept the account of his widow, Jane, events after Arthur Pole's death reveal the countess of Salisbury and Lord Montague acting in unison with ruthless determination to secure the position of Arthur's children.[70] As things stood at Arthur's death in the late 1520s, his son Henry was heir to the bulk of his grandfather's lands, and obviously the fewer children Jane had by other marriages the better. To ensure that matters stayed that way, Margaret and Lord Montague kept the news of Arthur's death secret for a month while they formulated a plan of action. Lord Montague finally broke the news of her husband's death to Jane on a Friday. On the Saturday Arthur was buried at Bisham Priory and on the Sunday, two days after she received the news, Jane took a vow of perpetual chastity and the mantle and the ring. According to Jane, testifying some ten years later, Lord Montague, with the support of his mother, pressurized her into taking a vow of chastity when she was 'in exceeding great heaviness and sorrow and almost besides herself'. She maintained that Montague 'did earnestly instigate, persuade and procure' her to take the mantle and ring with the excuse that 'she should take it for a time to avoid suitors and other dangers'. This unpleasant situation came to light when Jane eventually disregarded her vow and went on to marry Sir William Barentyne. Pointedly, this marriage took place in 1539 after Lord Montague had been executed and Margaret had been arrested. Jane acted the moment she felt secure from her in-laws' objections and interference, and it is a comment upon the personalities and influence of both Margaret and Montague that they were prepared, and able, to wield such stern authority over Jane, forcing her to remain a widow against her will. Nor was she as safe as she thought after the family's fall, for an objection to her marriage was immediately raised, which brought the situation before the consistory court of London, where sentence was pronounced on 15 December 1540. It declared Jane's marriage to Barentyne invalid and their son, Drew, illegitimate.[71] The Barentynes retaliated, stating in their defence the fact that Jane had been pressurized into taking the vow. Following the intervention of the king, matters were finally settled by an act of Parliament in 1543/4.[72] It decided against the Pole family, declaring that the Barentyne heirs should be considered legitimate.[73]

In addition to those with whom the Poles were connected by marriage, there were others to whom links were formed due to their blood relationship with the family. Among these was Arthur Plantagenet, Viscount Lisle who, as the illegitimate son of Edward IV, was Margaret Pole's first cousin. Despite the misunderstanding during the Lewknor dispute, Lisle remained on very good terms with the Poles. Both families were established in Hampshire and, as such, moved in the same circles, regularly retaining the same annuitants and employing the same officers. While relations with Margaret were undoubtedly amicable, it was with Lord Montague that a more relaxed familiarity was enjoyed, and it was important to the Poles that this relationship was successful in light of Lisle's position. Muriel St Clare Byrne has shown that Lisle's appointments as vice-admiral, gentleman of the privy chamber and councillor, warden and keeper of the king's forest and park of Clarendon, constable of Porchester Castle and keeper of the forest of Bere 'consolidated his position as the most important nobleman in Hampshire, with influence at Court and patronage to dispense locally'.[74] As a result of Lisle's appointment as lord deputy of Calais in 1533, the level of friendship between Montague and the Lisles can be gleaned from letters regularly exchanged between them. So familiar was Montague with them that he felt able to warn Lisle's wife, Honour, whom he described as 'my friend', of her husband's extravagance without offending them, advising her: 'for the love of God, look upon it in the beginning, now.'[75] In 1534 Honour sent Montague the personal gift of a token, while Montague at various times assured Lisle that 'of no kinsman he hath he shall be more assured of to do him pleasure', pledging himself as 'yours assured my life during', and most commonly signing himself 'your loving cousin Henry Montague'.[76] The letters were sometimes no more than an exchange of news and pleasantries, for instance when Montague thanked Honour for the three barrels of herring she sent for himself and Lord Bergavenny, and then informed her of the contents of a galley recently arrived.[77] In this letter, as in others, Montague passed on the Lisles' recommendations to his mother and vice versa, but because of their greater familiarity with Montague, they found it easier to approach him rather than his mother. In 1537 Honour, who was trying to place her daughter at court again, wrote to Montague to speak to his mother about it. Montague replied that, though he would do all he could, 'But and it please you to write a letter to my lady my mother yourself it will sooner take effect.'[78] Previously, in

1534, it was Montague they again solicited in the hope that he could persuade his brother Reginald to grant the next avoidance of the vicarage of Braunton to a relative of their associate Hugh Yeo.[79] The friendship certainly worked to the mutual advantage of both families. The lord deputy granted Montague a walk in the forest of Bere and apparently the use of his house at Soberton, for which Montague offered profuse thanks.[80] As a further mark of trust between them, Montague was nominated as one of Lisle's proxies in the House of Lords in 1536, and earlier, in 1535, when Montague fell seriously ill, the Lisles received bulletins on his condition from three different people.[81] In the opinion of John Husee, a man who knew the Lisles extremely well, Lord Montague was someone 'your lordship loved well'.[82] Although they enjoyed a pleasant and relaxed relationship, and evidence would certainly indicate that Montague was fond of his mother's elderly cousin, we can be excused for wondering how deep these feelings of friendship actually ran in Honour Lisle's case. There is something exceedingly unpleasant about Honour busying herself in an attempt to buy her 'lovyng cosyn's' carpets a few months after his execution and being told 'there was none sold but that which my lord of Sussex had. All the best was kept for the King, so that there will be no help for carpets that way.'[83]

There is no question about the genuinely affectionate friendship that existed between Montague and his slightly younger third cousin, Henry Courtenay, marquess of Exeter.[84] Most of the evidence concerning their social contact originates from the witnesses questioned in 1538 at the time of the Pole family's fall. John Collins, Montague's chaplain, heard his master praise the marquess of Exeter, describing him as a man of very good mind and courage. In Collins's opinion, Exeter would have been an 'assuryd frynd' to Montague.[85] Constance Bontayn, one of the marchioness of Exeter's ladies, witnessed great familiarity between Montague and Exeter, believing Montague considered him an 'assured friend'.[86] Letters passed between Montague and the Exeters regularly, especially in 1535 and 1536 when the marquess was ill and Montague was concerned about his condition.[87] In fact, so well did Montague know his cousin that he was able to remark that Exeter was a poor patient, having been 'the most passyonate and impacient man in his sykness that ever he knew'![88] Reginald, writing to Exeter's son in 1553, is specific about the friendship between them. He speaks of the 'affection and love' which Exeter always exhibited towards Montague and himself, explaining that they had been 'so linked by God in sincere affection throughout their lives, He would not at the last hour allow them to be separated, both dying together for the same cause'.[89] The most convincing piece of evidence revealing Exeter's loyalty to Montague is provided by Montague himself, who stated that the marchioness had written to inform him that Exeter had offered, in council, to be 'bownde bodie for bodie for hym', and at a time when it was becoming increasingly dangerous to be closely associated with the Pole family.[90] In 1535 Montague was among those enfeoffed with several manors to the use of Exeter and his wife, while Montague, Robert Chidley and Anthony Harvy were the probable means by which the reversion of the manor of Northam, Devon was purchased by Exeter.[91]

Montague also socialized with other members of the nobility and gentry among whom he acted as adviser, colleague, friend and financier. In July 1532 he was granted the manor of Stapul in Somerset from the earl of Northumberland as a means for Northumberland to meet the payments of a loan Montague had given him.[92] He was on familiar terms with Elizabeth Darell, daughter of Sir Edward Darell and mistress of Sir Thomas Wyatt, providing her with advice regarding certain lands and attempting to negotiate the repayment of £100 owed to her by Sir Anthony Hungerford.[93] He also advised the apparently estranged wife of Humphrey Tyrell, was named in the marchioness of Dorset's will as one of her feoffees and was appointed chief steward of Tewkesbury Abbey, obviously happy to maintain his ancestral links with an abbey which had been in the patronage of his grandparents.[94] Geoffrey Pole also had a circle of associates but these tended to be ecclesiastical personages such as George Croftes, chancellor of Chichester Cathedral, and John Stokesley, bishop of London.[95] It has already been shown that Reginald's attendance at Oxford University undoubtedly helped to create the links that existed between Margaret and the staff and graduates of that university but, compared with Montague, his brothers played minor roles.

It was not only in the social sphere that Lord Montague's contribution was important. Certain privileges and requirements associated with his mother's position were predominantly male.

For instance, the countess of Salisbury's male counterpart would be summoned to sit in the House of Lords, but, as a woman, Margaret was denied such a place. Therefore, as peeresses were able to transmit their right to sit in the Lords to their husbands and sons, Margaret's eldest son was summoned in her stead.[96] This was not the only time Montague acted upon his mother's behalf. As a female landowner Margaret could only partially fulfil the military requirements of her estates. She could supply the men but she obviously could not lead them into battle, and consequently Montague stepped in to discharge this duty. In 1523 Thomas Denys, Margaret's steward of Pyworthy, wrote to his cousin James Gifford concerning 'my Lady of Salisburys tenantts of Pyworthy'. Ten of these tenants had been appointed 'to serve the kyngs grace in his warres under the ledyng of my lord Mountague your master'.[97] Again, in October 1536, it was to 'our right trusty and wellbeloved the Lord Mountague' that the king sent a summons to put in readiness 200 men 'in case need shall require you may within a days warning, both advance with all your force to such place as shall be limited unto you'.[98] Montague also represented his mother on commissions of the peace.[99] Had Margaret been male, as a prominent landowner in the southern counties, there would have been no question about her inclusion, but as she was a woman Montague was again required to stand in her place. Montague's own lands lay in Buckinghamshire and, from 1532 when he acquired Stapul, Somerset. However, between 1528 and 1537 he was appointed to commissions of the peace for Dorset, Hampshire, Wiltshire, Somerset and Sussex on behalf of his mother. In theory, an individual's position on a commission tended to reflect his local status.[100] Significantly, Montague, as the representative of the countess of Salisbury, occupied a respectable position. In the commission for Dorset in 1528 he was placed third after Wolsey and the duke of Norfolk; the lowest he ever came was in the commission for Hampshire in 1531 where he was the eleventh named, behind four ecclesiastics, two dukes, one earl, Viscount Lisle, Sir Thomas More and Sir Edward Haward. His brother Geoffrey also sat on this commission, nineteenth on the list.[101] In addition, Lord Montague enjoyed a limited role regarding the estates of the earldom. Further to acting in an advisory capacity he was bound, with his mother, in the recognizance of May 1513 to pay the £2,333 6s 8d 'for the redeeming of Salisbury's lands'.[102] As the act of Parliament restored Margaret alone, Montague's involvement in the recognizance was probably to guarantee, in the event of his mother's death, that this initial payment would still be made. In 1538 Margaret sold the Wyke in Middlesex, of which she was the owner, to William Bower, but the agreement of sale was between Margaret and Henry, Lord Montague on the one part and Bower on the other.[103] This might be a result of the articles of marriage agreed between Margaret and Lord Bergavenny for the marriage of Montague and Jane Neville, which attempted to constrain what Margaret could dispose of out of the earldom. Therefore, her heir's permission might very well have been needed before any lands could be permanently alienated.

While it is true that many widows with large estates to run did feel the need to remarry in order to gain the support of a husband, Margaret, if she had felt that need, did not have to look towards remarriage. She enjoyed the help of a mature and sensible son who, in addition to providing advice and assistance, represented her in areas to which her gender denied her admission. Therefore, Margaret chose not to remarry. Although she was an intelligent woman capable of making decisions, she was also conventional and therefore did not mind that Montague was seen to be representing her in certain spheres. Of course, crucial to the success of this working partnership was the relationship between the countess and her son, and evidence indicates that they trusted, respected and were fond of each other. She addressed him as 'son Montague' and granted him the very generous annuity of 500 marks,[104] while in 1536 Montague wrote to Reginald that his book *De Unitate*, which formed an attack upon Henry VIII and the royal supremacy, had so upset him that he could not have grieved more had he 'lost mother, wife and children'. Montague had rooms set aside for him at Le Herber in London, as he would have had at all his mother's residences, and the evidence of 1538 often reveals him at Warblington visiting Margaret and taking supper with her.[105] He appears never to have harboured any resentment regarding his mother's pre-eminence and this might have been because he was able to play such an active and significant role. In fact, so prominent was he that Le Herber was sometimes described as his residence, while it was he and not his mother who was fêted by the ports of Dover and Southampton in 1526 when he was presented with gifts of wine.[106] His importance to his mother is neatly summed up by Lodovico Beccatelli, Reginald's secretary and close friend, who described him as 'the chief stay of his family'.[107]

Although Margaret relied on her son and consulted him on various matters, we must not make the mistake of thinking that Montague assumed more authority than his mother. It was a working partnership and, in areas from which her sex did not exclude her, she revealed herself to be an active and forceful personality. Indeed it was not her shy reticence or nervousness that prompted the earl of Southampton to describe her as 'rather a strong custaunt man than a woman'.[108] As head of her family she was primarily responsible for the marriage negotiations of her granddaughter Catherine, Montague's eldest daughter, to Francis Lord Hastings in 1531. The articles of marriage were concluded between herself and Montague on the one part and, in contrast, George, earl of Huntingdon, Francis's father only, on the other. Margaret agreed to pay for Catherine's wedding-day apparel, while she and Huntingdon were to stand equal costs for the meat and drink to be consumed over three days of feasting. Huntingdon pledged to settle lands worth 200 marks upon the couple immediately after the wedding, with the reversion of several other manors and a jointure worth 650 marks. Altogether, the annual worth of these manors amounted to the considerable sum of £900.[109] Margaret was also in an appropriate position to act as marriage broker to the princess's servants. Thus she intervened on behalf of Sir Giles Greville, Mary's comptroller, who wished to obtain the hand of Lady Anne Rede's daughter, by ascertaining the young lady's feelings towards the match.[110] Edward Labourne, local priest and schoolmaster of Wimborne, also had faith in Margaret's influence. In the summer of 1519 problems arose at Wimborne concerning 'a malicious parson' called Rikman. Although Reginald Pole was the dean of Wimborne, he was ill at the time and in his absence it was to his mother that Labourne wrote for help. He addressed her throughout the letter as 'your honor', and begged her to ensure 'that a diligent and An upright examenacion shulde be had in tyme, les it growe to wursse in short space'.[111]

Margaret did not shy away from initiating litigation when necessary either, and came before the Star Chamber on more than one occasion. In 1527 trouble flared in Yealmpton, Devon over certain lands held by Thomas Copleston and his sons, Francis and

John. According to Thomas, he was suffering persecution from Margaret's under-steward of Yealmpton, John Legg, who was continually bringing him before the manor court on false accusations and trying to deprive him of certain lands.[112] Copleston's sons also claimed that they were being forced out of their lands, this time by Edmund Mervyn, and had been unable to obtain justice, despite continual suit to Margaret and Mervyn himself.[113] Not surprisingly, Margaret's version was somewhat different. According to her, in March 1527 Thomas and Francis Copleston, with twenty other 'ryotous' persons, entered a court held by Henry Fortescue, the deputy of Margaret's steward, John Cobley, and assaulted him while menacing Margaret's tenants so that they would not give evidence against them. In addition, they went on to ambush Fortescue on his way home from the court. Again in December 1527, accompanied by armed followers, they broke into and illegally took possession of a corn mill.[114] Thomas denied this and he was supported by his servant John Crabbe, who claimed that Copleston and Fortescue had merely argued in court but no violence had taken place and they did not later ambush Fortescue. The ongoing altercation led to Margaret herself becoming actively involved and she personally interrogated several of the witnesses. Nine men between the ages of twenty and fifty-six sat before the countess's implacable gaze, causing John Crabbe to admit that he did not know whether Copleston had ambushed Fortescue later.[115] The outcome of the dispute is not known, but this was not the only instance of Margaret's involvement in such a case. In an undated draft of a complaint against certain persons who Margaret claimed had riotously entered one of her woods in Oxfordshire, she threatened, in couched terms, that she would have to resort to the same methods unless she received justice from the king. Possibly on the advice of her council, this dangerous course of persuasion was hastily crossed out. Nevertheless, she did send armed servants to the wood to try and prevent any more unlawful entries.[116]

As a substantial landowner, Margaret naturally enjoyed all the attendant feudal privileges and employed feodaries to ensure that these rights were enforced.[117] If one William Cobden is to be believed, Margaret pursued these privileges with zealousness. In October 1531 he accused Margaret of taking certain lands on the Isle of Wight into her hands as an escheat when, in fact, Cobden was the son and heir of the previous holder.[118] One of the most lucrative of feudal privileges was the right to wardship; for instance, in 1537/8 Margaret sold the wardship of one William Bokett's heir for £20.[119] The aristocracy also petitioned the king for the wardships of heirs and heiresses, either as marriage partners for their own children or with the intention of selling the wardship to someone else. In the meantime, they enjoyed the profits from the heir's lands. Margaret was no exception, and on 1 May 1520 the king granted 'to our beloved kinswoman Margaret Countess of Salisbury' the wardship and marriage of the seven-year-old heiress Elizabeth Delabere.[120] The Delaberes were a well-established Herefordshire family whose main seat was at Kinnersley Castle, and Sir Richard Pole had enjoyed an acquaintance with Elizabeth's grandfather, Sir Richard Delabere.[121] The Delabere family lands lay in Hereford and Gloucester and control of them would increase and augment the countess of Salisbury's influence in Wales. It is an important comment upon Margaret's role as 'good lord' that it was a member of her own affinity who ultimately purchased the marriage of the young girl from her. In 1529 Elizabeth Delabere married Michael Lister, son and heir of Richard Lister, who had been appointed Margaret's steward in 1513 and continued to serve her until her arrest in 1538.[122]

In addition to the marriages of her children which, it was hoped, would gain the Poles a foothold in Sussex, Margaret also purchased 240 acres of land, 20 messuages and 23s 4d rent in Marden Borne and Chamberleyns Marshe, Sussex, in 1533 and 1534.[123] Two further manors, Chalton in Hampshire and Aston Chevery in Buckinghamshire, bought in 1532, were intended to augment her existing presence in these counties.[124] Indeed, surviving evidence would suggest that the countess of Salisbury was an active and enthusiastic landlord. She personally oversaw the repairs at Clavering, signing and verifying all the receipts,[125] and in her manor of Easton, Northamptonshire, she took draconian measures to ensure that her copyhold tenants and tenants at will paid their 20s entrance fee promptly, threatening that if they did not discharge the debt within three months they would lose their tenancies.[126] Despite Margaret's conscientiousness, she did suffer arrears on certain manors, apparently amounting to £202 9d in 1538, but they were not very high.[127] For nineteen manors whose incomes we can compare in 1518 and 1538, twelve saw an increase in their annual incomes, while the incomes of only seven decreased.

In consequence, Margaret was receiving £82 26s 2d more from these nineteen manors in 1538.[128] Margaret's personal debts, however, were considerably more. By 1538 her loans, outstanding annuities and debts to various merchants and tradesmen amounted to the not insubstantial sum of £759 3s 1d, although it must be said that it was not unusual for members of the aristocracy to have debts.[129] Charles Brandon, duke of Suffolk had suffered indebtedness, as had the earl of Northumberland and the duke of Buckingham to astronomical proportions.[130] Undoubtedly, the successful management of a large estate depended not only upon the holder of the estate, but also upon the skill and reliability of the estate officials. An investigation into Margaret's most important officers will therefore allow us to assess the countess of Salisbury's success as an employer and landlord, while at the same time revealing the quality of administration that was at her disposal.

Barbara Harris has shown that, although the duke of Buckingham endeavoured to create ties with the gentry class, he tended to appoint dukes and earls as his stewards in order to strengthen his personal and political connections with other members of the peerage. He used these offices as a method of patronage, and this was his main concern rather than improving the management of his estates or maximizing his income from them.[131] However, Margaret's ideal officer was one who combined local prominence with genuine administrative ability. It was important that these men had influence locally in order to strengthen the countess's links with the area, ensure that her wishes were carried out and advise her accurately regarding their respective areas of operation. Margaret's appointments almost always strove to meet that ideal. The three most important estate officials whom Margaret employed were her chief steward, her surveyor and her receiver-general. The appointment of Richard Lister as chief steward is a perfect example of the type of man Margaret chose to welcome into her service.[132] Originally from Wakefield in Yorkshire, Richard Lister settled in Hampshire, where he gradually acquired property. He was a talented lawyer who in 1522 was made solicitor-general and in 1526 attorney-general and sergeant-at-law.[133] He represented Margaret in a legal capacity and was involved in her purchase of the manor of Chalton and in the negotiations for Lord Montague's marriage. Appointed receiver for Earlstoke in Wiltshire and Aston Clinton in Buckinghamshire by 1519, he was also trusted enough to be among those enfeoffed with the manor of Aston Chevery to the use of the countess and her heirs. Indeed, his talents were such that he maintained a successful career long after her fall.[134] Nicholas Harding, who was Margaret's surveyor until at least 1533, had a high profile in Bedfordshire, where he sat on a number of commissions. He was a justice of the assize for the Midland circuit in 1509 and 1510, and by 1546/7 had been appointed escheator for Bedfordshire and Buckinghamshire.[135] His successor as surveyor was John Babham, who was also the steward of Margaret's household.[136] Less is known about Babham but he was probably the same John Babham who entered Oxford University in 1513, especially considering Margaret's penchant for employing Oxford graduates.[137] Already a gentleman when he entered her service, he was locally prominent in Buckinghamshire where he sat on commissions of the peace and held the stewardships of several monasteries in the county.[138] Finally, the office of receiver-general, which was responsible for estate finances, was held by two men in succession. The first was John Skewes, who had been Margaret's first surveyor and continued to be retained as a member of her council along with Lewis Fortescue, a successful lawyer from Devon.[139] Skewes, who had attended Oxford University and Lincoln's Inn, was a prominent landowner in Cornwall where he sat on various commissions. One of the auditors of the duchy of Cornwall, he also served the marquess of Exeter, into whose family he had married and who described him as 'my cosyn Skewes'.[140] The indispensable Oliver Frankelyn, who replaced Skewes as receiver-general between 1527 and 1528, was one of Margaret's most prominent and devoted servants. Ironically, he is the one about whom we know least. Described as a gentleman in Margaret's inventory of 1538, he may have originated from Devon, where he held two manors at his death in 1546 in addition to Clyst St Mary, one of his mistress's manors which had been granted to him by Henry VIII in 1546. In 1511 he was clerk to Edward Chambre, auditor of the Exchequer, but it was in Margaret's service that he made an almost lifelong career. On 6 July 1514 he was receiving moneys owed to her from the manor of Ware and by 1519 was one of her revenue collectors for the counties of Somerset, Dorset, Hampshire and Wiltshire. By 1523 he had been appointed bailiff of Clavering, and thus he was involved in arranging all the extensive repairs that Margaret initiated there between 1523 and 1524. Three to four years later he had proved his ability sufficiently to be appointed receiver-general, an appointment that was formalized on 8 February 1530, when Margaret declared that she had 'yielded to my beloved servant Oliver Frankelyn' the office of receiver-general and feodary of all her manors, lands and tenements for life. Appointments still flowed Frankelyn's way, and in November 1528 he was appointed bailiff of Ware, Hertfordshire, and keeper of the park there, woodward of the manor of Cottingham, Yorkshire, and in 1533 he received the keepership of Donyatt Park, Somerset, in reversion to Philip Acton. Not only did Frankelyn occupy one of the most crucial offices on Margaret's estates, he was also one of her most important household servants, having been appointed comptroller. Following Margaret's fall, Frankelyn's talents allowed him to enter royal service, and he remained bailiff of Clavering and receiver-general of the Salisbury lands.[141] Although several of Margaret's officers also acted on her behalf in a legal capacity, the man she retained soley for that purpose was her solicitor, John Sawster of Steeple Morden, Cambridgeshire. Solicitor of causes-in-law, he was in receipt of 40s a year in 1538 and was also paid 6s 8d for divers writs and other processes made in law on Margaret's behalf in that year.[142] Admitted to the Middle Temple in 1519 at the age of twenty-two, he sat on various commissions for Hertfordshire and Huntingdonshire, and between 1535 and 1539 was steward of the monastery of Ramsey, from which Margaret was in receipt of £50 a year as its fee farm.[143]

Margaret employed eleven known stewards: Sir Thomas Boleyn, Sir John Carew, John Cobley, Sir William Compton, Christopher Conyers, John Corbet, Sir Thomas Denys, Thomas Hackluyt, Sir Thomas Heneage, Edward Montague and Sir Ralph Verney. Thomas Boleyn, steward of Bushey, Hertfordshire, was the father of Anne Boleyn, and his appointment is the only one we can equate to the type of appointments made by the duke of Buckingham.[144] John Carew and William Compton are in a class of their own, as they received their positions as joint stewards of all Margaret's manors in Dorset and Somerset in survivorship from the king prior to Margaret's restoration, positions she was obliged to honour.[145] The remaining eight stewards all appear to conform to Margaret's traditional requirements. John Cobley esquire of Brightley was steward of Margaret's manors in Devon and a well-established

Devonshire figure who was a neighbour of the Lisles, while Christopher Conyers, son of Lord Conyers and steward of Catterick, Aldborough and Hangwest Frendles in Yorkshire, was a member of a prominent Yorkshire family who had attended Lincoln's Inn.[146] John Corbet, steward of Brixton, Isle of Wight, was a member of one of the most important and influential families in Shropshire and possessed administrative expertise which had earned him employment with the duke of Buckingham as his receiver and forester of Caus.[147] Sir Thomas Denys, Margaret's steward of Pyworthy in Devon, was established locally and had received legal training, as had Thomas Hackluyt, steward of all Margaret's Welsh lands. Possibly a Herefordshire gentleman, Hackluyt was talented enough to begin his career as clerk of the king's council and, by 1527, was clerk of Princess Mary's council in Wales.[148] Sir Thomas Heneage, steward of Caister, Lincoln, who joined the king's privy chamber in 1528, was a Lincolnshire gentleman who had enjoyed local popularity at least until 1536, when he was attacked while trying to suppress the Cistercian abbey near Louth,[149] while Edward Montague, steward of Eston near Stamford in Northamptonshire, was a substantial Northamptonshire landowner who succeeded to the family estates when his elder brother died without issue. A proficient lawyer and an adviser of the countess by 1532, his standing was such that when he obtained the degree of sergeant-at-law a celebration followed lasting five days at which the king and queen were guests.[150] Finally, appointed steward of Aylesbury, Buckinghamshire by 1522, Sir Ralph Verney was nephew of Sir Ralph Verney, Eleanor Pole's husband, and a member of a well-established Buckinghamshire family whose members had served the crown before. In 1519 he was also among those enfeoffed with certain manors by Margaret to ensure the payment of her daughter Ursula's dowry.[151]

The countess's affinity also betrayed the influence of others. The overlap between the servants, annuitants and associates of Margaret and the Lisles has already been noted. However, in 1513 she had granted Thomas Wolsey an annuity of 100 marks and therefore expected him to advise her.[152] Consequently, certain members of her staff probably came to her on Wolsey's recommendation. For instance, John Skewes was a member of the cardinal's household and one of his most trusted councillors, serving him up until his fall,[153] while three of her stewards all had links to Wolsey. Sir Thomas Heneage had been one of Wolsey's gentleman ushers, and Sir Thomas Denys had been a member of Wolsey's household, serving as lord chamberlain in 1527 during Wolsey's visit to France, while Christopher Conyers might have been educated in the cardinal's household.[154] Margaret's household was also an obvious place to turn for those who had been associated with the executed duke of Buckingham. Therefore we find as her reeve of Earlstoke, Wiltshire, John Carter, who was most likely to have been the same John Carter who had been Buckingham's attorney at the exchequer between 1498 and 1509,[155] while John Corbet, steward of Margaret's manor of Brixton, has already been mentioned. William Cholmeley had been the duke's cofferer from 1503 and his clerk of the wardrobe from 1506. Both he and his wife, Johanne, became annuitants of the countess, and Johanne joined Margaret's household as one of her ladies-in-waiting. However, the Cholmeleys reciprocated the countess's favour by lending her considerable sums of money which, by 1538, had amounted to £66 13s 4d.[156]

That the head of this affinity was a woman is perhaps betrayed in the countess's significant employment of women in the administration of her estates. According to Shulamith Shahar, 'Reality generally matched the law. It matched it with regard to all offices not held as fiefs . . . Thus, women did not fill posts or perform functions on the manor.'[157] However, Margaret's appointment of women to offices on her manors disproves this. She employed two female reeves, one female bailiff and a female receiver. The two reeves were Margaret Frye and Agnes Jacob. Margaret Frye took over as reeve of Wilton after the death of her husband who had been the previous reeve, and there is no evidence that she employed a deputy.[158] Agnes Jacob the reeve of Swainston, Isle of Wight, did employ a deputy, Robert Whaddon, but, unlike Margaret Frye, there is no suggestion that she was replacing her husband.[159] In 1522 one of Margaret's bailiffs in Lincoln was a Lady Elizabeth Hanshert, who used the services of a William Astowgh as deputy.[160] The identity of Elizabeth Hanshert is unclear but her surname might have been Hanserd rather than Henshert, and she may have been connected to Anthony Hanserd who, apparently, was the receiver of Caister in Lincoln in 1522.[161] In 1521, Margaret's receiver of various manors in the counties of Hampshire, Hertfordshire and Lincoln was Jane Lister, wife of Margaret's chief steward, Richard Lister.[162] Receiving the rents with her was Oliver Frankelyn, and it is feasible that he was acting as her deputy. However, the document does not state that Frankelyn received the rents on her behalf, but that the rents were received 'by my lady Maister Lyster and Mr Oliver'.[163] Consequently, it is quite possible that Jane Lister was more than just a nominal receiver.

Being able to recognize and then attract competent and talented individuals into your service was one thing; retaining and enjoying a harmonious relationship with them over a long period of time was quite another. Not everyone managed it, and a breakdown in relations with servants could be disastrous, as the duke of Buckingham's experience reveals. The price of his litigious, vindictive and arbitrary behaviour towards them was the loss of their loyalty and affection, and three of his household servants played significant roles in his downfall in 1521.[164] It is a personal compliment to Margaret that relations with her servants appear to have been a success. Her surveyor and household steward, John Babham, enjoyed a warm relationship with his mistress and her family. Margaret granted him a generous annuity of £20, and he named two daughters after the countess and her daughter. Furthermore, Margaret's granddaughter Catherine gave Babham's wife the gift of a gold brooch.[165] Oliver Frankelyn, receiver-general and comptroller of Margaret's household, was devoted to his mistress. In addition to the fees Frankelyn received from his various offices, Margaret granted an annuity of £13 6s 8d for him and his wife, Johanne, who joined the household as one of Margaret's ladies.[166] He went beyond the call of duty by warning her about her son Geoffrey, and in his evidence given at the time of her arrest it appears that he tried to protect her. Although the longevity of service Margaret enjoyed from her servants cannot definitely indicate successful relations, it would tend to support rather than disprove such an assumption. By 1538, Oliver Frankelyn, Richard Lister, John Skewes and John Turner had served her for twenty-five years and Babham for at least six. We have evidence for five stewards, and of these Sir Thomas Denys and John Cobley served her for at least fifteen and eleven years respectively, Edward Montague for at least six and John Corbet for no less than twenty-one years. Of her lesser officers Thomas Geoffrey, reeve of Hunton, Hampshire, and John Apployn, reeve of Somerton, Somerset, served her for twenty years, while Andrew Hunte was succeeded as reeve of Clyst St Mary, Devon, by a relative, Richard Hunte, and thus the family's service with her also lasted twenty years.[167] William Legge, who rose to the positions of bailiff of Chalton, Hampshire, and yeoman of her chamber, was in the countess's employ for at least nineteen years,[168] while John Mounson, bailiff of South Kelsey and receiver and bailiff of Caister, Lincoln, served her in that capacity for sixteen years, as did Sir Nicholas Tyrwhitt, bailiff of Caister market. Sir Griffin Richard, clerk of the queen's signet from 1509 and Catherine of Aragon's receiver-general,[169] was appointed bailiff of Easton, Northampton-shire, by Henry VIII in 1509. Therefore his association with Margaret must have spanned twenty-five years.[170] Lastly, William Wintringham, deputy to Oliver Frankelyn and reeve and bailiff of Cottingham, Yorkshire, remained with Margaret for eleven years.[171]

Existing evidence certainly indicates that Margaret operated successfully as a 'good lord', while the fact that her officers were in the service of a woman never seems to have been an issue. She was a woman who could command men, but who could do so with diplomatic authority. Her noble ancestry inspired respect; her determination, sometimes to the point of ruthlessness, combined with energy and intelligence, encouraged obedience; and, most importantly, she made service to her worthwhile. She was well connected with other noble and gentry families and, at least until 1533, she possessed influence at court, which meant she was in a strong position to further the members of her affinity. Even after she lost the king's favour, few of her servants left her employ, and Frankelyn's devotion is a definite testament to her popularity. She chose the members of her administration with care and had no compunction about employing women on her estates if she felt they were 'the best man for the job'. Like Henry VII, Margaret tended to reward ability rather than status, and consequently she was well served. As countess of Salisbury she lived with lavish outward show, maintaining large, imposing, luxurious households which encouraged the respect and deference she was shown. She wielded patronage and sought it and, where her gender became an obstruction, sensibly utilized the services of her sons. She took on the responsibilities of the earldom of Salisbury with enthusiasm and, as countess, discharged them successfully within the boundaries imposed by her sex. It was an achievement any male counterpart would have found hard to surpass.

1. George, duke of Clarence, Margaret's father, 'a myghty prince semly of person and ryght witty and wel visagid'. At her birth in 1473 he stood third in line of succession to the crown of England. © *Geoffrey Wheeler, London.*

2. Margaret's son, Reginald Pole, who was consecrated archbishop of Canterbury in 1556. Vehemently and openly opposed to Henry VIII's religious changes, in 1537 he sent a message warning that if Margaret shared those opinions, 'mother as she is myne, I wolde treade appon her with my feete'. *By courtesy of the National Portrait Gallery, London.*

3. Margaret's granddaughter, Catherine Hastings, countess of Huntingdon, and her husband Francis, second earl of Huntingdon. In 1554–5 Queen Mary restored Catherine and her younger sister, Winifred, in blood and honours and granted them several manors which had once belonged to their grandmother 'in consideration of the service to the queen in her tender age of the said countess of Salisbury'. *Courtesy of Brian Robbins.*

4. William Fitzwilliam, earl of Southampton. Although sympathetic to
Margaret's youngest son, Geoffrey, he evinced a marked dislike for the
countess. During his interrogation of her in 1538 he declared: 'we have dealid
with such a one as men have not dealid with to fore us, Wee may call hyr
rather a strong and custaunt man than a woman.' *The Royal Collection
© 2002, Her Majesty Queen Elizabeth II.*

5. Warblington Castle, Hampshire. Commissioned by Margaret in 1517, it became her principal residence. Dismantled during the Civil War, today only one turret and an adjoining gateway survive. *Hazel Pierce*.

6. The Salisbury Chantry, Christchurch Priory, Dorset. Although built by
Margaret as her intended resting place, her remains were actually interred in
the chapel of St Peter ad Vincula at the Tower of London following her
execution in 1541. © *Geoffrey Wheeler, London.*

4

The Beginning of the End, 1519–1538

஺

'But Fortune with her smiling countenance strange,
Of all our purpose may make a sudden change.'[1]

The years 1519–38 encompassed monumental changes in the constitution of England, and the actions of the Pole family are highly significant, for it was inevitable that such a family would be drawn into the political machinations of this period. Margaret, a substantial landowner with a respectable claim to the throne and four politically active sons to whom she could transmit that claim, eventually found herself centre stage in a horrific and tragic drama. The closing scenes witnessed not only the execution of one of her sons, the attempted suicide and nervous breakdown of another and exile of a third, but Margaret's own brutal beheading at the age of sixty-seven. This chapter will chart the family's fortunes between these years, along with their attitudes and behaviour, which will serve as a starting-point from which to begin an analysis of their sensational fall in 1538.

The first blot on the family's hitherto spotless record came in 1519 when Arthur Pole, courtier *par excellence*, was possibly expelled from the king's privy chamber along with several of his colleagues. Historians continue to disagree over the motives behind the so called 'purge' of May 1519, some believing that Wolsey orchestrated the expulsion of the 'minions' under the guise of household reform because he feared their influence with the king might undermine his own pre-eminent position.[2] Another opinion holds that the 'purge' was provoked by the council as a result of the minions' increasingly obnoxious behaviour and overfamiliarity with the king following their return from a mission to Paris in

1518.[3] Although there is no evidence to prove that Arthur was removed, the known facts are ambiguous regarding his membership of the privy chamber after 1519. Nevertheless, at the Field of the Cloth of Gold in the summer of 1520 Arthur, described as a squire of the body, attended as a member of the king's chamber, and on 29 September 1520 was in receipt of a substantial annuity amounting to £33 6s 8d, again as a squire of the body.[4] Therefore, if Arthur was removed in 1519 it had not seriously damaged his position at court or his relationship with the king. Indeed, he remained at court and in 1526 could be found serving in the outer chamber still under the title of squire of the body. Attended by six servants, the honour of the position is clear in the requirement that he was to lie 'upon the Kinges palet'.[5] In 1519 it was to be two more years before the first serious storm appeared on the horizon. In these years Margaret continued to enjoy New Year's gifts from the king, bouche of court, which entitled her to eat at court, and in May 1520 the lucrative wardship of an heiress. By the latter date she had also been appointed governess to the Princess Mary, while the king's generosity had allowed her son Reginald to attend the University of Padua. In April 1519 Reginald wrote to Henry thanking him for his liberality and informing him of the great respect with which he had been treated by the magistrates at Padua due to his relationship with Henry VIII.[6] Meanwhile, Margaret's two eldest sons took part in all the major celebrations at court. In 1521 the sober Lord Montague, now aged twenty-nine, actually deigned to take part in that sport at which his younger brother excelled, and participated in the jousts and revels held at York Place on 11 and 12 February.[7] Two months later, however, the party atmosphere had changed; the duke of Buckingham, kinsman and friend of the Pole family, was executed, Margaret was removed as Mary's governess, Arthur was expelled from court, and Lord Montague was imprisoned in the Tower of London along with his father-in-law, Lord Bergavenny. Although historians tend to disagree over the seriousness of Buckingam's threat, most modern scholars believe that the duke's fate was of his own making. His alleged indiscreet conversations, which involved speculation on the succession and blustering rages during which he threatened to assassinate the king, would be unacceptable from anyone, let alone someone in Buckingham's elevated position. Barbara Harris, Buckingham's biographer, has charted the duke's blunders up until his arrest and feels that the king 'took reports that the duke threatened to alter the succession very seriously'.[8] Indeed, whatever the truth about Buckingham's intentions, the important fact is that the king believed the evidence and was genuinely afraid. Therefore, all those associated with Buckingham were in a very precarious position. The Poles' friendship with the duke had thus proved to be a double-edged sword.

The storm finally broke in April. On 8 April Buckingham was summoned to London, and by 16 April his servants were undergoing interrogations in the Tower. On 13 May Buckingham was tried and on 17 May he was executed, just over a month from his initial summons. Lord Montague and Bergavenny were lodged in the Tower sometime before 7 May, for on that date Sir William Fitzwilliam wrote to Wolsey from France: 'The French king and the Admiral tell me that the lords Bergavenny and Montague are taken.'[9] They were probably arrested in April, around the same time as the duke. Arthur's activities at this time can only be conjectured from two frustratingly mysterious pieces of evidence. The first of these are the well-known notes jotted in Latin by Richard Pace on the back of a private letter sent to him on 29 March 1521. As he wrote that the king 'believes' Buckingham will be found guilty they must have been written before Buckingham's trial on 13 May. The section of interest to us has proved difficult to translate coherently, but runs thus:

> Arthur Pole has been expelled from court. The Lord Leonard Grey has confessed that Arthur asked him to write concerning the imprisonment of the duke; he refused. He sent however his request to the brothers Henton to place Pole in . . . whom he did not find. Concerning the lady Salisbury the matter is under debate because of her nobility and goodness.[10]

It is difficult to be sure to whom Arthur was trying to persuade Grey to write, but a possible candidate is Reginald, who was studying at Padua University in Italy. The 'Henton brothers' refers to the Carthusian monastery at Henton, one of whose members unintentionally contributed to the duke's fall, but again the meaning is not clear. The second piece of evidence is equally inconclusive. Written in the third person it reveals that Arthur was trying to conceal the identity of a visitor he received at Dowgate:

Mr Arthur Pole did send a letter to the keeper of my lady of Salisbury's place before Dowgate instantly desiring him not to show the name of the person which spake with the said Mr Pole on Monday last, but in any wise to say it was a bailiff of his which come to pay money unto him, and to send him word wheder any such inquere were made or not.[11]

Unfortunately, this note is undated but is included in *Letters and Papers* as contemporary with Buckingham's arrest. If it was written at this time it does not necessarily mean that Arthur was engaged in anything sinister. The visitor might have been a messenger taking his earlier-mentioned request to Leonard Grey. Alternatively, it may have been an informer from the court apprising Arthur of the terrible situation. As his brother was a prisoner in the Tower facing possible execution it would be natural for him to try and find out what was going on. It must be remembered that nobody in 1521 could have predicted the Poles' restoration to favour, and therefore the dangerous position they were in should not be underestimated. Indeed, it appears that at one point the king was definitely convinced of their guilt. While Wolsey was putting on a brave face and informing the French that 'Bergavenny and Montague are loyal and were only sent to the Tower for a small concealment proceeding from negligence', the king warned the Venetian ambassador that the state must not continue to make too much of Reginald 'lest he prove disloyal like the others'.[12] Margaret was also removed from office, 'nobility and goodness' notwithstanding – certainly an indication of Henry's very real fears concerning the Pole family.[13]

Although the Poles' dynastic credentials left them vulnerable to Henry's suspicions, the extent of their guilt really does appear to be their innocent friendship with the duke. There is no evidence that they harboured any treasonable intentions at that time, that they engaged in any dangerous conversations with the duke or felt disenchanted with the policies of the government. The evidence put forward at Buckingham's trial does not even mention them, apart from the assertion that the duke did

grudge that the earl of Warwick [was put] to death, and say that God would punish it, by not suffering the King's issue to prosper, as appeared by the death of his son; and that his daughters prosper not, and that he had no issue male.[14]

Margaret's innocence in this whole affair must be accepted. She would never have done, or approved of, any act that would have been prejudicial to the interests of Princess Mary or her mother. In addition, Arthur Pole was enjoying a successful career at court and had no reason to make common cause with the duke. The member of the family who suffered the most serious punitive action was Lord Montague, but, as Margaret's eldest son, he was the most dynastically threatening of the family. Although no extant evidence links him treasonably with the duke, it might have been feared that he felt disgruntled with his position, for, although he was treated honourably and involved in all the important court ceremonials, his career, like Buckingham's, lacked political depth. More importantly perhaps, Montague enjoyed a close friendship with his father-in-law, Lord Bergavenny, who was mentioned in the evidence against Buckingham. He was indicted for misprision of treason for not reporting Buckingham's alleged threat that 'if the King should die, he meant to have the rule in England, whoever would say the contrary'.[15]

The Pole family did eventually recover from this débâcle, either because Henry realized their innocence in the affair or because he felt that Buckingham's execution had provided an effective warning shot across their bows. Certainly, Margaret did not regain her position as Mary's governess until four years later in 1525, but she was receiving New Year's gifts from the queen by 1522, and by 27 May 1522 Lord Montague was among those who were chosen to attend the king at his meeting with Charles V at Canterbury.[16] Significantly, Lord Bergavenny's name was struck out despite his pardon in March. By October of the same year Arthur Pole had regained the king's favour sufficiently to enlist his help against his father-in-law, Sir Roger Lewknor and the earl of Arundel, and in 1523 both brothers were involved in the ill-fated campaign in France. Serving under the duke of Suffolk, Henry was appointed a captain and on 1 November Arthur Pole was knighted by the duke.[17] Although the family had been restored to favour, the consequences of Buckingham's fall were long-lasting and left an unpleasant taste in their mouths. They could never again be confident of the king's trust and affection for them despite their kinship relationship to him. Moreover, the marriage between Ursula and Lord Stafford would not now produce the expected benefits. Margaret, still owing 2,500 marks of Ursula's dowry, would have to discharge the debt in the knowledge that her daughter would never become the duchess of Buckingham, nor would her husband inherit his father's vast estates.[18] Although Stafford was granted some of his father's estates in 1522 and 1531, they were the least valuable portions.[19] Despite holding manors in Staffordshire, Shropshire, Cheshire, Essington in Yorkshire and Caus and Hay on the Welsh marches, which produced an income of nearly £500 a year, Lord Stafford was constantly pleading poverty.[20] In 1537 he was reduced to petitioning Cromwell in order to purchase some dissolved monastic property, lamenting, 'I have twelve children and my living 40L a year less than it has been.' After desperately offering Cromwell £40 to allow him to buy it, he complained, 'if I have it not I must shortly leave this country.'[21] Ursula's fecundity, an asset to the duke of Buckingham's heir, had become a burden to Lord Stafford. The union of Ursula and Lord Stafford was not the only marriage to result in so much less than Margaret had expected. At some point after 1527 the wife of Lord Bergavenny, a man in his sixties, gave birth to a son and eventual heir, Henry.[22] In addition, two other sons and five daughters were born, and therefore Jane, Lord Montague's wife, was no longer co-heiress to her father's estates.[23] Even if her brothers had died, the inheritance would now have to be shared with at least six other female co-heiresses, and this is putting the most favourable light upon it. As Jane was only a sister of the half-blood to Bergavenny's three sons, she might not have been entitled to anything against the rights of their five sisters of the full blood. The only consolation for Margaret was the sum of money Bergavenny had agreed to pay in the event that he had male issue.

Arthur Pole's marriage to the heiress of Sir Roger Lewknor had also turned sour. Relations with his father-in-law appear to have been strained almost from the start, but the biggest blow came at some point after 1527, when Arthur died. In that year, on 20 March, he was included in a list of those assessed for the subsidy of 1524, and was one of those who could not be distrained for payment.[24] After this, he disappears from all records. The timing of Arthur's death is uncertain and, to date, only Frank Ward has looked into it, arguing that it occurred in the mid-1530s.[25] He bases his conclusion on the evidence provided by Arthur's widow, who stated that she took her vow of chastity before the prior of Bisham who was also the bishop of St Asaph. Although Ward correctly points out that William Barlow held both of these appointments, he is mistaken over Barlow's period as bishop of St Asaph. He states that Barlow was bishop from January 1535 until April 1536, but this is impossible as the previous incumbent, Henry Standish, did not die until July 1535. William Barlow was not, in fact, elected bishop of St Asaph until 16 January 1536, he was confirmed in February, but translated to St David's before his consecration on 10 April. This, therefore, would place Arthur's death somewhere between the middle of December 1535 (because Jane claimed that she took the vow a month after his death) and the beginning of March 1536. Although it is surprising that no comment survives concerning his death, it is particularly so at this time when Viscount Lisle was deputy of Calais and while letters were exchanged at regular intervals between himself and Lord Montague. The Lisles were kept well informed regarding the health of Montague and his mother and it is impossible to believe that no mention would have been made of Arthur's death in these letters. In addition, the identities of the priors of Bisham who preceded William Barlow are not known, and therefore Henry Standish, bishop of St Asaph from 1518 until his death in 1535, might have been appointed prior of Bisham at some point during those years. The most likely explanation is that Arthur died from the sweating sickness, an epidemic of which had broken out in 1526 and recurred in 1528. Likened to Spanish flu and highly contagious, it derived its name from the profuse sweating it caused, resulting in severe dehydration. Extremely virulent and fast-working, an individual could be 'merry at dinner and dead by supper'.[26] Indeed, the 1528 outbreak did strike the court, claiming Sir William Compton as a victim, with Anne Boleyn and Wolsey both contracting and recovering from it. Moreover, in 1527/8 Margaret made a new will, something that the death of one of her sons would have necessitated.[27] Arthur's death certainly left his children, Henry, Mary and Margaret, in a vulnerable position and, despite the efforts of Margaret and Lord Montague to safeguard their inheritance, Arthur's widow went on to marry Sir William Barentyne by whom she had a son, Drew. If this was not bad enough, Jane Lewknor's father had married, as his third wife, Elizabeth Messant by whom he had three daughters born between 1536 and 1544.[28] As a result of the wranglings over Sir Roger's estate after his death, Henry VIII became involved, finally settling them with an act of

Parliament in 1543/4. This firstly determined the jointure of Sir Roger's widow which after her death, along with the rest of his inheritance, was to go to Sir Roger's daughters and their heirs with 'a considerable award to Drew Barentyne and his heirs'.[29] Henry, Arthur's son, was not mentioned because by this time he had died; consequently, Margaret's two granddaughters would have received considerably less than she had envisaged. Clearly these marriages, that were initially full of such promise, did not produce anywhere near the expected dividends.[30]

Compounding these misfortunes was Margaret's involvement in a legal altercation with the king which became dangerously protracted as a result of her obstinacy. Hardly had she entered her estates than a dispute ensued with Henry VIII over lands that she claimed were part of the earldom of Salisbury, but which the king alleged belonged to the dukedom of Somerset. At some point after Sir William Compton's death in 1528, one of Margaret's council wrote to a member of the court pleading her case and asking him to move the king on her behalf. Cast as an innocent victim of revenge, Margaret's councillor explained that the late Sir William Compton,

> whos sole god pardon for that he obtenyd nott his purpose of her in maryage accordyng to hys sute and desyer surmysed unto the kyngs grace that the seyd manors of Canford and other lordships beforseyd of the seyd yerly value of 500 marks were parcell of the Dukedome of Somerset and nott parcel of the Erldome of Salysburye.[31]

Margaret, he continued, had of her own free will agreed to pay the king 5,000 marks, part of which was still outstanding, on the understanding that her restoration would include the lands that were now in dispute. Her councillor felt sure that if 'his grace were informed thereof accordyng to her ryght and tytle but his grace wold suffer her to enyoe them'. In that instance, he had overheard her say that she would be contented to pay the remainder of the 5,000 marks 'within convenient time of the payment thereof as his grace can think or desire'. The time within which she had originally agreed to complete the payment had expired in 1523.[32] The manors in question appear to have been: Canford in Dorset, Ware in Hertfordshire, the Wyke in Middlesex, Deeping in Lincoln, Charlton and Henstridge in Somerset and Alderbury, Crombridge,

Trowbridge and Winterbourne in Wiltshire.[33] Of these ten manors, Compton had been granted custody of the Wyke in tail on 13 February 1513 and held offices on four of the others.[34] On 11 April 1510 he was appointed bailiff of Ware for life, and on 6 March 1512 steward of Canford in survivorship with Sir John Carew.[35] Moreover, the grant of 1512 also appointed them stewards of Somerton, Chedzoy and Donyatt, manors to which Margaret was restored without dispute, and all the other lands in Somerset and Dorset called 'Salisbury lands' which included Henstridge and Charlton. Clearly, Compton was in a position to know about the descent of these lands; he had access possibly to the deeds and certainly to local knowledge. Margaret's refusal of Compton might believably have been delivered in tactless terms, but whether her rejected suitor walked away bent on revenge as a result is open to question. The fact that what he told Henry VIII concerning the descent of some of these manors was correct must cast some doubt upon Margaret's accusation and, significantly, she was careful not to attribute such a vengeful motive to him until safely after his death.

Margaret initially took possession of all these manors and began to enjoy the profits; she actually retained possession of the manors of Ware and of the Wyke.[36] However, the rest of the manors had been repossessed by October 1518 when Margaret promised, in the indentures of marriage between Ursula and Lord Stafford, to pay Buckingham a further 1,000 marks if she 'get back certain lands from the King'.[37] This was a result of the time it had taken Compton to discover weaknesses in Margaret's title and the king's subsequent investigation. As a consequence of the doubt cast by Compton upon the lands in Somerset and Hertfordshire where he held offices, the king probably launched a general inquiry into the rest of the countess's lands, discovering problems with estates elsewhere such as those in Lincoln and Wiltshire. At that point, she would have been told to vacate the lands pending a full inquiry. Both Margaret and the king advanced elaborate proofs of owner-ship of the manors extending back, in some cases, to the reign of Edward I. The only clear-cut case was that concerning Deeping, to which Henry had right by inheritance.[38] For the rest of the manors Henry's right hinged upon the words in the statute of Margaret's restoration which stated that Margaret was only to be restored to those lands held by her brother Edward, earl of Warwick at the time of his attainder. Consequently, although the manor of Ware had been inherited by Margaret's ancestor Thomas, earl of Salisbury, it had been granted to Margaret Beaufort in 1487, and she was in possession of it at her death in 1509.[39] Technically, therefore, Henry's claim to Ware was the better, although he allowed Margaret to retain it, perhaps hoping that it would be an incentive for her to relinquish the other manors. Indeed, possibly in a further attempt to placate the countess, he granted her the fourth part of the lordship of Cottingham in 1516/17 worth £133 a year, and Aldbrough, Catterick and Hang West Frendles, parcel of the lordship of Richmond, Yorkshire, in 1522/3 worth £62 a year.[40] Unfortunately Margaret was not to be bought off by these grants. She claimed the Wyke as the descendant of Richard and Alice Neville, earl and countess of Salisbury, who had been granted the manor in fee simple by a John Wolston and Richard Philyp.[41] No claim can be found for Trowbridge, which was parcel of the Duchy of Lancaster, while the descent of Alderbury and Crombridge is uncertain. Regarding the five remaining manors,[42] neither Henry nor Margaret had any legal right to them as their claims resulted from the illegal actions of their respective ancestors.[43] These lands had legally escheated in 1429, after which they had been purchased by Cardinal Beaufort in order to endow the hospital of St Cross, Winchester. Due to delays, the endowment did not take place before Richard Neville, earl of Salisbury took possession of them in right of his wife in 1461. However, in 1492 Cardinal Beaufort's heir, Margaret Beaufort, presented a bill to Parliament which explained clearly how these manors had been illegally possessed and that Edward, earl of Warwick was not therefore entitled to them. Her bill was correct, but the legal heir should have been St Cross Hospital for which they were purchased. Again the hospital's rights were ignored, and this time Margaret Beaufort appropriated them. She held these manors until 1506, when she relinquished them to Henry VII for a life interest in Canford.[44]

Ignoring the illegality of both claims, the king's is certainly the stronger. Margaret's, at least regarding Canford, is ill researched and blatantly wrong, claiming, as it does, that Henry VII's only interest in Canford prior to her brother's attainder was due to Edward's minority and Henry's position as guardian, and that Henry VII only had possession as a result of Edward's attainder. It ignores the fact that first Henry VII and then his mother held the manor in their own right before the earl's attainder, therefore proving their interest pre-dated Edward's forfeiture.[45] Nevertheless, despite her weak case Margaret refused to admit defeat. Initially, the king would have expected Margaret to put forward a case, and thus it did not affect her appointment as Mary's governess in 1520, or in 1525 either, by which time the dispute had been going on for approximately eight years. However, at this point Henry expected the matter to rest. In that year he granted Winterbourne to his queen, and Canford and Deeping to his illegitimate son, Henry Fitzroy, upon his elevation to the dukedom of Richmond, a clear indication that as far as he was concerned the matter was at an end.[46] However, not even this deterred Margaret, who immediately proceeded to involve the young duke himself, laying her rights to Canford before him.[47] In 1528, she took advantage of Compton's death to inject fresh impetus into her suit, her councillor writing that the 'matter as yet depends and is before the juges undeter-myned', continuing defiantly: 'albeyt it is thought and advertised cleerly by her counsell that she hath as good ryght therunto as she hath to any other londs of the seyd Erldome'.[48] It appears that she even gained or, perhaps more accurately, bought the support of John Incent, master of the dispossessed St Cross Hospital, Winchester. Apparently, Incent had various charters and writings in his possession appertaining to Canford which he consistently refused to relinquish to the duke of Richmond.[49] In a case brought against him in Chancery by Richmond, Incent dishonestly stated that the manors had been forfeited due to John, earl of Salisbury's attainder, when they had, in truth, legally escheated. After reminding the court that Alice, countess of Salisbury had entered the lands and reiterating Margaret's descent from her, he declared that he possessed certain charters and evidences and was ready to do with them what the court decided. He ended by requesting that Margaret be called into court to interplead with the duke of Richmond.[50] Understandably, by 1531 Margaret's machinations had exhausted the king's patience. Among his instructions to Cromwell in September of that year was 'a communication to be had with my Lord Montague for the clearing of certain lands given to the Duke of Richmond'.[51] However, if the documents in Cromwell's custody in 1533 are dated in that year, then Montague had not succeeded. Among them are 'Articles devised for making sure of the manor of Canford'.[52] The gross folly of Margaret's actions is made very clear when compared to the reaction of several fellow peers who had also been forced to relinquish lands to the king. In 1532 John, Lord Lumley had to give up five manors in Westmorland to the duke of Richmond, receiving an annuity of £50 in return. Again in 1532, Henry, Lord Scrope of Bolton was informed that the king wished to have Pisho in Hertfordshire, owned by Scrope's family since 1393. Despite being unwilling to sell and then, following his death, his son's request that he should be recompensed by lands of equal value, the manor was duly sold to the king for £1,000. In 1532 John Bourchier, Lord Berners, was forced to give up his lease of Petty Calais, his London residence, to the king despite having spent considerable sums of money on repairs and drainage.[53] Although both these men initially wrote in defence of their rights, both avowed total submission to the king's will, Bourchier declaring: 'the kynges grace may do as yt shall plese hym ffor all that I have ys and shall be at hys commandment.'[54] Moreover, Bourchier had capitulated within a year and Scrope within two. In 1533 the king also forced an exchange of lands upon his boon companion and brother-in-law, the duke of Suffolk.[55] The exchange was detrimental to Suffolk, who strove to obtain certain concessions, such as the reversion of some de la Pole estates and confirmation of recent leases he had made on the manors he was to lose. Although the duke initially tried to negotiate, he also offered complete submission to Henry's will. However, Henry was not pleased with Suffolk's behaviour, seeing it as a sign of 'som ingratitude and unkyndenes'. He warned Suffolk that it would be unwise to cause him 'to conceyve any jalousie or mistrust in him'.[56] Richard Rich was instructed to remind Suffolk that he had 'attained this degree only by the king's advancement' and trusted that the duke would part with the lands 'without looking for other recompense than the King's liberality', which, Rich was ominously ordered to explain, 'will be more beneficial to him than ten times as much land as the reversions amount unto'.[57] We can only imagine how much more disenchanted the king must have been with Margaret, who, despite the generous terms of her restoration and the weakness of her claims, had continued to argue her case against him for over fifteen years! Although Margaret's actions were extremely unwise, they were, to an extent, understandable. Worth 500 marks a year, these manors were valuable and, apart from Deeping, they all lay in the southern counties, an area where Margaret was attempting to increase her presence. In addition, her dogged determination in the face of Henry's growing disapproval might have been a manifestation of the resentment she felt, but never openly expressed, over the fate of her brother and her own impecunious circumstances following the death of her husband. Naturally, when she found herself in a position to regain her family's lands she felt justified, even duty-bound, to try and retain everything to which she believed she was entitled. However, anything other than sycophantic gratitude and utter submission to Henry's will would always provide fertile ground in which to sow the seeds of the king's suspicion. Despite the warning Buckingham's fall had provided in 1521, Margaret had continued to underestimate the king. However, after the events of 1533 the cold realization that the security she believed their bond of kinship and past friendship gave her actually meant nothing, if it proved an obstruction to Henry's chosen course of action, became all too frighteningly clear.

From 1525 to 1533 Margaret held the position of governess to the Princess Mary. These years saw Henry VIII move inexorably towards the repudiation of Catherine of Aragon, marriage to Anne Boleyn and the eventual break with Rome. It was inevitable that Margaret, as Mary's governess and a close friend of Catherine, would be drawn into the crucial events of this period. However, during the nineteen months Margaret and Mary spent in the marches the possibility of Catherine's repudiation was not an issue, and those years must have been enjoyable ones for both of them. Princess Mary's household was necessarily impressive and several residences were made available for her use in the marches. Apart from Ludlow Castle there was Thornbury, the former seat of the duke of Buckingham, Tickenhill in Shropshire and Hartlebury in Worcestershire.[58] Margaret, of course, was familiar with two of these residences and her return to them must have been somewhat poignant. Ludlow Castle was where her husband had spent a great deal of his time and where her friendship with Mary's mother had begun, while the irony attached to Thornbury was bitter, for Margaret had expected that one day her own daughter would have been mistress there as duchess of Buckingham. Although based in the marches, Mary was not confined there, and travelled quite extensively, making ceremonial entries into the various places she visited. She also visited and corresponded with her parents. Catherine wrote regularly, and in a letter of 1525, in which she encouraged Mary in her studies, she ended with the request to 'recommend me to my lady of Salisbury'.[59] The year 1527 opened with serious discussions between England and France concerning the marriage of the eleven-year-old princess, and Margaret was ordered to bring Mary to court in April to meet the French envoys.[60] The prospective bridegrooms were Francis I's second son, the duc d'Orléans, and Francis himself; at thirty-three years of age he was only three years younger than Mary's father and an inveterate lecher.[61] Despite the conclusion that marriage was out of the question for the next three years because Mary was 'so thin, spare and small', she was formally contracted, no doubt to the relief of both Margaret and Catherine, to the duc d'Orléans on 18 August in the treaty of Amiens.[62] Although the treaty was indeed ratified, in July of the same year rumours began to surface concerning the king of England's intention to repudiate his wife.

By 1527 events had conspired to render Catherine's marriage to Henry considerably less valuable and useful than it had once been. Catherine's nephew Charles V, the Holy Roman emperor, had proved an unreliable ally when, after his capture of Francis I at Pavia in 1525, he had failed to gratify Henry's greatest wish of carving up France between them. Henry's disappointment was compounded by the fact that after eighteen years of marriage, Catherine had been unable to bear him a living son. The dynastic upheavals of the Wars of the Roses were still fresh in the memory; in fact Richard III's usurpation had taken place a mere forty-four years earlier. Henry genuinely believed that the security of England and the smooth accession of his heir could only be guaranteed if that heir was a son. Catherine, however, believed that she was Henry's wife as a result of God's will, and nothing could persuade her otherwise. This conviction dictated her refusal to retire to a nunnery, which would have guaranteed Mary's place in the succession while allowing Henry to remarry. Catherine, previously obedient to all Henry's wishes, refused point-blank to accept that her marriage was invalid, and stood firm in her beliefs despite eventual separation from her daughter and banishment from court. Margaret's main concern throughout this difficult period was to cocoon Mary as much as she could from the growing tension between her parents. With sons prominent at court who were ostensibly advancing the annulment of the king's marriage to Catherine, Margaret was well aware of what was going on, and the strain of trying to ensure that Mary remained as untouched as possible by all this must have been considerable. Nevertheless, in the hope that Henry's actions were being directed by his temporary infatuation for Anne Boleyn, Margaret tried to keep everything as normal as possible for Mary. In 1528 Mary's household was reduced and she was recalled from the marches, but Margaret's position was unchanged and the reduction merely revealed that the king was still undecided as to his daughter's future.[63] Indeed, the princess spent Christmas at court in 1529 and 1530 and continued to receive gifts from her father.[64] In June 1530 she sent the king a buck, and in June the following year he visited her at Richmond and made 'great cheer'.[65] However, by 1531 it had become impossible for Margaret to continue shielding her charge from the painful truth. Mary was fifteen years old, with a sharp, intelligent mind, and could no longer be deceived by equivocating explanations. When Henry finally left Catherine in July 1531 after twenty-two years of marriage, Mary would have been all too aware of it. Although publicly Mary remained calm in the face of such provocations, in the privacy of her own chamber her demeanour was quite the opposite. The injustice of her mother's treatment, and her own, provoked an emotional crisis which could not have come at a worse time. Coinciding with the onset of Mary's puberty, this combination no doubt increased her susceptibility to fearful hysterics, tantrums and depression.[66] Of course, Mary was not the only one to lose her self-control during this highly charged period. Anne Boleyn, whose hot temper is well known, often ranted unguardedly at court, on one occasion proclaiming that she would prefer to see Catherine hanged 'than have to confess that she was her queen and mistress'.[67] Even Catherine herself was affected, her dignified exterior being seriously ruffled when the king asked her to return her jewels in 1532. She snapped back that it 'would be a sin to allow her jewels to adorn "the scandal of Christendom"'.[68]

Up until 1533 no direct action had been taken against Mary, and the king's mind was not finally made up until September, when Elizabeth was born. The birth of another daughter meant that Mary's status had to be clarified once and for all.[69] Nevertheless, as early as the summer of 1533 moves were initiated which no doubt alerted Mary and her supporters to what might follow. Cromwell, on the king's orders, informed Mary's lord chamberlain, Lord Hussey, to place Mary's jewels in the custody of Mistress Frances

Elmer. As a result, Margaret was put in a position where she was forced to make a choice, either unquestionable obedience to Henry or, as she saw it, the defence of Mary's position. For Margaret, conscience, not political expediency, prompted her actions. Therefore, the stand she took was dictated by her loyalty to Mary and devotion to the old faith, but it was one contrary to her own interests. Throwing herself firmly into the fray, Hussey's attempts to carry out his orders were hindered at every turn by Margaret. Upon his request to the countess that an inventory of the jewels should be produced along with the jewels themselves, 'non could be had or founde for to charge hyr that had the custody of them and her executors'.[70] In fact, when the inventory was finally drawn up, it was drawn up by Margaret herself, who then made Hussey and the cofferers sign it. More than that, despite all Hussey's entreaties, she was not prepared to do; 'in no wyse she wyll as yete deliyver to Mistress Frances the jewells for anything that I can say or doo onlesse that yt may please you to obteyne the kyngs letters unto hyr in that behalf.'[71] Margaret, frustratingly implacable, left Hussey with no alternative but to 'beseche' Cromwell to send him the king's letters. Shattered by his confrontation with the countess and the unsavoury nature of his task, he wrote impassionedly to Cromwell: 'wolde to god that the kyng and you dyd knowe and se what I have had to doo here of late.'[72] Unfortunately for Hussey, hard on the heels of this letter came further orders from Cromwell, this time instructing the hapless gentleman to send 'certen parcells of plate' which he believed were in Hussey's custody. Replying on 27 August, Hussey apologetically informed Cromwell that they were not in his custody, nor in the custody of the clerk of the princess's jewel house, but 'with my lady Governesse'. Naturally, the plate was not produced, Margaret informing Hussey that it was in use 'at all suche seasons as the princesse is diseased' and could not possibly be spared unless 'suche like newe plate shulde be bought'. However, she had made her point and Hussey was at least able to tell Cromwell: 'she saith that if it so stande with the king's highness pleasur to have the same, she will at all tymes be redy upon hir discharge to make thereof delivery.'[73]

The difficulty Henry was experiencing in retrieving Mary's jewels and plate was compounded by Catherine's utter refusal, at the same time, to surrender her christening robe to Anne Boleyn, declaring that it had not pleased God that 'she should be so ill advised as to grant any favour in a case so horrible and abominable'.[74] Following Elizabeth's birth on 7 September 1533, Mary was informed that her household was to be reduced, as she was no longer princess of Wales.[75] The size and composition of the new household was not seriously affected, and a number of Mary's long-standing associates remained, including Lord Hussey, Dr Fetherstone and Margaret.[76] However, following a visit from a deputation headed by the earl of Oxford, Mary made her position clear. She did not accept her illegitimacy nor, consequently, the loss of her title of princess. Henry's anger and loss of patience at this point is revealed in his decision to dissolve Mary's household completely and place her in Elizabeth's establishment. The importance of Mary's nonconformity should not be underestimated. Not only did it cast an embarrassing public slur upon the Boleyn marriage and its issue, but it was also dangerous. Mary could become an important focus for disaffection as 'disloyalty to Henry did not seem like disloyalty when it was thought to be support for the rightful heir'.[77] Although Henry was angry with Mary she was still his daughter and he was fond of her; consequently it was much easier for him to believe that others were behind her obstinacy. According to Chapuys, when Norfolk arrived in December 1533 to inform Mary that her household was dismissed, Margaret 'offered to follow and serve her at her own expense, with an honourable train'.[78] Chapuys attributed the refusal of Margaret's dramatic offer to sinister motives. With the countess by her side, Chapuys explained:

> they would no longer be able to execute their bad designs, which are evidently either to cause her to die of grief or in some other way, or else to compel her to renounce her rights, marry some low fellow, or fall prey to lust, so that they may have a pretext and excuse for disinheriting her.[79]

In reality, Margaret's offer was rejected because, without her by Mary's side, Henry hoped his daughter would be induced to accept the new situation. Although Henry never explicitly blamed Margaret for encouraging Mary's disobedience, as he did Catherine,[80] he no doubt suspected that the truculent countess was among those inciting his daughter's intransigence. The resulting antipathy he felt towards Margaret is evident from a discussion he had with Chapuys in February 1535. Upon Chapuys's request that

Mary should once again be placed under Margaret's care Henry exploded, declaring that 'the countess was a fool, of no experience, and that if his daughter had been under her care during this illness she would have died, for she would not have known what to do'.[81] Over a year later Henry's anger had in no way diminished.

Margaret had been a major part of Mary's life for the last eight years, and the psychological trauma of their separation in such circumstances should not be underestimated. Margaret had been a support to Mary through the most crucial and formative years of her life, she had watched her grow up, had been her confidant, and, according to Chapuys, was regarded by Mary 'as her second mother'.[82] But now Mary was to be placed in the household of her half-sister among individuals who, Margaret feared, might not be as understanding or indulgent of her particular needs. Margaret's concern about how Mary would cope under this new arrangement, and her distress at being separated from her charge, is revealed by her offer to follow and serve Mary at her own expense. The situation of the past few years which had entailed first trying to protect Mary from the truth, then trying to console her when that truth was known, followed by her defence of Mary's position in the face of Henry's growing anger, had taken its toll on Margaret both physically and mentally. It is not surprising that after her dismissal as Mary's governess, which left her feeling that she had failed her charge, the sixty-year-old countess suffered some sort of collapse. Barely two months after her removal from Mary's household her son Lord Montague wrote to Honour Lisle: 'My lady my mother lies at Bisham, to whom I made your ladyship's recommendations. I assure you she is very weak, but it is to her great comfort to hear of my lord and your ladyship.'[83]

Henry's perception of Margaret's unsuitability to continue as Mary's governess was compounded by her implication in the unsavoury scandal of the Nun of Kent. This whole affair has been seen by some historians as a mere pretext for moves against the queen and her more prominent supporters. This idea no doubt originates from one of Chapuys's dispatches: 'Many think, and even believe, that those who now have the Nun in their power will make her accuse many people unjustly that they may thus have the occasion and the means of revenging themselves upon those who have supported the Queen.'[84] According to A. Denton Cheney, 'Cromwell was exceedingly anxious to involve as many as possible of the adherents to Queen Catherine in a supposed conspiracy', while Garrett Mattingly believed that Cromwell was not so interested in the Nun herself because he 'aimed at larger game than monks and friars. He aimed at the Marchioness of Exeter and the Countess of Salisbury, Catherine's two chief friends among the ladies of the higher nobility.'[85] Furthermore, J. J. Scarisbrick has suggested that it might very well have been the king himself who 'turned an assault on the nun into a purge of more illustrious opponents'.[86] Certainly, many eminent individuals were implicated in the affair including John Fisher, who was accused of misprision of treason, and Thomas More who only escaped by a hair's breadth. However, both of these, upon their own admission, had actually met the Nun and heard her revelations at first hand. Margaret's implication came via Father Hugh Rich of the Observant Friars, who claimed to have repeated to Margaret the Nun's prophecies 'concerning the King and his reign'. He had apparently told the same prophecies to the queen, Princess Mary, the marchioness of Exeter and Lord and Lady Hussey among others.[87] The Nun of Kent's prophecies concerned the consequences of Henry's marriage to Anne Boleyn, 'that then within one month after such marriage he should no longer be king of this realm, and in the reputation of god should not be a king one day nor one hour'.[88] The prophecies also included the promise that 'the Lady Mary, the King's daughter, should prosper and reign in this kingdom and have many friends to sustain and maintain her'.[89] These predictions were obviously explosive, and the whole affair was taken very seriously by the government, not least because the Nun, Elizabeth Barton, was held in the greatest esteem. The perceived accuracy of her prophecies, combined with a devout and irreproachable life, gave her considerable influence. Many genuinely believed that her messages were sent from God himself, John Fisher reminding Cromwell that 'God never acts without first warning his prophets'.[90] Indeed, so renowned was Barton that she was informed by the papal nuncio of the king's suspended excommunication before the king himself had been told.[91]

A. Neame has successfully highlighted the tense atmosphere that must have prevailed during the month of countdown to Henry's 'deposition' as predicted by the Nun. Understandably, the promulgation of these predictions had to be stopped, and Henry's grave concern is reflected in the severe action that was taken against

Barton. Included among the accusations was one that claimed she had 'fortified Princess Mary's obstinacy', an obstinacy to which Henry believed Margaret had contributed. Moreover, Barton had done this by predicting that 'no man should put her from her right that she was born unto', which had encouraged Mary's supporters 'to rebel or make war against the King's Grace upon trust of good success according to the said revelation'.[92] Margaret's implication in such an affair put her in an extremely dangerous position, especially following so soon after the incident over Mary's jewels and plate. Nor should her involvement be taken simply as the result of a government 'frame-up'. Hugh Rich was the guardian of the Observant house next door to Richmond Palace which had been Mary's main residence since her return from the marches.[93] Furthermore, Rich moved in the highest social circles and, as such, had spoken to Thomas More about the Nun, was in contact with Thomas Abell, Queen Catherine's confessor, and, more importantly, had visited the queen herself.[94] Therefore, it is quite likely that Margaret had met him and no doubt heard his tales of wonder regarding 'the holy maid'. Fortunately, it seems certain that Margaret never met the Nun herself. No doubt Catherine, who steadfastly refused to allow Barton an audience, instructed Margaret that on no account was she to allow Mary to see her either. Margaret followed Catherine's cautious example and avoided personal contact with Barton. Nevertheless, she may have been questioned regarding possible contact with the Nun, for among Cromwell's remembrances of 1533 is one to 'send for my Lady of Salisbury and Lord Hussey'.[95] Once more, Margaret's name had been linked to treasonable activities, and again activities which involved a dynastic element.

After the traumatic events of 1533, and having done all she considered she could for Mary, Margaret sensibly decided to maintain a lower profile. Little is heard of her during the next three years except for a brief episode in 1535 which found her in conflict with Thomas Cromwell. Characteristically unable to put common sense before conscience, she became involved in the opposition to William Barlow's appointment as prior of Bisham. This is not surprising as Barlow enthusiastically supported Catherine's repudiation and enjoyed the patronage of Anne Boleyn and Thomas Cromwell, who both desired his appointment.[96] Although Margaret had been opposed to the previous prior, whose resignation she had sought, upon learning that Barlow was to replace him she did her utmost to ensure that he would not now resign despite his being 'very unmette to contynue'. She was still proving herself a force to be reckoned with, and Nicholas Carewe, who had also become involved in the affair, wrote miserably to Cromwell: 'I wold I hade spent a hundred pounds I had never spokyn in it ffor somewhat it toucheth my pore honestie.'[97] Despite her being one of the most powerful figures in the vicinity of Bisham Priory, Margaret's protest proved ineffective against the combined efforts of Cromwell and Anne Boleyn, and Barlow was duly appointed. Apart from this episode, the rest of Margaret's activities were conducted well outside the political sphere, with the only other sour note being the sudden departure out of the realm of her personal chaplain, John Helyar, in 1534, of which the bishop of Winchester ominously wrote to Cromwell, 'in such fashion and maner as I like not'.[98]

On 7 January 1536, at about two o'clock in the afternoon, Catherine of Aragon died, possibly from the effects of a heart attack.[99] Exiled from the court at Kimbolton Castle in Huntingdonshire, one of the last letters Catherine dictated was to Henry, 'My most dear lord, king and husband', whom she pardoned everything. She ended the letter with 'this vow, that mine eyes desire you above all things'. According to the imperial ambassador, Chapuys, upon hearing the news of her death the relieved Henry declared: 'God be praised, the old harridan is dead, now there is no fear of war.'[100] What Margaret felt we can only imagine. Their friendship had spanned thirty-five years, and the tragedy of Catherine's end was poignant. Nevertheless, there seemed to be a glimmer of hope for an improvement in the current state of affairs with the events of May 1536. That month saw the sensational fall and execution of Anne Boleyn. Anne had married Henry in January 1533 but, like Catherine, her failure to provide Henry with a male heir, coupled with the political atmosphere of the time, contributed to her equally tragic downfall. As Henry's desire for an imperial alliance grew, so did Cromwell's need to remove Anne who, just by being Henry's queen, was a serious obstacle to the conclusion of such an alliance.[101] Although Cromwell considered Anne to be a woman of 'intelligence, spirit and courage',[102] he nevertheless temporarily joined forces with her opponents and engineered a *coup d'état* which led not only to her death, but also to the deaths of her brother, Viscount Rochford, Francis Weston, Henry Norris and William Brereton, all friends of the king and members of his privy chamber. The remaining victim was the hapless Mark Smeaton, a court musician. Anne was executed on 19 May, and eleven days later Henry married Jane Seymour.

Jane Seymour had been an admirer of Catherine of Aragon and therefore encouraged a reconciliation between the king and his daughter. Although this eventually took place, it was only after Mary's complete acceptance of all that Henry had done regarding the break with Rome and his marriage to Anne Boleyn. She was left in no doubt about the king's genuine commitment to the Royal Supremacy, and the conservatives' victory over the Boleyn faction was thus a hollow one. However, these circumstances allowed for Margaret's tentative return to court. In June 1536 the bishop of Faenza wrote: 'On the return of her [Mary's] governess to Court . . . it being supposed that the Princess was in her company, a crowd with 4,000 or 5,000 horses ran to meet her.'[103] Furthermore, in the same month Margaret's influence was considered such that Honour Lisle wrote to her in the hope that she could forward the appointment of her daughter to the new queen's household. One of the reasons behind this cautious return to court might have been the king's conviction that Margaret's son Reginald was about to announce his support for the Royal Supremacy. From 1532 Reginald had been studying in Italy, avoiding the issue of Catherine's repudiation. However, in February 1535 the king ordered Thomas Starkey to write to Reginald requesting his opinion regarding the Boleyn marriage and the pope's authority.[104] W. Schenk points out that Reginald's 'reassuring letters' convinced Starkey that his response would be favourable to the king.[105] Indeed, on 28 October 1535 Reginald wrote to Cromwell begging him to

> assure his highness of my readiness to do him service at all times; for I count whatsoever is good in me next to God to proceed of his grace's liberality in my education, which I esteem a greater benefit than all the promotions the King ever gave to any other.[106]

Reginald's 'letter' duly arrived at the English court in June 1536, the very month of Margaret's return to court. It was also the crisis month during which Mary faced condemnation as a traitor before her final capitulation to Henry on 22 June. Both the timing and the content of the 'letter' could not have been worse. Fiercely opposed to the king, it was delivered in the strongest and most vehement of terms. Likening Henry to a wild beast and accusing him of being incestuous, Reginald also called him 'a robber, a murderer, and a greater enemy to Christianity than the Turk'.[107] He encouraged Charles V to invade England, drew Henry's attention to the likelihood of Francis I also launching an attack, used Scripture to prove the innocence of his uncle, Edward, earl of Warwick, and declared that the king would never succeed in repudiating Princess Mary.[108] Thomas Starkey's description of it is understandable: '[This is] the most frantic judgement that ever I read of any learned man in my life.'[109] The king's rage was no doubt inflamed by the fact that he had been led to expect quite the opposite. The arrival of *De Unitate* put Margaret and her sons in a very difficult position and, unfortunately for Margaret, the news of the letter's arrival and content was revealed to her by the king himself. The interview would not have been pleasant, and Margaret immediately conferred with her eldest son, Lord Montague, who advised her to proclaim Reginald 'a traitor to their servan[ts], that they might so report him when they came in to their countries'. According to Margaret, this is what she did, declaring to them that she 'took her said son for a traitor and for no son, and that she would never take him otherwise'.[110] A further message from the king, delivered by Lord Montague, prompted a letter to Reginald. No doubt intended to be seen by the king's council, it rebuked Reginald for his behaviour. Seeing him in the king's 'high indignation', she wrote: 'I am not able to bear it', and she urged him 'to take another way And serve our master as thy bounden duty is to do unless thou will be the confusion of thy mother'. She reminded Reginald of how much he owed the king, warning him, if he did not use his learning to serve him, 'trust never in me'.[111] Although the letter was sent to admonish Reginald, it describes his actions merely as 'folly' and clearly could have been delivered in much stronger terms. The letter is not dated, but was probably written around the same time as Lord Montague's letter to Reginald which was written on 13 September at Bisham. Apparently, Lord Montague knew nothing about the content of *De Unitate* until he received a letter from his brother in July. After speaking to Cromwell, he was advised to approach the king himself who, Montague wrote to Reginald, 'declared a great part of your book so to me at length'. With a similar theme to Margaret's, Montague's letter is longer and some-what stronger. It appears that while the letter was being composed, Montague was informed of Reginald's intention to spend the winter with the pope. This latest information seems to have elicited genuine exasperation: 'if you should take that way then farewell all my hope. Learning you may well have but doubtless no prudence nor pity.' He warned that should Reginald continue with that course of action, 'then farewell all boundes of nature not only of me but of mine, or else in stead of my blessing they shall have my curse'.[112] Montague's irritation is understandable, for this was not the first time he had been placed in an awkward position with the king due to Reginald's actions. In 1530, Henry was prepared to offer the archbishopric of York to Reginald on condition that he made his opinion clear regarding Henry's and Catherine's marriage.[113] Initially Reginald thought he had 'found a way to satisfy his Grace' and told both Lord Montague and Edward Fox. Relieved, they informed Henry forthwith who excitedly sent for Reginald. However, when Reginald came before the king, 'my mind changed from what I had intended and ran upon nothing else but how I could find it in my best to confirm [him] in what, in my opinion, was dishonour'.[114] The king was understandably in-censed, again compounded by the fact that he had been led to expect the opposite by the unfortunate Lord Montague.

In the summer of 1536 Margaret finally withdrew from court altogether. Her reappearance might have been prompted by the expectation of serving Mary once more, but this was not to be the case. The composition of Mary's household was being discussed towards the end of June, when she was asked for her suggestions for potential members, and, significantly, Mary did not include Margaret's name in her list. It is true that the new establishment was not as grand as that of 1525, and lacked both a lady governess and a lord chamberlain. Moreover, at twenty years of age Mary did not require the services of a governess. Nevertheless, David Loades has shown that, of the twenty-four members, twenty-one had been in Mary's service before, revealing 'that both Henry and Cromwell were willing to accept Mary's desire for the support of old friends'.[115] Consequently, Margaret's exclusion is telling. The advice Mary was receiving from Cromwell at this time obviously did not include the recommendation to reinstate Margaret, and

Mary probably realized that such a proposal would be extremely provocative. Henry and Cromwell no doubt feared that Margaret would be too disruptive an influence upon Mary, and probably suspected that she shared Reginald's views. In addition, Mary herself might not have wished to resume her friendship with Margaret, at least not at the level of closeness it had once been. Her capitulation to Henry had been complete, after which she went on to enjoy a genuinely close relationship with Jane Seymour. This friendship was safe and had the stamp of her father's happy approval, a situation she did not want to threaten by resuming her association with Margaret. There might also have been an element of shame. Deep down, Mary believed she had betrayed her mother and perhaps found the prospect of continually facing the woman so closely associated with Catherine's, and her own, initial stand against her father too difficult. Although respecting Mary's wishes, Margaret did attempt to maintain some contact with her former charge, sending her New Year's gifts for 1537 and 1538, but clearly there was nothing left for her at court.[116] She no longer attended any of the major court ceremonies, such as Prince Edward's christening, and after 1533 evidence suggests that no more New Year's gifts were exchanged with the king. From 1536 until her arrest in 1538, Margaret spent most of her time at Warblington where, in addition to overseeing the administration of her estates, she busied herself with the upbringing and education of her five granddaughters.[117] Although her two sons paid frequent visits to Warblington, the king made a point of staying away. Those halcyon days when the countess of Salisbury lavishly entertained her king and queen had come to an end.

The behaviour of Margaret's sons throughout these years is also significant. Reginald's actions are so well known as not to require detailed rehearsal here. Initially an active supporter of the divorce,[118] by late 1530 he had changed his mind, having developed qualms about the king's intentions. Apprising Henry of this in 1530, he was finally granted permission to leave the country in 1532. According to Chapuys, this was because Reginald had informed the king that 'if he remained here he must attend Parliament, and if the divorce were discussed he must speak according to his conscience. On this, the King immediately gave him leave to go.'[119] In fairness to Henry, despite the provocation, he did allow Reginald to keep his income and benefices. However, after the arrival of Reginald's letter in 1536 the breach between Henry and his cousin was rendered irreparable, with Reginald's actions becoming openly treasonous in the following year. Lord Montague's conduct throughout this period was, excluding his misplaced endorsement of Reginald in 1530, apparently beyond reproach, while Geoffrey Pole's favour with the king fluctuated mostly as a result of his financial difficulties. However, up until 1532 Geoffrey's career progressed as successfully as his brother's, with both ostensibly supporting the annulment of Henry's marriage to Catherine in every way. Lord Montague was first appointed to a commission of the peace in December 1528 for Dorset, and in January of the following year he was appointed for Hampshire, Somerset and Sussex, for the last of which his brother also sat at the same time.[120] Indeed, both brothers continued to sit on commissions of the peace, Lord Montague more frequently than Geoffrey, until 1538. The year 1529 also marked Henry Pole's first summons to Parliament as Lord Montague, and he was the fourth lord to enter the chamber, following his friend Lord Delaware.[121] Geoffrey also attended this Parliament as MP for Wilton and was knighted during its course at York Place.[122] The emergence of the Pole brothers onto the political stage in this way must be seen as part of the king's attempt to muster support over the sensitive issue of Catherine's repudiation, and it certainly appeared that he enjoyed that support from Lord Montague. In July 1530 Montague was among those 'Spiritual and Temporal Lords' who put their names to a petition addressed to Pope Clement VII 'praying him to consent to the King's desires, and pointing out the evils which arise from delaying the divorce'.[123] Montague's name headed the list of signatures under the section for barons. In 1532 Montague was also one of those appointed to accompany the king and Anne Boleyn to Calais for their meeting with Francis I, while in the following year he enjoyed a position of honour at the coronation of Anne Boleyn when he was appointed carver to his new queen.[124] Moreover, his son-in-law, Francis, Lord Hastings was dubbed a knight of the Bath at the same coronation.[125] Summoned back to Parliament in January 1534, Montague subscribed his name to the controversial oath to the Act of Succession.[126] In April of the following year he was appointed to a commission of oyer and terminer for Middlesex regarding the trial of the prior of the Charterhouse and, three months later, for the trial of Sir Thomas More.[127] His involvement in the trial of More must have caused Montague considerable anguish, as Thomas More was a man he admired. After his death, Montague obtained all his books and 'dyd moche take pleasure [rea]ding of them'.[128] The ordeal of the trial and execution of More took its toll on Montague, and on 7 July, the day after More went to the block, John Husee wrote to Lord Lisle that the 'saying is that my Lord Montague is sore sick or dead', while Leonard Smyth wrote on the same day that Montague 'is sore sick and like to die'.[129] Ironically, the next trial in which he was involved, more welcome than that of Sir Thomas More, was the trial of Anne Boleyn on 15 May 1536.[130] Montague continued to show the king scrupulous obedience and, in October 1536, was summoned along with Geoffrey to attend the king himself against the rebellion known as the Pilgrimage of Grace, Montague bringing 200 men and Geoffrey 20.[131] In the following year Montague played a prominent role at the christening of Prince Edward, where he supported the earl of Sussex, and at the funeral of Jane Seymour, where he assisted the grieving Mary, the chief mourner.[132] With such a demonstration of loyalty, it is easy to understand Alan Neame's misconceived claim that Montague's sympathies lay very definitely with the king and Anne Boleyn.[133] Despite his mother's lapses and Reginald's extreme behaviour, Montague's obedience went some way towards ensuring that the king's anger towards the family was somewhat assuaged, and the New Year's gifts he received in 1532 and 1533 were certainly honourable.[134]

While Montague maintained a consistent presence at court, carefully toeing whatever line the king drew, Geoffrey was not quite so circumspect. Lacking his elder brother's composure and quiet intelligence, Geoffrey was at times foolish and irresponsible. Albeit ambitious, he was considered unsuitable for any serious government office, apart from that of justice of the peace, and, although he was charming and well liked by those who knew him, that charm was not combined with the finesse and acumen necessary for a significant court appointment either. His lack of judgement is glaringly revealed when he forcibly entered Slendon Park with ten or twelve of his servants armed with bows and arrows in 1536 and dispossessed the tenants of Lord Maltravers, son of the earl of Arundel with whom he had clashed before. Despite a letter from the king commanding his immediate removal, he stubbornly

insisted on staying one extra night, which resulted in his indictment.[135] Ironically, this obstinate streak brought him the nearest
thing to a compliment he ever received. In 1535, James Hawkes-
worth informed Lord Lisle of the rough treatment Ralph Rigsby,
keeper of the forest of Bere, was receiving from Thomas Uvedale,
constable of Winchester Castle. He therefore wished that Lisle had
matched Uvedale 'either with Sir Gefferay Paulle or else with
Master Browne, and either of them would have holden him short
enow; for I can see no kindness in Master Thomas towards mere
servants.'[136] Geoffrey's problems seem to have started in earnest
around 1530 when his financial difficulties were such that he
approached his friend, William Friend, schoolmaster of Chichester
prebendal school, for a loan. With his fondness for puns, Geoffrey
wrote: 'Mr Frynd I hartily commend me unto you and pray you be
so fryindly unto me at this tyme as to lend me the sum of five
pounds sterling to the fest of Mychelmas . . .'.[137] At some point
between 1530 and 1532 a warrant was issued for him which
probably related to his indebtedness and appears to have resulted
in Geoffrey's first expulsion from court.[138] In a desperate letter to
Cromwell on 20 April 1533, Geoffrey begged for his help 'to be a
meane that I may be able to contynew my dewty that I owe farther
to hys hyghnes'. Although he understood that, due to all
Cromwell's grave affairs and business, it was no wonder that he
had forgotten him, he continued hopefully: 'I havyng trust of your
goodnes to me . . . do leve my servant to wayt on yow to remembre
you somtyme off me.'[139] The letter must have succeeded, because
he was appointed a server at the coronation of Anne Boleyn a
month later.[140] It is even possible that Cromwell himself was
lending Geoffrey money to keep the king at bay, for in July of the
same year Geoffrey received £40 from Cromwell for no specific
reason.[141] In November 1534 Geoffrey had the honour of being
appointed to the commission of sewers for Sussex[142] but by 1537 he
was out of favour once again, possibly in relation to the Slendon
Park affair as much as his continuing debts to the king. Indeed, in
February 1537 he was warned by Thomas Starkey that 'Mr
Gostwyke looks for you for the King's money'[143] and on 14 August
1537 he signed an obligation to pay an outstanding debt of '£8 18d'
to the king owed for various chattels, grain and utensils bought of
the royal commissioners from the monastery of Durford at its
dissolution. This debt was to be discharged by 1 May 1538.[144]

Writing to Sir Thomas Audeley, the lord chancellor, on 5 April 1537, he thanked him for his goodness: 'the last time I was with you when my heart was full heavy; I take patience, trusting to have the king's favour again.' He went on to seek the chancellor's advice about approaching Cromwell to obtain permission to attend court the next time he was in London for 'I have business this term for myself and if as desired by my Lord Privy Seal and the others before whom I was present, I should come to London and not, as wont, come to the court, men would marvel.' He ended by asking to be allowed to buy 'stuff' from the local suppressed abbeys for £30 payable in instalments. Not surprisingly he added: 'but if ye be hasty on me now I cannot do it.'[145] This time, however, Geoffrey's pleadings did not work. Ignoring Cromwell's instructions to stay away from the court, he suffered the humiliation of being refused entry. Sir Thomas Palmer reported to Lord Lisle that on the day of Prince Edward's christening 'lord Montague's brother came to Court to do service, but the King would not suffer him to come in'.[146] It must have been extremely embarrassing for Lord Montague, who was officiating at the christening. Indeed, Geoffrey's situation had reached the stage where he was considering fleeing the realm to escape his debts, which by now amounted 'to a great sum'.[147] At this, George Croftes advised John Collins to warn Lord Montague to 'se[e the said Sir] Geoffrey Pole's debts paid . . . lest that should be a great occasion for him to [flee]'.[148] Montague assured Collins that he had 'provided a stay for that matter well enough, for the said Sir Geoffrey was discharged of many of the said debts'.[149] It is quite likely that Margaret's sale of the Wyke in Middlesex to William Bower in 1538 was the means of discharging these debts.[150] Although Geoffrey was back on commissions of the peace by 1538, the king was understandably unimpressed with his general behaviour.

The situation in which the Pole family consequently found itself by 1538 was clearly not enviable. Margaret had lost the king's favour as early as 1533 and, except for the brief hiatus in 1536, had effectively been forced to withdraw from court at that time. Geoffrey had revealed himself to be not only extravagant but foolishly obstinate, which stretched the king's patience to the limit, while assassins prowled Europe in search of Reginald, for whom Henry seethed with hatred. By 1538 only Lord Montague was able to represent the family at court, and any reconciliation with the king must come through him. However, Montague's loyalty and acquiescence to the king's will was a mere façade, and that façade, while skilfully constructed, was unable to withstand the ill-considered behaviour of his two brothers.

5

The Fall of the Pole Family, 1538

'*Son Montague . . . This is the gretist gift that I can send you for to desire god of his helpe wich I perceave is great need to pray for.*'[1]

On 14 August 1538 Margaret Pole was sixty-five years old; two weeks later on 29 August her youngest son Geoffrey was arrested and taken to the Tower of London.[2] It was to be nearly two months before Geoffrey's first official examination, which took place on 26 October. Following this, however, events moved swiftly with intensive activity throughout November during which numerous witnesses were examined and their depositions taken. On Monday, 4 November Lord Montague and the marquess of Exeter were arrested and joined Geoffrey at the Tower, with Sir Edward Neville following on 5 November.[3] On 12 November Sir William Fitz-william, earl of Southampton and Thomas Goodrich, bishop of Ely arrived at Warblington to interrogate Margaret, and three days later she was escorted to Southampton's residence, Cowdray, where she was kept in confinement.[4] By the end of November multiple examinations had taken place, Geoffrey alone having endured seven separate interrogations, and by the beginning of December all was prepared for the trials. On 2 and 3 December Lord Montague and the marquess of Exeter respectively stood trial, and the following day Sir Edward Neville, Sir Geoffrey Pole, George Croftes, clerk, John Collins, clerk, and Hugh Holland, yeoman, stood before the bar.[5] Although Montague, Exeter and Neville pleaded not guilty, guilty verdicts were passed unanimously on all. On Monday, 9 December, in bad weather, Lord Montague, the marquess of Exeter and Sir Edward Neville went to the block on Tower Hill, while Croftes, Collins and Holland faced a less swift fate at Tyburn.[6] All in all, approximately twenty-four witnesses and suspects were questioned, resulting in the arrest of thirteen people. Of these thirteen, seven were executed, four received pardons, one disappeared mysteriously in the Tower, and we lack evidence for the fate of the remaining one.[7] In just over three months two of the wealthiest and most prestigious families in England had been destroyed. To understand how this débâcle occurred, it is necessary to look firstly at the numerous depositions taken and the evidence produced in order to piece together the sequence of events that took place in 1538.

The first arrest to take place had been that of Hugh Holland, one of Geoffrey Pole's servants. According to the popular story, Holland was arrested and taken up to London with his hands tied behind his back and his legs beneath his horse's stomach. On the journey, Geoffrey Pole supposedly met him and, with his fondness for puns, asked half-jokingly where he was 'bound' to go. Holland allegedly replied that he could not say himself, but told Geoffrey to 'kepe on his way, ffor he sholde not be long after'.[8] Although some historians have accepted the authenticity of this story,[9] it actually originated from local gossip, and evidence suggests that it was not true as Holland was most likely to have been arrested at Bockmer, Lord Montague's seat, while both Montague and his brother were in residence. The scene was not pleasant, for Holland did not go quietly and a scuffle ensued, which prompted Lord Montague to confide in Geoffrey that he had burned many letters at Bockmer.[10] Unfortunately, we are not told the date of Holland's arrest, but we know that Geoffrey Pole dispatched John Collins, Lord Montague's chaplain, from Bockmer to Lordington to burn certain letters he kept there, and that this probably occurred on 21 June 1538.[11] According to Constance Pole, Collins came to burn the letters between Whitsun and Midsummer, while Jerome Ragland, Morgan Wells and Collins himself stated that he was sent at Corpus Christi time, Collins adding that it was a Friday.[12] As Easter Sunday in 1538 fell on 21 April, Corpus Christi must have occurred on Thursday, 20 June, dating Collins's urgent dispatch to Friday, 21 June. It is not unreasonable to assume that this was provoked by Holland's arrest and Lord Montague's subsequent comment to Geoffrey. The arrest of Holland, one of his most trusted servants, would have alerted Geoffrey to the necessity of removing any incriminating evidence. Hence, we can place Holland's arrest at some point in the third week of June, possibly only a day or two before Collins was sent to burn Geoffrey's letters. Obviously, it is

X Is it not more likely that Holland's arrest would have been very quickly followed by that of Sir Geoffry — which we can date to August?

necessary to understand why Holland was arrested, and Gervase Tyndall may very well provide the answer.

A sometime schoolmaster who had attended Cardinal's College, Oxford, Tyndall arrived in Hampshire in the summer of 1538.[13] Apparently suffering from ill health, he found it necessary to stay at a surgeon house near Warblington which was maintained by Margaret. Its surgeon, Richard Ayer, naturally enjoyed an association with the Pole family, and it was from Ayer that Tyndall learned a great deal about what was going on in Margaret's household and of contacts between the Pole family and Reginald. This information was duly passed on by Tyndall to Cromwell. Consequently, Tyndall's arrival in Hampshire poses some important questions: was it by chance that he picked up this information from idle conversations with the gossiping Ayer, or can a more sinister explanation be proposed? Had Tyndall been sent into Hampshire by Cromwell to investigate the activities of the Pole family? Certainly, Tyndall, a firm proponent of the New Learning, had direct contact with Cromwell and apparently had acted as an informer before, when he wrote to Cromwell in 1535 that a doctor named Stanley had delivered a sermon against the Royal Supremacy at a church in Grantham.[14] His relationship with Cromwell continued, and by October 1537 a Mr Tyndall, who had been appointed schoolmaster of Eton, was described as 'Cromwell's true scholar and beadman'.[15] Tyndall also seems to have had a connection with Richard Morisyne, one of Cromwell's most loyal adherents and the future author of the *Invective*, claiming to have attended Oxford at the same time as Morisyne. Moreover, Tyndall told Ayer that he could arrange an interview between Ayer and Cromwell if Ayer was prepared to talk, assuring him that 'my lord wold geve hym gret thankes yn th[at] behalff, and do mor for hym than ever my lady w[old]'.[16] Clearly, Tyndall was actively seeking information against the Pole family, and from the evidence discussed it seems most likely that he was a member of Cromwell's spy network. So why was Tyndall sent to Hampshire in the summer of 1538?

After Geoffrey Pole's arrest in August the neighbourhood buzzed with gossip about the family, with Ayer once again at the centre of it. He supposedly told Laurence Taylor, a harper of Havant and one-time servant of Geoffrey Pole's colleague John Gunter, that if Geoffrey had not been apprehended he would have sent a band of men over to Reginald in March the following year and that Holland was suspected of carrying letters overseas.[17] Certainly, Morgan Wells, a loyal servant of the Pole family, was aware that Ayer was prepared to inform on the family, declaring in his evidence that it was 'spoken at Bokmar that the said Ayer shuld open the sayd hollands going oversees'.[18] John Collins corroborated this, stating in his testimony that he

> hard att bockmar of hugh hollands being beyond the sees, And that the Rumour was thatt he shuld go over with lettres to Cardinall poole . . . And thatt the discosing of his often going beyond the sees was made by one Ayer to Tyndall, And by Tyndall to the prist of havant.[19]

Given Ayer's loose tongue, and the sensational nature of the rumours, it is almost certain that dangerous gossip about the Pole family was prevalent before Geoffrey's arrest and Tyndall's arrival at the Warblington surgeon house. Cromwell's importance in Hampshire was not inconsiderable, and Ronald Fritze has revealed that even before 1531 Cromwell's influence had started growing, eventually challenging that of the absent bishop of Winchester, Stephen Gardiner. Indeed, Southampton looked to Cromwell as patron, and he formed friendships with the inhabitants and took them into his service.[20] Consequently, it is easy to understand how scraps of sensitive information about the Poles and Hugh Holland might have found their way to the ears of the lord privy seal. Furthermore, Hugh Holland was the type of character to attract gossip. Described in evidence as a 'knave' and crafty fellow, he had been involved in serious piratical activities in 1533, although on that occasion he escaped imprisonment.[21] Therefore, the most likely sequence of events is as follows: Ayer had been gossiping about the family and their correspondence with Reginald for some time; Cromwell, due to his connections in the locality, became aware of the gossip and sent Tyndall on a surreptitious visit to the source of these rumours, Ayer. Cromwell was not to be disappointed with either Tyndall or Ayer.

Richard Ayer seems to have had leanings towards the New Learning and was genuinely disgusted at what was going on in Margaret's household. From his statements, and the general whispering of her servants, the countess was portrayed as a 'godfather' figure heading a Mafia of priests. Nothing was done in the county 'bout my Lady dyd knoe yt', for the local priests informed her of what they learned from the confessional.[22] At Easter 1537, ten or twelve of Lord Montague's servants went to Chichester to be confessed 'with the which thyng [my] lady was not a lytyll dyscontent',[23] presumably because by their going to Chichester she would be unable to discover the content of their confessions. The priests were able to justify this betrayal because they believed it was 'for the sole helthe off the partys yn that my Lady was off g[ood mind] and wold se secret reformatyon and feyn as thowe sche dyd [know] be sume other mens'.[24] Ayer was furious that the curate of Warblington had betrayed even his confession to the countess, and was understandably not appeased even though the curate 'askte hym forgevunes afterward off hys knes'.[25] Despite this, there appears to have been no animosity directed towards Margaret as it was believed she was being misled by her priests, especially by her chaplains, Mr Newton and Mr Nicholson, 'for thes be the ryngleders [of] my ladys error all together'.[26] Furthermore, Ayer described the curate of Havant as 'skasly the kyngys [fr]end'.[27] Apparently, Tyndall's arrival in the neighbourhood was not quite as covert as he had hoped, and once his religious leanings were known, Margaret ordered Ayer to send him away from the surgeon house. On Tyndall's refusal to go, she instructed Ayer to send all the patients away. Again, Ayer believed her priests were behind this and affirmed that he could tell the lord privy seal a 'tale that wher worth t[ell]ynge'.[28] Upon Tyndall's offer to set up an interview with Cromwell, Ayer revealed more sensitive information, this time concerning Hugh Holland. According to him this 'knave' Holland 'begenythe nowe off late [to act] the marchant mane and the broker, for he go[yth over] the see and convays letters to Master Helyar ower [parson] her off Warblyntune'. Moreover, Ayer continued, Holland 'playthe the knave off thother [hand] and convaythe letters to Master Poole th Cardy[nall, and] all the secretes off the rem off Ynglond ys k[nowyn to the] bychope off Rome as well as th[ough he] wer her'.[29] Ayer also pointed Tyndall in the direction of a disgruntled ex-member of Margaret's household who, he promised, 'wyll tell more then thys'.[30] This gentleman, possibly a Peter Wythends,[31] had seemingly been put out of Margaret's service due to his adherence to the New Learning. This Peter was anxious that Tyndall should convey all he told him to Cromwell, for on telling

Master Cotton[32] he had been told to leave the matter well alone for 'other men schold do yt welynowhe yff the mychgt parsa[ve them to] be trewe thus'.[33] According to Peter, Margaret's council had forbidden her tenants to have the New Testament in English or any of the new books sanctioned by the king. He also provided more information about the flight out of England of John Helyar. Helyar apparently told Peter that the bishop of Rome had as many friends in England as he ever had, and may also have claimed that he was supreme head over all the Church of Christ.[34] When Peter replied that Helyar's remarks were treasonous, the vicar took fright and fled to Portsmouth where he lodged for six days with one of Holland's infamous piratical associates, Henry Bykley, until he gained passage on a ship to France. On Cromwell's discovery of this, Helyar's goods were sequestered but, Peter continued, Geoffrey Pole and Sir William Paulet 'mayd suc[h] scheft that the matter was clokyd and hys good[es re]stauryd again'.[35] If, Peter promised, he could talk to Cromwell he would show him the truth. He also advised Tyndall on how Cromwell might best extract information from Holland, Bykley and Thomas Standish, clerk of Margaret's kitchen. Being such 'crafty felows', 'my lord schold never get nothy[ng of] them, except he had ther concell and went [more] wysly to worke'.[36]

Margaret was not the only one to be concerned about Tyndall's appearance in the neighbourhood. Although the document is mutilated, it seems that the local priests may have believed him to be an Observant friar and sent a friar from among them to try and discover the truth. When Tyndall realized what was afoot, he declared that he was 'no suche parsne and defyde them all which are frers'.[37] At this, the locals' suspicions not being allayed, the curate of Havant, a Sir William 'Wantlatyn', accompanied by the local constable, visited Tyndall and questioned him. Tyndall eventually lost his temper and warned the curate to remember Ayer's words that he was scarcely the king's friend. Immediately the local constable, 'yn a gret fewme', pledged that he himself and twenty more would testify in support of the curate, and ranted that 'yt was mery yn thes contry [be]for suche felowys came, which fyndythe suche fawtes with ower honestes prestes'.[38] Unfortunately for them, Tyndall, with his high connections, was not to be intimidated and turned the interrogation back upon his examiners. He found it incredible that the constable did not want to question him further to ascertain the veracity of his information against the curate. He also asked him what he meant by Hampshire being merry before such fellows came to find fault with the local priests. The constable replied that he meant Hampshire was a quiet country before, but by now was alarmed enough to go straight to Sir Geoffrey Pole the following day. After telling Geoffrey all that Tyndall had said, Geoffrey, who was also a local justice of the peace, summoned Tyndall before him and assured him that he could speak all he knew for he was the king's justice and friend. At this, Tyndall told Geoffrey what he had heard, adding defiantly that he might well say so 'for yt ys truth'.[39]

Upon hearing such serious accusations, and realizing that Holland's trips were being so widely gossiped about, Geoffrey became extremely concerned, and turned for advice to Oliver Frankelyn, comptroller of Margaret's household and her receiver-general. Frankelyn admonished Geoffrey to take Holland and Ayer and go at once to Cromwell to explain. This Geoffrey did, and reported to Frankelyn that 'the lorde Pryvey Sealle was good lord to hym, And had dyspachyd the said Ayar and holland'.[40] However, the accusations explained by Geoffrey to Cromwell only concerned letters to John Helyar.[41] From this it would appear that Tyndall had not revealed to Geoffrey, or the locals of Havant, the full extent of his knowledge. However, when Tyndall sent Cromwell his full report, probably shortly after Geoffrey's visit,[42] it contained the allegations concerning Holland's conveyance of letters to Reginald and the dissemination of England's secrets to the bishop of Rome. Upon receiving this, Cromwell decided to strike, resulting in Holland's arrest in June. Although Margaret had been implicated over her aversion to the New Learning, her priests' activities and letters to Helyar, for which Geoffrey had also been implicated, Holland's supposed activities were far more serious, and his arrest immediately followed. Holland's testimony was crucial, determining as it did the government's next move; it therefore requires close examination.

Although Holland's interrogation was conducted on 3 November 1538, as with Geoffrey Pole's first examination on 26 October, it was merely the formal record of evidence which the government had already gained from him. Holland's testimony is very extensive, seven pages long and detailed. Indeed, one of the most disturbing things about it is Holland's apparently excellent memory of the verbal messages he had carried between Geoffrey and Reginald. From his evidence, it is clear just how involved both he and Geoffrey Pole were in the flight of John Helyar. Helyar was the countess of Salisbury's personal chaplain from 1 May 1532.[43] He was also the vicar of East Meon and rector of Warblington, a living to which he was presented by Margaret in 1533.[44] An admirer of Reginald, he wrote to him in July 1537 encouraging his stand against the religious changes in England and suggested that the pope should call a three-day fast and general communion to ask for God's mercy on England.[45] Thomas Mayer has noted the potential Helyar possessed to become another hostile propagandist abroad and, at a time when it was feared Reginald might publish his *De Unitate*, this was a possibility the English government did not relish.[46] Naturally, Helyar's departure was viewed with great seriousness. According to Holland, Helyar first asked him whether he would take him overseas at the beginning of the summer in 1534 or 1535.[47] Holland agreed providing his master, Geoffrey Pole, would give him leave. Geoffrey himself then approached Holland, desiring and commanding him to take Helyar to Paris where, he explained, Helyar was going to study. He promised Holland that Helyer 'shall honestly recompense you'.[48] Thus Holland hired a French ship and took Helyar over from Portsmouth at the end of the summer, which corroborates the evidence given by the informer Peter. Having escorted Helyar and his servant Henry Pyning to Paris, Holland left them there and returned to England. Upon his return he informed Geoffrey of Helyar's safe arrival, at which Geoffrey thanked him and promised he should 'not lacke as longe as I lyve'.[49] Holland's interrogators were particularly interested in any conversation Holland might have had with Helyar during the journey, and this Holland also remembered. Helyar told him he had left England because he feared that if he stayed he would be put to death because he believed the ordinances of England were 'agenst godd's lawe'.[50] Explaining the secrecy of Helyar's flight, Holland diverged from the informer Peter's testimony and attempted to vindicate Margaret. It was due, Holland said, 'partely because my lady of Salisbery wolde geve hym no lyevee'.[51] Geoffrey continued to correspond with Helyar, although Holland was not always the messenger. He counted at least three occasions when letters passed between them; the last was about twelve months before when Helyar had left Louvain to join Reginald.[52] Holland further testified that when he was sent by Geoffrey to Helyar after the vicar's benefices had been sequestrated, he also brought back replies to Sir William Paulet, Dr Stuard, chancellor to the bishop of Winchester, and Helyar's brother-in-law, John Fowell. Sir William Paulet, in an attempt to help Helyar, sent Fowell to Louvain to obtain a certificate from the university proving Helyar's attendance in order that the sequestration might be released.[53]

Holland's next testimony was utterly damning for Sir Geoffrey Pole, alleging undeniable treason. Apparently, around Easter 1537 Geoffrey, hearing that Holland was going to Flanders to sell some wheat, asked him to visit Reginald who was in the area on his first legation. He requested Holland to convey a long verbal message to Reginald. This message included Geoffrey's wish to be with Reginald and willingness to join him if his brother would have him, in addition to criticisms of England's religious policies: 'shew hym the worlde in England waxeth all crokyd, godd's lawe is turnyd upsedowne. Abbes and churches overthrowen and he is taken for a traytor, And I thinke they wyll caste downe parisshe churches and all att the last.'[54] He sent word to Reginald that a Mr Wilson and Powell were in the Tower and warned him that assassins were 'sende from Englond daylye to dystroye hym' and that Francis Bryan and Peter Meotes had been sent to France to kill him with a hand gun 'or other[wise as] they shall see best'.[55] The day before Holland embarked Geoffrey suggested that he should go to Reginald himself, but Holland refused, as not even he was prepared to take that risk. After selling his wheat at Nieuport, Holland caught up with Reginald at Awne Abbey, as he had already left Cambrai on his way to Liège. Initially vetted by Reginald's right-hand man, Michael Throckmorton, Holland was finally summoned before Reginald following Mass. After listening to his message Reginald responded with smug sarcasm that, despite all the king's efforts to turn the French king against him, 'yett I was receyvyd into Parys better then some men wolde'.[56] Already aware of Bryan's and Meotes's mission, he doubted that his death lay in their power or Cromwell's. After discussing the merits, or otherwise, of the bishops of London and Durham, Reginald instructed Holland to convey several messages to his family. He commended himself to his mother by the token 'that she and I loking appon a wall togethers redd this, Spes mea in deo est [my hope is in God], and desire her blessing for me. I trust she wylbe gladd of myne allso.' But, Reginald added, should she be 'of the opinyon that other bee there, mother as she is myne, I wolde treade appon her with my feete'. He remembered himself to Lord Montague by the token 'In domino confido' [in the Lord I trust], while Geoffrey was commended by being told to 'medle lytle and lett all things alone'.[57] This, Holland declared, was the extent of the messages he took to and received from Reginald. Unfortunately, Lord Montague was more seriously compromised by his supposed contact with Michael Throckmorton. Holland remembered that while he was there Throckmorton 'desyryd hym to commende hym to the lord Montacute by the tokne that [they had] communyd togethers att his laste beyng in Englonde' in a place which Holland could not remember; 'And bydd hym styrre nott, or bydd hym be contentyd . . . unto his comyng into Englonde'.[58] However, Holland asserted that, on Geoffrey's instruction, he told only Geoffrey of the messages, not Margaret or Lord Montague because Geoffrey feared that 'lord Montacute, was owte of his mynde and wolde shewe all to the lorde Prevey Seale by and by'.[59] Following Holland's visit to Reginald, Geoffrey continued to request that Holland should take him overseas, believing that if he could get to the bishop of Liège 'he showlde have money inough and he trustyd ons to kysse the pope's foote, and made many large promyses to this examinatt'.[60] Nevertheless, Holland always refused his requests. Continuing the examination, Holland admitted telling Lord Montague that Geoffrey was 'very desyrous to goo oversee', at which Montague instructed Holland to 'medle not with that in any case'.[61] In May 1537, at exactly the same time that Holland was visiting Reginald at Awne Abbey, John Hutton, the English ambassador in Brussels, informed Cromwell that he had gained information from two spies that Throckmorton was about to take, or had taken, letters to several of Reginald's friends in England.[62] Of course, now the government knew that Holland could have taken these letters, but more worryingly, despite one of the informers having heard at Awne Abbey that Throckmorton was to go to England with letters, Holland's visit had succeeded in passing completely unnoticed.

Holland was examined on two more occasions, 11 November and at some point afterwards. This information the government might not have had prior to Geoffrey's arrest, but it concerned Helyar informing Geoffrey that he could write to him via a servant of the imperial ambassador, and Holland asking Thomas Standish, clerk of Margaret's kitchen, to inform Montague of Geoffrey's wish to go overseas. Holland also told Standish that he had visited Reginald, and that Geoffrey had told him that Lord Montague 'wolde as fayne be over as he'.[63] Furthermore, he confessed that Margaret's steward, John Babham, had visited him and asked: 'have you spoken with that traitor my Lady's son?' Holland denied that he had but admitted speaking to Throckmorton, at which Babham advised him to 'keep that secret; it may hap to cost you your life else'.[64] This completed Holland's testimony. Although several people had been implicated, Geoffrey had been irretrievably compromised and it is no surprise that his arrest followed. Some historians, no doubt with hindsight, have alleged that Geoffrey was chosen as a witness due to his weak character and the government's belief that he could be intimidated and manipulated into telling all he knew and what they wanted to hear. Muriel St Clare Byrne described the 'emotionally unstable' Geoffrey as being selected by the government 'as somebody who could be made to talk', while S. T. Bindoff believes that the 'government had picked on the weakest of its suspects'.[65] However, it has been shown that this was not the case. Holland's evidence had incriminated Geoffrey Pole, and Geoffrey more seriously than anybody else. Consequently, it was Geoffrey who was arrested as a result, and it is difficult to imagine what other course of action the government could have taken.

Geoffrey's arrest proved something of a minor sensation locally, serving as a trigger for more gossip as the tension mounted. On 2 September Sir Thomas Denys, steward of Margaret's manor of Pyworthy in Devon, and John Rowe, sergeant-at-law, sent the sayings of a Breton priest, Gulphinus Abevan, to Cromwell, having examined him on the day of Geoffrey's arrest. Abevan's assertions were somewhat bizarre and at best confused: for instance he believed that Geoffrey had already 'lost his head'.[66] More incredible was his claim that he had sailed over to England and landed at Rye with Reginald in September 1537, in order for Reginald to 'attempt secretly amongst his friends to obtain the King's favour'. While in England Reginald met the marquess of Exeter and lodged first with Geoffrey, then with his mother, but did not lodge 'in one place above one night'. If Reginald, who was still in England, could not obtain the king's favour then, he told Abevan, he would leave before September 1538 from either Dartmouth or Plymouth. Due to his connection with the countess of Salisbury, it was imperative for Denys to demonstrate scrupulous loyalty to the king. Therefore, he took these ravings seriously and earnestly informed Cromwell that he had 'warned the officers of the western ports to suffer no suspect person to pass under any disguise, either as monk, friar, beggar, hermit, pilgrim, or such like'.[67] September was also the month in which more gossip originating from Richard Ayer, and this time Laurence Taylor, came to light. As discussed, this concerned the comments relating to Holland's meeting with Geoffrey after his arrest, Geoffrey's intention to send a band of men over to Reginald in March 1539 and the suspicion that Holland was carrying letters overseas. In addition, there was the added comment that if Margaret had been a young woman, the king and his council would have burnt her when they were last in Sussex.[68] This gossip passed from Richard Ayer through five people and eventually reached the ears of the local justice of the peace, John Gunter.[69] As a result, Gunter imprisoned one of the gossips, Johanne Sylkden, for claiming that Geoffrey Pole 'wolde have sent over the sea a band of men, to his broder Cardinall Poole if so bee, that he had not beene taken before with oder words'.[70] Here the matter might have ended had not the gossip's husband gone over Gunter's head and approached Sir William Fitzwilliam, earl of Southampton, for help. Ironically, when Sylkden's husband approached Fitzwilliam, he was hawking with the earl of Arundel and Lord Delaware, the latter of whom would also be arrested during the course of the investigations due to his connection with the Poles. Naturally, with Geoffrey Pole's arrest only three weeks earlier, such an accusation which seemed, in Fitzwilliam's words, 'to emplie maner of high treson' could not be ignored.[71] Thus he immediately sent for Gunter, the pertinent depositions and Alice Patchet and her daughter Johanne Silkden, who repeated their accusations. Obviously, Fitzwilliam expected Laurence Taylor, Patchet's source, to be in custody and was flabbergasted to hear that he was in fact attending a wedding in Wimborne! It transpired that after examining him Gunter had let him go. Fitzwilliam, knowing Taylor to have been a servant of Gunter, angrily accused him of acting 'lyke an untrue man'. Gunter, realizing the dangerous position he was in, 'sodenly chaunged countenance, waxeng paale, and with tears and sobbing pitifully besought me to be good unto him, recognising his indiligence, and slacknes'.[72] To make amends, he pledged to make diligent search for Taylor in order to 'serve the king in this mater truly and loyaullie'.[73] It would seem from this incident that Gunter, a colleague of Geoffrey Pole, had tried to protect him. He had not made any attempt to bring this evidence to the attention of the authorities, but had imprisoned the gossip possibly in an attempt to stifle the damaging rumour. This makes Geoffrey's attack on Gunter two years later, in the belief that he had betrayed him, all the more sad. If Gunter had repeated secret conversations to Fitzwilliam, as Geoffrey was to allege, it was due to fear and not malice. His first reaction had been to cover up for his friend.

As in the case of Hugh Holland, Geoffrey Pole languished in the Tower for nearly two months before his first official examination, although he had been questioned prior to this.[74] Not surprisingly the first questions, numbers one to thirteen, concerned Reginald.[75] The government wanted to know which of Reginald's acts Geoffrey liked, how he knew of them, whether he had discussed them with family and friends, and whether he or his family had exchanged any letters with Reginald. Next they turned to John Helyar and in questions fourteen to twenty-six wanted to know what opinions Helyar held concerning the bishop of Rome, what role Geoffrey had played in Helyar's departure, and whether Helyar had sent any letters or messages to him or anyone else.[76] Moreover, showing that they had taken the gossip of Alice Patchet and her associates seriously, they questioned Geoffrey about his intention to visit Helyar at Louvain: why he was going; whether he was taking any men with him, and if so, how many; whether he intended to go on and visit Reginald; where he was going to embark; and with whom he had discussed the victualling of the ship. The questions end with an attempt to find out with whom Geoffrey had discussed wishing for 'a change of this world', how he intended to achieve it, who were prepared to advance it and whether he had received any letters supporting this project. Out of fifty-nine questions, twelve concerned Reginald, thirteen Helyar, thirteen wanted to know who else wished for a change, and nineteen concerned Geoffrey's going overseas with a band of men.

Geoffrey's actual responses, however, reveal that he was only asked questions about those with whom he had discussed a change of this world.[77] It is clear that by this point, 26 October, the government was very anxious to discover who else was involved in this possible conspiracy. A substantial amount of evidence against Geoffrey Pole had been provided by Holland, but little against anyone else. Montague had been slightly compromised by Holland, but the government was unclear as to his total involvement and unaware of just how extensive this network of disaffected individuals was. This line of questioning does not prove that the government was deliberately trying to implicate those it had decided to destroy. The evidence against Geoffrey was extremely serious, and his actions, by informing Reginald, posed a threat to national security. Consequently, almost the whole of Geoffrey's first examination concerned the involvement of others. Although he obligingly mentioned ten names, he strove to vindicate them from any treason. He admitted discussing a change of the world with Lord Delaware, George Croftes, Mr Friend and Mr Langley, but did so without meaning any hurt to the king.[78] Moreover, he continued, Delaware and Montague were more indifferent to such opinions now, while he had not spoken to the marquess of Exeter for two years. He admitted that Edward Neville had trusted the world would amend one day, John Stokesley complained that heretics preached at St Paul's Cross, and Mrs Roper and Mrs Clement disliked the pulling down of abbeys and also wished for a change.[79] However, the government was not to be deflected and demanded to know the meaning of the word 'indifferent' used in relation to Montague and Delaware, and what the nature of the change was. To this, Geoffrey replied that 'they waar nott so much affectionate to thatt part as they war att the former conferences', and that the change referred to the 'pluking down of Abbys Images and pylgremages and this maner of preaching to be changyd, but nott the King's person'.[80] By implicating these individuals, no matter how innocently, Geoffrey had made a rod for his own back. Now sure that others were involved, the government was determined to discover everything. It may have been to further that end that Geoffrey was threatened with torture at the end of the interrogation,[81] for he sent a desperate plea to Henry VIII via his examiners, beseeching the king

that he may have good keping and cherisshing and thereby somewhatt comfort hymself and have better stay of himself, and he sayd he then wold truly and fully open all thatt he ded know or may remember whomsoever it touch, whether it bee mother, brother, uncle or any other whatt se ever he bee.[82]

There is certainly an element of hysteria evident here and much has been made of Geoffrey's collapse. Although some historians might view Geoffrey with contempt as a weak man who betrayed his own mother and brother in order to save his own neck, others, such as the Misses Dodds, take a very sympathetic view of him. G. R. Elton's general description of Geoffrey was of an 'unstable and unhappy man', but this was with hindsight. Geoffrey was indeed unstable and unhappy after his arrest, but not before, as Elton implies.[83] Although Geoffrey was not happy about the religious changes that had been introduced in the 1530s and was worried about his debts, he was not alone, for these were concerns that many others shared. There is no evidence that Geoffrey was suffering from depression or exhibiting any signs of instability prior to his arrest. True, he lacked sound judgement and was often foolishly impetuous, traits that both Montague and Reginald recognized, but despite this he was well liked by most people who knew him. A jolly fellow with a sense of humour and a penchant for puns, Henry VIII showed more patience over his repeated misdemeanours than he deserved, while John Gunter and Richard Cotton, his friends and colleagues, both tried to protect him. Even the implacable Fitzwilliam was moved to pity for him, writing to the king on his behalf in 1540. It is not surprising, then, that he was totally unprepared for the situation in which he found himself in 1538. With the stark realization that this time neither his mother nor brother could help him as they had in the past over his debts, he collapsed, hysterical with fear. In fact, word reached his wife that 'he was in a frenzy and might utter rash things'.[84] Even worse, he could still reason through his anguish and knew that this was exactly what he was going to do, and thus his first suicide attempt was made immediately after his first formal examination.[85] This reveals, as nothing else, his unhinged mental condition. For a man of Geoffrey's religious beliefs suicide meant the damnation of his soul; yet it was a course of action he attempted to take as the only way to avoid the betrayal of his family.

Geoffrey underwent two more interrogations on 2 and 3 November before his brother and the marquess of Exeter were arrested on 4 November. His examination on 2 November corroborated more concisely Holland's visit to Reginald, adding that Reginald had sent a message that both he and Montague should remain in England and 'hold up yea and nay th[ere, for] he would do well enough'.[86] He also admitted that it was Elizabeth Darrell and Lord Montague who had told him that assassins had been sent to kill Reginald and that Thomas Starkey had warned him that 'the lord Pr[ivy] Seall, if the King war nott of a good nature, for one Pole's [sake] would destroy all Poles'.[87] This second examination was accompanied by a grateful pledge of Geoffrey's loyalty to the king, possibly prompted by the knowledge that he would not now suffer torture:

> . . . now especially in my extreme necessity, as I perceive by my lord Admiral and Mr Controller, your goodness shall not be lost on me, but surely as I found your Grace always faithful unto me, so I refuse all creature living to be faithful to you.

It ends with complete abasement, 'Your humble slave, Geffrey Pole'.[88] Geoffrey's third examination, which took place on the following day, was far more compromising for his brother and implicated more fully Elizabeth Darrell and Gertrude, marchioness of Exeter.[89] Apparently, Holland's message from Reginald included the instruction to remind Montague of their communication at Reginald's departure and Throckmorton's offer to fetch Montague when he was ready to come overseas.[90] Geoffrey also alleged that while he served the king Montague 'regardyd hym little' and commented in disgust that only 'flaterars' served at court and 'none sarvyd the King butt knaves', but, after he was forbidden the court, Montague 'made more of hym' and began to confide in him.[91] During the course of his interrogations Geoffrey also revealed that Montague had received letters from Gertrude, or Elizabeth Darrell, informing him that Reginald had escaped Henry's assassins, and letters from Gertrude telling him that when Montague had been discussed in council, her husband had 'offred hymself to bee bound bodie for bodie for hym'.[92] Moreover, Geoffrey confessed that he had repeated all Reginald's messages to Montague, but had not told him the identity of the messenger.[93]

In addition to Geoffrey's evidence, by 28 October the government had the detailed testimony of Jerome Ragland, another witness who unwillingly gave evidence. Described as Montague's

'Right hand',[94] this country bumpkin was no match for seasoned interrogators and, like Geoffrey, he was gradually worn down into revealing the most damning of allegations against Lord Montague.[95] These included personal criticisms of the king, revealing Montague's dislike of and lack of respect for Henry VIII. Montague was disgusted that the king did not keep his promise to hold a Parliament at York at the time of the Pilgrimage of Grace[96] and complained that 'he hath seyn more gentylnes and benygnytie yn tymys past at the Kyng's hands than he hathe nowadays'.[97] At Bisham in 1536, Lord Montague told Ragland that Henry had threatened the lords that he would go with the 'Lubekks' unless they complied with what he wanted, at which Montague remarked to Ragland 'that we shuld be well ryd of hym',[98] evidence which is corroborated in Geoffrey's seventh examination on 12 November.[99] Montague also noted disdainfully that 'the Kyng ys ffull of flesse and unweldy, and that he can not long contynue with hys sower legge', and reflected that if he was sent over sea on the king's business he would be tempted to remain there until England was 'yn a better estate'.[100] Indeed, Ragland continued, that very summer Montague had wished that he himself, his son and six other persons were overseas. Furthermore, Montague criticized the Treason Act, believing it to be too severe and, as Geoffrey also said in his evidence, complained that 'knavys ruylll about the kyng'.[101] He lamented Lord Bergavenny's death, understandably as he was very fond of his father-in-law, and at the time of the Pilgrimage of Grace claimed that Bergavenny, if he were alive 'were able to make a gret nombre of men in Kent and Sussex'.[102] However, as Höllger notes, Montague may have meant that they would have been raised in support of the king.[103] Ragland also testified to the friendship and contact which existed between Montague and Exeter, stating that Montague had 'great trust' in the marquess and described him as a 'nobyll man.'[104] In addition, Ragland had heard Montague say in the last year that he thought Reginald was 'ordeayd of god to do good'[105] and that Montague's servant, Perkyns, spoke favourably of a marriage between Princess Mary and Reginald.[106] Not surprisingly, the evidence gleaned from Geoffrey Pole by 3 November and Jerome Ragland by 28 October guaranteed the arrest of Lord Montague on the evening of 4 November along with the marquess of Exeter. Exeter's wife, Gertrude, was possibly arrested at the same time and conducted with her son Edward to the Tower, to which Montague's young son Henry was also conveyed. On the following day, 5 November, Sir Edward Neville joined his friends at the Tower, and at some later date John Collins and George Croftes also suffered arrest.

Geoffrey's next four examinations, from 5 to 12 November, continued to implicate his elder brother even further. He claimed that Montague had a dream that the king was dead, but within two days declared that the king was not dead but will one day die 'sodenly hys legg wyll kyll hym and then we shall have jol[ly] styrring'.[107] While discussing the Pilgrimage of Grace, Montague exclaimed, 'Twysshe Geoffrey, thow hast no cast with [thee the lord] Darcye played the foole he went abowt [to pluck away the] counsayle he shuld fyrst have begoon [with the head but I beshrew] them for leaving of so soon.'[108] Montague also warned Geoffrey, most probably after Holland's arrest and with amazing foresight, 'never to open any thyng if it shulde happen hym to be examined for if he opened one all must neds come out'.[109] Geoffrey further asserted that Montague only wished him to serve Catherine and not the king.[110] Geoffrey also claimed that both Montague and the earl of Huntingdon complained at the Parliaments of what was being determined there, asserting that only knaves and heretics agreed to what was being accomplished, and mostly out of fear.[111] Furthermore, Montague apparently declared 'that he never lovyd the king from chyldhood and that kyng Henry the viith had none affecion not fansye unto hym',[112] and predicted that 'the kyng wolde be out of his wytts'.[113] Obviously, the careful Lord Stafford, circumspect with the example of his father before his eyes, was concerned about Montague's increasingly treasonous remarks. Apparently confiding in Geoffrey that he was afraid to converse with Montague, he warned him: 'ye foll[ow] so moche the lorde Montacute that he wyll bee yor undoyng one day.'[114]

Another revelation which emerged during the course of Geoffrey's examinations was that he had surreptitiously gone to France in 1532 in disguise, and that Exeter was also apparently aware of this.[115] Keeping 'hymself secretly in hys brothers chamber' during the day, he ventured out only at night and, while there, Geoffrey heard his brother say that the French king was a 'hardyer man than the king our master'.[116] Afterwards, Montague sent him to Catherine to assure her that nothing had been done regarding the king's marriage to Anne Boleyn, 'And that the king had doon the best he cowd, but the frenche king wolde not assent therunto'.[117] In addition, on his return from Calais he delivered letters from Montague to their mother who was then in Kent.[118] Geoffrey also provided most of the evidence against Sir Edward Neville, claiming that he had heard Sir Edward 'many tymes most abhomybly deprave the king saying that his highnes was a beast and worst than a beast'.[119] He told Geoffrey that they should not be seen talking together due to the suspicion in which they were held, but reassured him 'it forsyth nott we shall doe well inough one day'.[120] Another time, when the court was at Westminster, Neville, during an outburst of frustration and disgust, ranted to Geoffrey:

> godds bloodd I am made a fole amongs them, but I laugh and make mery to dryve forth the tyme, the king kepeth a sorte of knaves here that we dare nother look nor speke, And [if I were] hable to lyve, I wolde rather lyve any lief in the world [than] tarry in the pryvey chamber.[121]

Montague's bearing during his incarceration could not have been more different from Geoffrey's. He exhibited the same cool exterior that all but his most trusted associates ever saw. Even after Geoffrey's arrest he ostensibly carried on business as usual, visiting Elizabeth Darrell concerning a loan she had made to Sir Anthony Hungerford[122] and paying a call on his sister-in-law, Constance Pole. On being informed by Constance that her husband 'was in a frenzy and might utter rash things', Montague nonchalantly replied: 'It forceth not what a madman [speaketh].'[123] In fact, there seems to be an air of resignation about Montague more clearly revealed in his mournful observation that 'he hath lyvyd in prison all this vj yeres'.[124] Montague's evidence, obtained from only one interrogation, was characteristically restrained as he strove to provide his interrogators with nothing too incriminating. He declared that Edward Neville had only ever sung songs that contained 'meriy things', nothing political, but did confess that he had burned letters.[125] He also admitted that it was Thomas Starkey who told him Peter Meotes had been sent to assassinate Reginald, a fact which Montague related to Elizabeth Darrell.[126] His evidence also made clear the propensity of Exeter and his wife to confide in him, confirming that Gertrude had informed him that her husband had offered to be bound body for body for him. He also revealed that Exeter had told him of Cromwell's inquiries regarding William Parr, Exeter's bearward. Parr had been convicted of treason in February 1537, possibly for uttering seditious words, and executed with another of Exeter's servants, John Payne.[127] Cromwell was keen to discover who had apprised Exeter 'of his servant that was then in prison',[128] to which Exeter replied that 'he wold never open or disclose his ffrend if it touchyd nott the king'.[129] The marquess also warned Montague of the danger they were in, explaining that 'he was advertiseyd by certayn ffrends of his to kepe no company with hym, And therfor prayed this examinate contentyd to forbear his company'.[130]

John Collins, Lord Montague's chaplain, was also pressed into revealing additional fragments of damning information.[131] Some of his evidence tallied word for word with that given by Geoffrey and Ragland, for instance that Montague had said that knaves ruled about the king, that he hoped the world would amend and that the world would come to stripes. Moreover, Montague described Exeter as having a 'very good mynd' and being 'a man of very good corage'. In Collins's opinion, if there had been any change, Montague 'shuld have hadd a very assuryd frynd of the lord Marquess'.[132] Collins's examination also reveals the government's sinister attempts to ascertain the involvement of Montague's young son, for he was asked 'whether the lord Montacute's soon dyd know anything of the letters of which he spak befor or nott', to which Collins replied that he could 'nott tell saving thatt he dydd know att thatt tyme this examinatt went to the sayd Sir geffreys howse'.[133] In addition, Collins confessed that he and Montague had discussed a letter that Reginald had sent to the king, Cromwell and the bishop of Durham, and that Montague showed him letters sent to himself and his mother in which the cardinal vindicated them from any responsibility for his actions.[134] He testified to Montague's disenchantment with the new Treason Act,[135] claimed that he heard Geoffrey say that Mary should marry Reginald, and that Geoffrey believed that if there was a change then Mary should have a title to the crown.[136] He also signed his own death warrant when he admitted telling Geoffrey and Montague that 'both the king and the lord pryvey seall wold hang in hell' for the plucking down of the abbeys.[137] What also might have come to light was the fact that Collins was on very warm terms with John Helyar, apparently writing to him after his flight. In one of these letters, Collins describes Helyar's letters to him as his 'only defence against the evils of this pestilent age'.[138]

George Croftes, chancellor of Chichester Cathedral, provided further information regarding his friends, Geoffrey Pole and Thomas West, Lord Delaware. He testified to Geoffrey's dislike of the Royal Supremacy[139] and insinuated that Geoffrey intended to desert from the royal forces if it came to fighting during the Pilgrimage of Grace.[140] Croftes also alluded to Lord Delaware's conservative leanings,[141] his dislike of the Statute of Uses[142] and that he advised Croftes not to flee the realm, 'for if he should flee he would be had again wheresoever he were'.[143] Croftes admitted that, being unable to dissuade Geoffrey from leaving England, he gave him twenty nobles for the journey. However, the following day he managed to persuade him to stay[144] and it was at this point that he approached Lord Montague to find a remedy for Geoffrey's debts.[145] Croftes also revealed that Delaware warned him about Sir Henry Owen, who was openly speaking against him, and advised him what to do about it.[146] There does seem to have been some animosity between Owen and Delaware, this incident with Croftes no doubt contributing to it, for Owen was only too willing to inform upon Delaware. Although he was Delaware's brother-in-law, he was also the son of Sir David Owen and thus a kinsman of Henry VIII. According to Croftes, Owen had supposedly bid a Thomas Alen to inform Cromwell that Croftes 'could te[ll marvellous t]hings of a great confederacy between the lord Mar[qu]es of [Exeter], the lord Montacute, the lord Chamberlain[147] and lord [De]laware'.[148] Alen, Croftes continued, refused to repeat such things for he knew they were spoken of malice. Not surprisingly, on 13 November, the same day as Croftes's second examination, Sir Henry Owen underwent interrogation, during which he declared Lord Delaware's dislike for the dissolution of the monasteries and his friendship for the marquess of Exeter.[149]

In addition to these witnesses, a further host of servants and associates were questioned. Elizabeth Darrell claimed Geoffrey Pole swore to stab and kill Peter Meotes even if he were 'att the king's heles',[150] while Morgan Wells admitted that he himself had declared openly his intention to slay Meotes 'with a hand goon' and anyone else 'whom he shold know to kyll the cardinall pole And thatt he was going over sees for thatt purpose'.[151] George

Tyrell, Montague's servant for the past three years, testified to
letters and messages sent between Montague and Exeter and his
wife,[152] while Gertrude admitted that Neville sang in her garden
'thatt he trustyd this world wold amend one day, And thatt honest
men shuld rule one day'.[153] At her fear for her husband's safety
during the Pilgrimage of Grace, Neville said: 'Madam, [be not]
afeared of this, nor of the second, but beware of the third.'[154]
Clearly, Lord Montague and Geoffrey were at the centre of a hot-
bed of gossip as the family, their friends and servants grumbled
angrily and profusely about the state of the realm.

The evidence against Exeter comes almost entirely from
Geoffrey Pole. Apart from testifying to the contacts and letters
between Exeter, his wife and Montague, Geoffrey asserted that
once at Horseley when Exeter gave Cromwell a summer coat and a
wood knife he winked at Geoffrey, saying: 'peas knaves rule abowt
the king', then, holding up and shaking his fist continued: 'I trust
to give them a buffet one day.'[155] On accepting abbey lands, Exeter
assured Geoffrey that they were 'good inough for a tyme, they must
have all agayn one day'.[156] Geoffrey also made the standard
accusation that Exeter liked well the proceedings of Reginald and
misliked the proceedings of the realm,[157] that 'nother the lord
Mountegue nor the lord Marques ever lykyd any doyngs of the
king',[158] while Montague preferred the west parts to Warblington
for 'my lord Marquis of exeter is strong ther'.[159] A far more grave
allegation, however, was that Lord Montague had told Geoffrey
'that many tymys the kyngs pryvye councell weare att theare wytts
ende in such matters as they had in hand' and, Geoffrey continued,
'that the lord Montague knewe all thatt was done in the councell
when the lord Marques was theare'.[160] If Exeter was informing
Montague of the secrets of the Privy Council and Montague was
telling Geoffrey, this was very serious. The government was aware
that Geoffrey had been in contact with Reginald through Holland
and, as Richard Ayer told Tyndall, as a result of Holland's
messages to Reginald, 'all the secretes off the rem off ynglond ys
k[nowyn to the] bychope off Rome as well as though he wer her.'[161]
Certainly, the questions drawn up for the marquess[162] concerned
his communications with Lord Montague, whether he had told
him about the arrest of his bearward and 'Whether you showed
Lord Montacute that the lord Privy Seal had sent Mr Richard
Cromwell to you at the King's being at Oking to be frank and plain

in certain things.'[163] This visit occurred whilst the king was in residence at Woking, Surrey, and so must have taken place between 20 and 28 July, and after Holland's arrest.[164] Clearly, Exeter was being given the chance to tell the king all he knew about the Poles' activities, and possibly save his life. By refusing to do so, Exeter had chosen to protect his friends rather than the king. All this, combined with Exeter's conservative leanings and his proximity to the throne, illustrated in the rehearsal of the Kendall affair, made his arrest inevitable.[165]

In residence at Warblington throughout the investigation, the countess of Salisbury realized the peril in which her son Lord Montague stood, and in September wrote to him:

> as to the case as I ame enformid, that you stand in Myne advise is to enser you to god principally, and upon that ground so to order you both in word and deed to sarve your prince not disobeyeng goddys comandments as far as your power and life woll serve you.[166]

The head of the family herself was, however, the least implicated of all the suspects. Geoffrey Pole's evidence did not compromise his mother at all, and George Tyrell, Lord Montague's servant, when asked if he had heard any conversations between Margaret and Montague, answered that he had not as he was never present when they took supper together.[167] In his evidence, Margaret's comptroller and receiver-general, Oliver Frankelyn, actually strove to protect his mistress. He admitted warning her that Geoffrey might cause her displeasure and said that she replied: 'I trowe he is not so unhappye that he wyll hurte his mother, and yett I care neyther for hym, not for any other, for I am true to my prynce.'[168] In her own evidence, Margaret stated that she only answered: 'nay nay . . . he will not bee so unhappe.'[169] Margaret's own examination began on 12 November when Sir William Fitzwilliam and Thomas Goodrich, bishop of Ely, arrived at Warblington. Her interrogation lasted for two days until 14 November and continued at Cowdray, to which she was conveyed on 15 November.[170] Each page of her answers is signed in her own hand, firmly and legibly with no hint of nerves or sign of age. Despite being relentlessly examined virtually all day from early morning into the night on 13 November, 'sometime with doulx and mild words now roughily and asperly', the 65-year-old countess was staunch in the defence of herself and her sons, declaring 'that if ever it be found and proved in her, that she is culpable in any of those things, that she hath denied, that she is content to be blasmed in the rest of all the articles laid against her'.[171] With two sons in the Tower along with the marquess of Exeter, her courage was remarkable in the face of Fitzwilliam's bullying, and his frustration is obvious: 'we have dealid with such a one as men have not dealid with to fore us, Wee may call hyr rather a strong and custaunt man than a woman . . . She hath shewed herself so ernist, vehement and precise that more could not bee.'[172] She took the king himself to witness that she did not want Reginald to go overseas, 'ffor she desired his grace that her sonne might no more goa over the sea'.[173] She knew nothing of Helyar's flight, a fact which Hugh Holland in his evidence corroborated, and never received any letters from Reginald. During his interrogation John Collins confessed that Montague had shown him letters sent by Reginald to himself and his mother vindicating them from any responsibility for his actions.[174] Nevertheless, this does not prove that Margaret was lying to her interrogators, as Montague may not have shown her the letters.

As the examination continued, Margaret prayed God 'she may bee torne in peaces' if she ever heard that her sons wished to go to Reginald, and 'prayeth that she never see god in the face' if she heard they wanted to go to the bishop of Liège either.[175] She denied burning letters which concerned the king, had never heard that her sons had burned any and asserted that she had not heard her son say that the world was turned upside down, would come to stripes, that he wished for the king's death or 'mention any stiring, or motion or thing like days of her life'.[176] She had never heard Montague say he preferred the west parts to Warblington[177] or that he beshrewed the Lord Darcy for leaving off so soon at the time of the Pilgrimage of Grace 'upon her damnacion',[178] and believed that her son Montague was 'verie sore belied'.[179] It is no wonder that Fitzwilliam exclaimed 'that [either] her sons have not made her pr[ivy] ne participant of the bottom and pit [of] their stomachs, or else is she the [most] arrant traitoress, that ever [lived]'.[180] Margaret also described her reaction to Reginald's *De Unitate*. After being apprised of its content by the king himself, she bemoaned to Lord Montague the misfortune of having such a child. As a result, he counselled her to declare Reginald a traitor before their servants so that they might so report him when they returned to their counties, which she did.[181] She did admit, however, that her sons had told her of Reginald's escape from the king's assassins, 'wherfore for motherly pietie she cold not but reioysce'.[182] She also confessed that she knew Geoffrey had slipped over to France in October 1532 with the royal entourage, but both she herself and Montague had discovered this only after Montague had arrived in Calais. Moreover, if it had not been for Montague sending him back to England, she continued, Geoffrey would have gone in warfare.[183] Margaret's exasperation with Geoffrey and keenness to vindicate Montague is apparent here. The story of Montague's restraint of his brother need not have been included, except that it served to protect Montague while inevitably further incriminating Geoffrey. Clearly, there was little from this examination, and indeed from any of the other interrogations that had taken place, to implicate Margaret seriously. Her innocence is further implied by the confidence and exactness of her answers: using 'most stiff and earnest words', she was 'so precise aswell in gesture and words that wonder is to be'.[184] Therefore, it is not surprising that when Fitzwilliam announced that her goods had been seized and she was to be removed to Cowdray 'she seemeth thereat to be somew[hat] appalled'.[185]

The final examination to take place was that of John Collins on 20 November, and three days later the first of the special commissions was issued to receive indictments in Surrey, Sussex and Buckinghamshire.[186] Although it was approximately five months since Holland's arrest and three months since Geoffrey's, the majority of the examinations had taken place in November with feverish activity on the 12th and 14th, when seven and five individuals were interrogated on each of the days respectively. By the end of that month the government was ready to proceed to trial, and the first, that of Lord Montague, took place at Westminster Hall on 2 December, the marquess of Exeter's on 3 December and that of Geoffrey Pole, Edward Neville, Holland, Croftes and Collins on 4 December. Found guilty, the full penalties were to be exacted on all the condemned at Tyburn, but the king relented regarding Montague, Exeter and Neville. The first to go to their deaths on 9 December were Croftes, Collins and Holland, who were hanged, drawn and quartered at Tyburn, their heads set on London Bridge and their quarters 'on divers gates about London'. Immediately following their executions, Montague,

Exeter and Neville were beheaded at the Tower, and 'theyr heds and bodyes were buryed in the chapel within the Tower'.[187] On 2 January 1539 Geoffrey Pole was pardoned, and his life was spared. A week later, on 9 January, Chapuys reported Geoffrey's fate to the emperor: 'I am told his life is granted to him, but he must remain in perpetual prison; also that on the 4th day of the feasts he tried to suffocate himself with a cushion.'[188]

6

Assessment

❧

'The marquis of Exeter and lord Montague are committed to the Tower for horrible treasons, known, not by light suspicion, but by proofs and confessions.'[1]

Henry VIII and Thomas Cromwell have both suffered criticism over the fall of the Pole family and the marquess of Exeter. Many motives have been ascribed to them, Henry's dynastic fears and desire for revenge against Reginald Pole being the most popular. Against such prevailing opinions, is it possible to vindicate Henry and Cromwell for their actions? What is clear is that the situation in 1538 was complex, and no single cause in isolation can explain the events of that year. Chapter 5 has revealed the copious amount of evidence produced during the course of the investigation. Equally important are the international situation, and the influence and resources of the Pole family. This chapter will attempt an assessment of the families' fall and, by doing so, will hope to illuminate not only the government's motives but the guilt or otherwise of those condemned.

The arrests and executions of 1538 were, not surprisingly, something of a *cause célèbre*. In England it would have been unwise to exhibit any signs of disapproval. Thus letters of congratulation winged their way to Cromwell. Hugh Latimer exclaimed: 'Blessed be God of England that worketh all, whose instrument you be!'[2] Sir Thomas Wriothesley enthused: 'How joyful tidings it must be to all Englishmen to know that such great traitors have been punished, and their attempts frustrated.'[3] A calmer Robert Warner wrote to Lord Fitzwalter: 'It is for Lord Montague's brother, who is with the Bishop of Rome and is an arrant traitor. They would have made foul work in England.'[4] Reactions abroad were far more unfavourable. While on 31 August Chapuys attributed Geoffrey's recent arrest to the fact that he had 'corresponded with or received letters from him [Reginald] without showing them to the king, which is here considered a crime of lèse majesté',[5] in January 1539 he reported Sir Nicholas Carewe's arrest, writing cynically that 'the principal thing that had been required of him since his imprisonment was to testify something against the Marquis; for since the testimony of young Pole is not sufficient, these men . . . want to form the process after the execution.'[6] Louis du Perreau Castillon, the French ambassador in England, wrote to Anne de Montmorency, constable of France, on 5 November that he believed the arrests were a fulfilment of Henry's promise to 'exterminate the house of Montague, which is the remains of the White rose and the house of Pole to which the Cardinal belongs', a promise Henry had informed Castillon of 'a long time ago'. Consequently, he continued, 'It seems that he is seizing every occasion that he can think of to ruin and destroy them'.[7] Meanwhile, the emperor's ambassador in Rome, the marquess of Aguilar, wrote to his master on 20 July 1539 of his disappointment that Charles had not forbidden commerce with England, reporting in disgust that 'the King of England continues in his misdeeds and cruelties, and has now sentenced to death the mother of Cardinal Pole'.[8] Reginald himself imputed his family's downfall to their devotion to the Church, thus casting them in the role of martyrs. To Francis I's letter of condolence he replied that the 'calamities' of his family 'are connected with those of the Church, and of the [Catholic] religion'.[9]

Such adverse foreign reactions, at a time when England's relations with both France and the Empire were extremely tense, prompted the government to put forward its side of the story. On 31 December 1538 Castillion wrote to Montmorency reporting Cromwell's claim that Reginald had written to his brothers and Exeter telling them to do nothing 'until he should come hither'. This refers to Geoffrey Pole's evidence in which he stated that Reginald instructed both himself and Montague to remain in England and 'hold up yea and nay the[re]'.[10] Cromwell went on to explain that their intention was to drive out Henry VIII, for Exeter and the Pole brothers were very powerful. This must refer to the recurring accusation throughout the evidence that the three of them wished for a change. However, by 9 January the government's claims had descended into a farrago of nonsense. Remonstrating with the French ambassador in Henry's defence, Cromwell declared: 'one who punished traitors by law did not deserve to be called a tyrant', and announced that Exeter had planned to marry Mary to his son and usurp the kingdom.[11] By the following month things had deteriorated further when Wriothesley made it known in Brussels on 5 February that Exeter had been a traitor for the last twenty years, planning to take Henry's place and kill all his children. On 13 February Henry ordered Sir Thomas Wyatt to inform the emperor that both Montague and Exeter had plotted to murder the whole royal family, including Mary, and 'usurp the whole rule, which Exeter had meditated these last ten years'. Moreover, these facts had been disclosed by Geoffrey Pole and 'openly proved before their faces'.[12] Naturally, few were convinced by these outrageous accusations, which merely revealed the government's desperation to stem the hostile foreign reports.

The views of modern scholars are no less varied than those expressed by contemporaries. The first detailed account of the fall of the Pole and Courtenay families was completed by the Misses Dodds as part of their two-volume work on the Pilgrimage of Grace in 1915.[13] According to them, once Reginald's letter, *De Unitate Ecclesiastica,* arrived and Reginald accepted the pope's invitation to Rome, the family's fate was sealed: 'the King would bide his time, but in the end he would strike.'[14] Their 'few careless words' gave the king that opportunity.[15] The Dodds' inference is that by 1536 Reginald's actions had already doomed them, their innocence or guilt notwithstanding. They do admit, however, that their ruin might have been hastened by the threat of invasion which hung over England in 1538.[16] This is a view shared by Helen Miller who, noting Exeter's power in Devon and Cornwall, interprets their fall as a precaution in the event of a Catholic invasion.[17] According to Joyce Youings, Exeter's execution 'was in accordance with a long-term policy of exterminating all possible Yorkist claimants to the Tudor throne'.[18] Mortimer Levine maintains that Henry VIII had harboured a 'long meditated aim of annihilating the house of York' which, Barbara Harris believes, was behind the king's decision to prosecute the duke of Buckingham in 1521.[19] Alan Neame also makes much of this, feeling that while he remained sonless Henry remained vulnerable. Without a male Tudor heir, 'However loyal, however discreet, these close relations of his stood to gain a great deal if things remained as they were.'[20] According to R. B. Merriman, the apparent difficulty Cromwell had 'in trumping up any plausible charges against his victims, would seem to show that no adequate proof of any really disloyal intent could be found',[21] while Sir Arthur Salusbury MacNalty takes the view that the Poles and Courtenays were among many who met their fate due to Henry VIII's abnormality of mind, incidentally a condition alluded to by Lord Montague in 1537.[22] According to MacNalty, the severe pain of Henry's leg 'certainly helped to bring out the evil that a saner mental disposition would have controlled'.[23] G. R Elton, however, believes that Henry 'had a reality to react against'. He notes the substantial amount of evidence pointing to the fact that 'treason was contemplated if not plotted', and, while their incompetence earns them pity, it 'does not disprove their intention to plot'. Elton is one of the few historians who is convinced that both families were 'not only disaffected but revolving ways of giving disaffection teeth'.[24] Certainly, Thomas F. Mayer has sought to prove that Reginald's legation of 1537 had the potential to pose a real threat to Henry VIII's security, and while G. W. Bernard disagrees with this he does accept that Henry's actions, in the serious international climate of 1538, were understandable.[25]

Christoph Höllger has conducted an examination of the so-called 'Exeter Conspiracy' as part of his study on Reginald Pole's legations of 1537 and 1539. He firmly believes that the family's fate was directly related to Reginald's activities on the Continent. He links up every move against them with every act of opposition to Henry VIII perpetrated by Reginald in Europe: 'Henry tried to use the Poles as hostages to secure reasonable conduct by Reginald Pole, and he destroyed them as his policies did not work with the cardinal.' While admitting that the trials were technically legal, he believes that evidence was in some cases forged and 'on most occasions flimsy if not dubious'. Thus, he reaches the firm conclusion that 'the government had used English law as an instrument with which to commit judicial murder'.[26] While maintaining that the Poles suffered for Reginald's behaviour, the marquess, he believes, went to the block purely as a result of his proximity to the throne. The only aspect upon which most scholars do agree is that, whether guilty or innocent of conspiracy, the Poles and Courtenays were never a serious threat to Henry's security. So let us examine each of these motives in turn, starting with Merriman's and

Höllger's allegations that the evidence was weak and, in parts, forged.

It has been shown in the previous chapter that many accusations were corroborated by several different witnesses. Although the interrogators would not be averse to using a point raised by one witness to press another into agreeing with it, on the whole the veracity of the testimonies should be accepted. For instance, it is hard to argue for Geoffrey Pole's innocence since, by his own confession, the detailed testimony of Hugh Holland and the corroboration of others, we know that Geoffrey sent messages and betrayed secrets of the realm to a known traitor. Höllger specific-ally claims that the comment, 'this world will change one day, and then we will be merry. We shall have a day upon these knaves that rule about the king',[27] attributed to Edward Neville in the indict-ments, was forged because it cannot be found, word for word, in any of the evidence against Neville.[28] However, Geoffrey Pole, in his testimony, claimed that Neville 'trusted the world would amend one day', while Gertrude supported this by adding that he also hoped 'honest men should rule one day'.[29] She also stated that Neville 'trusted knaves should be put down and lords reign one day'.[30] The sentiments expressed in the indictment, and in the testimonies of Geoffrey and Gertrude, are so similar that it would be otiose to forge this piece of evidence against Neville. Höllger further feels that there is no reason to believe that the papers con-cerning Geoffrey Pole are incomplete, and so Neville's comment in full should be there. Equally, there is no way to be sure that Geoffrey's papers are complete. Geoffrey may very well have made a further statement that has since been lost or destroyed, and indeed some of these documents are already in a poor state of pre-servation. Turning to the evidence against Montague and Exeter, there is a distinct difference which accurately corresponds with their personalities. Montague had never been close to Henry VIII, and by the 1530s revealed a marked dislike for him. With the king's treatment of Catherine and Mary and the execution of Thomas More, a man he admired, Montague found it easy to think the worst of Henry VIII, and the evidence clearly reflects this. Mont-ague reserved his greatest insults for the king rather than for Cromwell, and even suggested that Wolsey would have been a better man had he had a better master. It was the king Montague blamed rather than his ministers. The marquess of Exeter, however, was fond of Henry VIII. This is not surprising as he had enjoyed many years of friendship with him and Henry had been very generous towards him. Therefore he, unlike Montague, found it difficult to think badly of Henry, and it was the ministers rather than the king whom he chose to blame. Exeter's indiscretions concerned threats and insults against those about the king, especially Cromwell, but not one criticism did he utter against Henry VIII.

So how serious was the evidence against the accused? Was it flimsy as Höllger suggests, and trumped up by Cromwell as Merriman claims? With the exception of Geoffrey Pole and Hugh Holland, the Misses Dodds believe that the rest of the accused were only guilty under the new laws, meaning the Treason Act of 1534, not under the old treason laws, as the case against them rested on words only.[31] This is not quite true, as the accused's comments did bring them within the bounds of the 1352 statute against treason. Moreover, words had been sufficient to indict for treason before Henry VIII's statute. The declaration in the 1352 statute that it was treason 'to compass or imagine the death of the king' was used to indict for what were considered malicious words or writings against the king.[32] In the second half of the fifteenth century the king's lawyers explained their extension of the clause by stating that such behaviour was 'intended to destroy the cordial love which his people had for the king and thereby shorten his life by sadness'.[33] Indeed, at the trial of the duke of Buckingham in 1521, Chief Justice Fineux explained the difference between felony and treason. While felony required an act to be committed, 'merely to intend the king's death was high treason and such intention was sufficiently proven by words alone'.[34] As J. Bellamy makes clear, 'If the words did not suggest a direct intent to bring about the king's demise then they were held to do so indirectly and the accused found guilty of treason just the same.'[35] Montague's alleged statements that he approved of Reginald's proceedings, wished to be overseas,[36] feared the world would come to stripes[37] and that they would lack honest men when the time came,[38] were explained as an indication of his intention to confirm Reginald in his treacherous opinions and to deprive the king of his dignity as Supreme Head of the Church.[39] The sayings of Geoffrey Pole and the marquess of Exeter that they too approved of Reginald's doings[40] were also taken as an indication of the same treachery. Such a protestation of approval for the actions of Reginald, by 1538 a recognized traitor to Henry VIII, could be seen to fall under the old treason law of 1352 which stipulated that it was treason to 'adhere to the king's enemies and be provably attaint of it by men of the offender's own condition'.[41] Montague's prediction that the king would die suddenly resulting in jolly stirring,[42] was used as proof that Montague wished and desired the king's death.[43] This did fall under the Treason Act of 1534, under which to wish or attempt bodily harm to the king could be expressed by words, writing or deed.[44] Montague's hope that Henry would carry out his threat to leave England,[45] that he never loved Henry VIII from childhood and that one day the king would be out of his wits,[46] were described as traitorous declarations, while his statement that Wolsey would have been an honest man if he had had an honest master[47] was seen as an indication of his intention to have a day upon the knaves about the king.[48] His desire to dwell in the west parts, his regret that Lord Bergavenny had died and his criticism of Lord Darcy's failure to pluck away the head[49] were also rehearsed. In addition to his support of Reginald's actions,[50] and his disapproval of the king's,[51] the marquess was indicted for saying that he hoped to have fair day upon the knaves and pledged to give them a buffet,[52] and hoped to see a change of the world.[53] These words were widely interpreted as a manifestation of his desire to procure the death and destruction of the king.[54] Edward Neville's indictment rested on his description of the king as a beast,[55] his hope that knaves should be put down, lords reign one day and that the world will amend.[56] He also supposedly assured Geoffrey: 'this world will change one day, and then we will be merry. We shall have a day upon these knaves that rule about the king.'[57] The indictments against Geoffrey Pole were obviously more clear-cut, involving his threat to desert during the time of the Pilgrimage of Grace[58] and, most obviously, his message to Reginald, for the conveyance of which Holland was indicted.[59] The accusations against Croftes and Collins concerned their opposition to the Royal Supremacy[60] and Collins's prediction that the king would hang in hell for pulling down the abbeys.[61] Clearly, all these comments, of which there were many, were serious enough to fall under one or both of the Treason Acts of 1352 and 1534.

Although admitting that the trials were technically legal, Höllger is in no doubt that judicial murder had been committed. He has criticized the procedure of these trials, especially that of the marquess of Exeter because in treason trials it was usual for the accused to make a plea in their defence. There is no record of a plea in Exeter's trial, which Höllger interprets as an indication that the government was desperate to keep him from speaking. However, no pleas appear to be recorded at any of the other trials either. Apart from the documents in the Baga de Secretis and Wriothesley's account of the executions, the only account of the trials is by Richard Morisyne. Commissioned by the government to explain its version of events, his *Invective*, published in 1539, included an account of the conduct of Exeter, Montague and Neville. In treason trials the accused were not apprised of the evidence beforehand, and Morisyne gives the impression of three flabbergasted men. They stood stiff at the bar but 'with castyng up of eies and handes, as though those thynges had ben never herd of before, that thenne were laid to theyr charge'. The marquess, Morisyne continued,

> stack hardest, and made as though he had ben very clere in many poyntes, yet in some he staggered, and was very sory so to do, nowe chalangyng the kynges pardon, now takynge benefytte of the acte, and when al wolde not serve, he began to charge Geffrey pole with frensye, with foly, and madnesse.[62]

Morisyne's account does have an air of truth about it; the three men's surprise and bewilderment, the marquess's sometimes clumsy attempts to refute evidence for which he was totally unprepared and, at the last, his accusation of madness against Geoffrey Pole.[63] Exeter was, Morisyne continues, allowed to confront Geoffrey, but the account loses credibility at this point by reporting a persuasive rebuttal by Geoffrey who, although not usually an accomplished speaker, was granted temporary eloquence from God for the purpose of his speech. Nevertheless, even Morisyne reports no pleas from the accused. Certainly, Buckingham had been allowed a plea, as had even the dangerously persuasive Thomas More and Anne Boleyn, so it is hard to understand why Exeter and Montague were denied the opportunity. It is just possible that they refused to make a plea in disgust, knowing that it was useless, although this does seem less likely for Neville.[64] Although the matter of the plea is unclear, the trials themselves do appear to have been fair, or at least as fair as sixteenth-century treason trials could be.

G. R. Elton has shown how treason trials could be rigged against the accused. For instance, the lord steward's court, before which Montague and Exeter were tried, was theoretically composed of all peers. In practice, the peers were appointed 'by selective summons', and clearly the opportunity for rigging the panel of lords triers existed.[65] However, Montague and Exeter were tried before twenty-eight peers, over half of the nobility,[66] and several of these peers were connected to them through marriage, kinship and friendship, while the rest carried no known grudges against them. Indeed, the earl of Arundel, a peer with whom the Pole family had experienced problems, was omitted from the panel. Of those who sat, the duke of Suffolk was an annuitant of the countess, Thomas, earl of Rutland was the grandson of Anne Plantagenet, Edward IV's eldest sister, and George, earl of Huntingdon's son was married to Lord Montague's daughter. Henry, Lord Morley was married to Alice St John, the daughter of Richard Pole's cousin John. Charles, Lord Mountjoy was Exeter's brother-in-law, while William, Lord Sandys had enjoyed a long association with the Pole family, to whom he was distantly related.[67] Finally, the brother of Andrew, Lord Windsor, Sir Anthony Windsor, was closely connected to John Helyar. He had administered Helyar's parish after his flight from England, for which he received letters of gratitude from Helyar.[68] In addition, Geoffrey Pole's daughter Margaret married a brother of Lord Windsor.[69] Clearly it was not a panel of enemies rigged to the detriment of the accused. Nevertheless, it must be remembered that such men would be particularly keen to demonstrate their loyalty to Henry VIII in order to avoid any implication themselves, especially as some had been compromised in the evidence against the two families. Accordingly, although both Montague and Exeter pleaded not guilty, the guilty verdict was unanimous.[70] The composition of the commission of oyer and terminer before which Neville, Pole, Holland, Croftes and Collins were tried was equally unremarkable, and again the guilty verdict was unanimous, with only Edward Neville pleading not guilty.[71]

According to Christoph Höllger, 'Montague was not killed by his quick tongue, but simply because someone had to suffer for the annoyance caused to the king, by the rebellious cardinal.'[72] Each new affront that Reginald committed against Henry's authority was, he claims, followed by action against his family. When Reginald first went to Rome they were threatened; when Reginald accompanied the pope to the peace negotiations at Nice, Geoffrey was arrested; when Reginald went to meet the emperor on his second legation, Montague was executed; and when the threat of this second legation reached its climax, Margaret's and Reginald's own attainder followed.[73] Their trials 'had been staged only to gain a pawn against Reginald Pole',[74] while Henry's predetermination to exterminate the Poles is revealed in Castillon's letter to Anne de Montmorency in November 1538. Firstly, Henry did indeed feel Reginald's treachery keenly. His betrayal was not only of his king and his country, but of his own kinsman. The education Henry had so generously provided for Reginald had now been turned against him, while Reginald's actions not only posed a danger to Henry but were a source of great embarrassment. Not surprisingly, although the family of such a traitor was bound to fall under the betrayed king's suspicion, it has been shown that the arrests in 1538 followed a logical sequence independent of Reginald's activities. For instance, Geoffrey had been arrested, not because Reginald went to Nice with the pope, but because he had been irretrievably compromised by the evidence of Hugh Holland. Montague was executed because a week earlier he had been tried and found guilty of treason. As to the charge of premeditation, this hinges on Castillon's letter in which he claims that Henry VIII told him 'quite some time ago' that he intended to destroy the family.[75] Castillon came to England between November 1533 and April 1534 and again in June 1537. Höllger places his conversation with Henry VIII in 1537 in the aftermath of the arrival of *De Unitate* and Reginald's elevation to the cardinalate, when Henry was sufficiently angry to make such a threat.[76] Although this is a year after *De Unitate* arrived and six months after Reginald was made a cardinal, it is a more likely time than between 1533 and 1534, when Henry still had genuine hope that Reginald might support him. However, we must be careful not to make too much of this letter and Henry's alleged remark. The king's volatile temper is well known, and in June 1537 he was still smarting from the abject failure of his attempts to have Reginald assassinated. A furious outburst such as this would be understandable under the circumstances. Also, the fact that he said it to the French ambassador is significant. In the summer of 1537 Reginald had been allowed into France, much to

Henry's chagrin. Therefore the remark was probably intended to reach Reginald's ears and serve as a punishment and threat, while his anger was probably directed as much at the French as at Reginald. Hence, it would be dangerous to conclude from this one remark, spoken in the heat of the moment, that Henry had definitely decided to kill Reginald's family. It is true that Henry was capable of harbouring resentments, but what of the letter dashed off by Wriothesley to Sir Thomas Wyatt on 12 November 1538? Reporting the arrests of Montague and Exeter, he observed: 'yet the kings maiestie loveth them so well and of his great goodness is soo loth to proced against them that . . . yt ys doubted what his highnes woll doo towards them.'[77] The premeditation of which Henry is accused by Höllger goes only so far as keeping Reginald's family under surveillance once the cardinal's true colours were revealed, and the family themselves were aware of it. Montague likened the past six years of his life to being in prison once doubt was cast upon Reginald's adherence to Henry's cause. Exeter had been warned to avoid Montague because of the suspicion their friendship excited, and Neville was advised by the king himself, in Cromwell's presence, to shun the marquess's company,[78] while Tyndall's arrival at the Warblington surgeon house has been shown to be more than mere coincidence. Nevertheless, such surveillance merely points to the government's good sense rather than to any malevolent intentions. Only when the first fragments of gossip about the Poles began to reach Henry's ears did he order a thorough investigation, and he did so as a result of genuine fear for his security.

Some historians have portrayed Henry as a king whose terror of potential rivals to his throne resulted in the executions of 1538. However, this charge is again hard to defend for, if Henry was that afraid, why did he approve the Pole family's marriages? Although at Mary's birth in 1516 Henry had optimistically declared that, with God's grace, sons would follow, in the autumn of 1517 Catherine suffered a miscarriage and in November 1518 the thirty-three-year-old queen was delivered of a stillborn child. While the situation was not yet as desperate as it became by 1524 when Catherine's barrenness was obvious, the miscarriages, stillbirths and lack of a male heir would have been a cause for concern by 1518, after nine years of marriage. Yet it was in that year that Ursula's marriage to the duke of Buckingham's son took place and united two strong claims to the throne.[79] In addition, Montague's wife, Jane Neville, was descended from Joan Beaufort, the daughter of John of Gaunt,[80] while Montague's son-in-law, Francis, Lord Hastings, was the son of Anne Stafford, daughter of the duke of Buckingham. Indeed, Montague's grandson was to be regarded as one of the principal claimants to the throne during the reign of Elizabeth I. In addition, if the Pole family and the marquess had succeeded in overthrowing the Tudor dynasty, the resultant situation would have been most confusing, a fact of which Henry could not have been ignorant. The marquess of Exeter's claim was as the grandson, through the female line, of Edward IV. Although Lord Montague's was only as the grandson in the female line of Edward IV's younger brother, Montague's mother, unlike Exeter's, had never been declared illegitimate, a fact Chapuys considered an impediment to Henry VIII's claim. Therefore, should Montague's title prevail, then the countess of Salisbury, like Margaret Beaufort, would have to set aside her own claim in her son's favour. Furthermore, the situation would test the friendship between Montague and Exeter to the limit, as one would have to agree to relinquish his claim in favour of the other. M. L. Bush has constructed a convincing argument which suggests that there was no vendetta against those of the blood royal under Henry VIII, a conclusion with which David Starkey concurs.[81] Bush has noted the prosperity enjoyed by several royal relatives under Henry VIII, which, in addition to the Poles, Courtenays, Arthur Plantagenet, and the earls of Rutland and Worcester who have already been mentioned, included the Bourchier peers, that is, Lord Berners and the earls of Bath and Essex.[82] Bush also correctly notes that those members of the blood royal who fell during the reign of Henry VIII had all compromised themselves.[83] Clearly, the idea that Henry VIII was desperately afraid, and had been for some time, that either Montague or Exeter was successfully going to advance his claim to the throne, and destroyed them because of it, must be viewed with caution.

In reality, what the government did seem to fear in 1538, and a far more understandable fear it was, was a rising in support of Princess Mary. The testimony of witnesses during the accumulation of evidence against the Poles reveals that they were being questioned about this very possibility. Ragland admitted hearing Lord Montague's servant Perkyns say that 'it were a mete maryage of Reynolde pole to have the lady Marye the kings daughter',[84] while John Collins claimed he had heard Geoffrey Pole himself say that Reginald should marry Mary. He also added that 'when communication hath byn of change' he believed it referred to the possibility that 'the sayd ladie Mary shuld have a tytl to the crown one day if such change shall happen'.[85] The idea of Reginald marrying Mary was also supported by Chapuys.[86] Certainly, the devotion of the Poles and Courtenays to Mary was no secret. Margaret's loyalty to her had been proved in the face of Henry VIII's anger, while in 1535 Chapuys wrote to the emperor that the marquess 'only regrets that he has no opportunity of shedding his blood in the service of the Queen and Princess'.[87] During the crisis of June 1536 when Mary faced prosecution as a traitor, Exeter was expelled from the council due to his partiality for her. Moreover, in order to facilitate the endorsement of Margaret's attainder in the Lords in May 1539, Cromwell produced a tunic allegedly found in one of her coffers.[88] The symbolism clearly denoted Reginald's intention to marry Mary and restore papal authority to England.[89] So associated with Mary were the Poles, that Cromwell chose to present evidence he considered was plausible enough to convince the Lords of its authenticity.

Mary's restoration was a far more credible banner behind which to march than any dynastic claims of the Poles and Courtenays. Indeed, one of the demands issued by the Pilgrims in 1536 was that Mary should be made legitimate again and restored to the succession.[90] Unlike any other claimant, Mary might also enjoy the support of the emperor, who would naturally prefer to see his own cousin on the throne of England than a member of the Pole or Courtenay families. It is significant that in May 1538 Mary was warned by Cromwell 'not to give her father grounds for suspicion, particularly by entertaining strangers in her house'.[91] Mary was unable to deny the presence of these 'strangers', merely responding that their presence had been reported 'to the worst'.[92] Although Henry had been blessed with a son in 1537, it can be argued that by 1538 the succession was still not secure. Edward had been born while England was in schism. Thus, to those who still believed in papal authority, the young prince could be considered illegitimate. Compounding these fears was Edward's age: in 1538 he was only a baby while Henry, at forty-seven, was well into middle age. In May of that year, when Edward was only seven months old, Henry VIII actually fell seriously ill after one of the fistulas in his leg stopped, causing a blackening of the face and loss of speech.[93] With the usurpation in living memory, perpetrated by the countess of Salisbury's uncle, the fate of his baby son in the event of his death was a fear constantly on Henry's mind, especially should a religious split occur in the country. It is therefore clear that the devotion of the Poles and Courtenays to Mary is what gave Henry real cause for concern, far more than any worries he might have had over their own dynastic claims.

Should the Pole family have decided to take action against Henry VIII, how substantial a network of support might they have been able to muster? This was undoubtedly a question the king would have contemplated, especially in light of Reginald's assurance to Charles V in *De Unitate* of 'an English fifth column of "whole legions, lurking [*latent*] in England"'.[94] It has been shown in chapter 3 that many of Margaret's officers were local men from the southern counties, and from most of them she enjoyed longevity of service, but would that loyalty have extended to supporting her and her family against the king? Thomas Mayer certainly believes that there were a number of candidates who would have been ready and willing to support Reginald Pole should he have taken military action against England. However, he places too much importance upon lesser figures like Hugh Holland, Morgan Wells, George Croftes, John Collins, Michael Throckmorton, Bernadino Sandro, John Walker, Jerome Ragland and John Helyar, who cannot really fit the description of 'foot soldiers and clergy in some numbers' upon whom Reginald could call.[95] Mayer's claim that Sir William Fitzwilliam, earl of Southampton might also have rallied to the call is debatable too. His evidence for this is Fitzwilliam's exclusion from the council in 1536 along with Exeter; his attempts to cover up the first signs of Geoffrey Pole's crimes as well as those accusations levied against Margaret; and his enthusiasm at Cromwell's fall some years later. His expulsion from the council probably had more to do with his support of Mary than any links to Exeter, while he was the first to inform Cromwell of the gossip concerning Geoffrey Pole in September 1538, and was more than diligent in his investigation of it. The sole proof that Mayer offers for his supposed cover-up on Geoffrey's behalf is that when Fitzwilliam wrote to Cromwell concerning the gossip that originated from Laurence Taylor, he explained that the only evidence 'came from an old woman, a midwife, and a young woman with a small baby'.[96] However, what Fitzwilliam actually said, in the context of the letter, was that because Laurence Taylor had confessed the words attributed to him by Alice Patchet 'who bee the toue of them an old woman, and a midwife and the toodre a yong woman haveng a child sowking on her brests. I think it not mutch necessarie to deteigne, or molest them ferdre'.[97] Fitzwilliam was a man who prided himself upon his loyalty and service to the king[98] and although he took pity on Geoffrey Pole in 1540[99] he revealed a marked dislike for the countess of Salisbury, describing Reginald as a 'whoreson' to her face in March 1539.[100] There might also have been an element of revenge here as Fitzwilliam had every reason to resent Margaret's wealth and position. His mother, Lady Lucy Neville, was a daughter of John Neville, marquess Montague but, due to the acquisitiveness of Margaret's father and her uncle Richard, duke of Gloucester, Fitzwilliam's family had been deprived of Montague's estates to the benefit of the two dukes.

Mayer is, however, correct to draw our attention to the Poles' connections and thus their potential supporters. It becomes clear that, in addition to Chapuys, the Poles had a further connection to the imperial court. Elizabeth Darrell, friend of both Lord Montague and Geoffrey Pole, was the mistress and true love of Sir Thomas Wyatt, English ambassador to the imperial court. Elizabeth did not shrink from repeating snippets of information passed on to her by Wyatt. Jerome Ragland confirmed that in the summer of 1538 Elizabeth told him about a poison Wyatt had discovered in Spain, and that he had asked Henry VIII if he should bring some to England, to which Henry had replied 'nay'.[101] Indeed, Edmund Bonner, Wyatt's enemy, took advantage of the tense and suspicious atmosphere to write letters of complaint from the imperial court to Cromwell. One reported that Wyatt had instructed John Mason to make contact with Reginald.[102] Although this was an attempt on Wyatt's part to gain information 'that were worthe the kynges knowledge',[103] Bonner naturally preferred to infer a more sinister intention. Although Cromwell was confident of Wyatt's innocence, after the minister's fall these charges were again raised against Wyatt, resulting in a short spell in the Tower in January 1541.[104] The Poles' link to the French court was through Sir John Wallop, one of the ambassadors to Paris in 1532, who had also received the lieutenancy of Calais in 1530. He made a good impression on Francis I, whose favour he enjoyed,[105] and also reaped the benefits of Henry VIII's generosity, receiving land and manors in Somerset and Devon, augmenting his already substantial inheritance in Hampshire.[106] Sir John had married as his first wife Elizabeth, widow of the eighth earl of Kildare and a kinswoman of the Poles. Daughter of Oliver St John, Elizabeth was Sir Richard Pole's first cousin, and it emerged from the evidence of 1538 that it was to Wallop that Lord Montague had sent his dependant Thomas Nanfant to learn the French tongue. Fortunately for Wallop, what the government did not discover was a letter written by Cardinal Ridolfo Pio Carpi, bishop of Faenza and papal legate to France to Signor Ambrogio, the papal secretary, in March 1537 describing Wallop as 'a great friend of the Legate [Reginald]'.[107] Certainly, the fact that all the government's plans to kidnap or assassinate Reginald were revealed to the cardinal seriously unnerved the king, who must have wondered just where Reginald's information was coming from. Furthermore, Wallop had been in France as ambassador during Geoffrey Pole's surreptitious visit in 1532, and by 1538 his brother Oliver had been appointed constable of the countess of Salisbury's castle at Christchurch, Hampshire. Significantly, Wallop was arrested in 1541 at almost the same time as Wyatt due, as Chapuys put it, 'to his having said something in favour of Pope Paul'.[108]

In the mid-1530s Cromwell was experiencing problems in Calais with another potential Pole ally, Lord Lisle. Cromwell was concerned that Calais under the conservative Lisles was a potential weak spot and thus a danger 'if either French or Imperial forces were placed at the Pope's command against Henry VIII'.[109] These fears were exacerbated by Cranmer's constant complaints that Lisle was hindering the furtherance of the Reformation in Calais.[110] Cromwell's attempts to mediate between the two proved useless and by 1537 resulted in a breakdown of relations between the lord deputy and Cromwell himself. Indeed, Lisle was arrested in 1540 under suspicion of having communicated with Reginald in order to deliver Calais up to him.[111] Lisle's conservative leanings, kinship to the Poles and strategic office would be enough to raise doubts as to his loyalty if the Pole family took action against the king. Another name to conjure with is that of William, Lord Sandys, who had enjoyed a long connection with the Pole family. A colleague and distant kinsman of Sir Richard Pole, he had been appointed constable of Christchurch Castle for life in 1499[112] and presumably held it for some years during Margaret's possession, before relinquishing it, possibly due to ill health.[113] A religious conservative whose sister, Edith, had been Lord Darcy's first wife, he was described by Chapuys in 1535 as 'one of the most experienced soldiers of this kingdom'.[114] By the 1530s, disgusted with the goings on at court, he quietly withdrew. However, his conservatism was known, and when one of his servants criticized a sermon by Hugh Latimer, the king was seriously offended.[115] In August 1537 Lord Lisle apparently tried to block an investigation by John Butler, commissary at Calais, into Lord Sandys's activities,[116] and during the investigation of the Poles in 1538 he was accused by Sir Henry Owen of being involved in a 'great Confederacy' with Exeter, Montague and Delaware.[117] Sir Thomas Denys, Margaret's steward of Pyworthy in Devon, was another possible danger man. Hailing from a local Devonshire family, Denys was recorder of Exeter and had been pricked sheriff five times.[118] In 1537, however, he was accused by Thomas Cromwell of hanging at the Courtenays' sleeve, while in the same year it was discovered that he had assisted a fellow JP (justice of the peace) to conceal a robbery carried out by a member of that JP's own family.[119] In addition to men like these, there were also all those to whom the Poles were connected by kinship, marriage and service, which amounted to a substantial group of not uninfluential individuals. Added to this was the extent and location of the countess of Salisbury's lands.

Among her manors, Margaret held one in Cornwall, three in Dorset, six in Devon, eight in Somerset, eight in Hampshire and the Isle of Wight, and properties in St Nicholas parish, Calais. In addition, Geoffrey Pole held moieties of the manors of Gatcombe and Calbourne on the Isle of Wight. Of the two manors she held on the Isle of Wight, Swainstone and Binstead, Swainstone, which stretched from the Solent to the Channel, was the largest estate on the island. Moreover, at some point Margaret had granted the tenure of it to the notorious Thomas Standish, her clerk of the kitchen.[120] The extent of Margaret's manors in Hampshire, along with her main seat, the fortified castle at Warblington which was barely a mile from the sea, made Margaret a considerable figure in the locality. Further along the coast towards Dorset lay Christchurch, one of Margaret's richest manors, which in 1538 still boasted a substantial medieval castle with a keep 50 ft by 45 ft 6 in. and walls 9 ft 8 in. thick under the constableship of Oliver Wallop.[121] As noted, Margaret also held several other riverside and coastal manors stretching from Dorset through Devon and down into Cornwall. Furthermore, in 1538 the most powerful family in the west of England was the Courtenay family, headed, of course, by the marquess of Exeter. The dominant landowner in the Exe valley,[122] his estate was eclipsed only by that of the Duchy of Cornwall, of which he was steward.[123] Thus substantial areas of the south and the southern coast, areas over which diligent control needed to be exercised, lay under the influence of Margaret and the marquess of Exeter.

The sensitivity of the Isle of Wight was made glaringly obvious seven years after the arrest of the Poles. In 1545 the French launched an invasion fleet and troops actually succeeded in landing on the island in July. In Hampshire R. H. Fritze has revealed the lack of any serious resistance to the dissolution of the monasteries, but he has also shown that the area was not without its problems, admitting that 'sporadic and unorganised resistance' did occur.[124] A case of 1538 reveals how local officials were prepared to aid conservative clergy in their attempts to resist the enforcement of reformation statutes,[125] while in April 1539 there were rumours in Sussex 'that the King's enemies were arrived at Haylyng in Hampshire'.[126] Cornwall was the scene for a rising in 1497 which, with support from Devon and Somerset, marched all the way to London.[127] Retaining their own language, which enhanced their separatism, the Celtic Cornish had maintained links with their Celtic brothers in Brittany. Good trade relations existed between them and many Bretons lived in Cornwall, while in 1530 Leland testified to the large number of Irishmen in Padstow.[128] Julian Cornwall maintains that the Cornish, conscious of being a conquered race, had always remained 'antipathetic to their English neighbours',[129] and in 1537 Dr Simon Heynes, Reginald's replacement as dean of Exeter, wrote to the king: 'This is a perilous country. For God's love let the king's grace look to it in time.'[130] Although Joyce Youings believes that Heynes's report was undeserved and, due to Cornwall's relative tranquillity since 1497, would fail to convince the king, how can we be sure that Henry, with a propensity for suspicion, would not be alarmed by such a remark? Certainly, in March 1539, as part of his provisions for the security of the realm, Cromwell charged Norfolk to be responsible for the north of England, and Bishop Rowland Lee for south Wales and for the coasts of Somerset, Dorset, Devon and Cornwall, and a team of twelve knights prominent in the four counties was appointed 'to search and defend the coast'.[131] In addition to the militia and royal officers, Cromwell also recognized the importance of having 'sad and expert men in every shire near the sea to view the coasts'.[132] The south and south-eastern coasts were particularly vulnerable due to their proximity to France, and Henry was well aware that any weakness in these areas could be fatal as it might provide an entry point for a foreign army or allow the inception of further risings against the Crown. By 1538 it is clear that the king felt he had genuine cause for concern.

By early 1539 England's political isolation had reached a desperate stage. In June 1538, a ten-year treaty between France and the Empire had been signed. The following December Pope Paul III confirmed the suspended bull of excommunication against Henry VIII, and two months later both the French and imperial ambassadors were recalled from England. Furthermore, it was believed that an invasion force was mustering off the Dutch coast.[133] The government's concern at the possibility of a Catholic invasion is illustrated by the extensive defensive measures taken. Forty warships as well as impounded merchantmen were prepared for action, while musters were held and men and armour assembled. A survey of coastal defences was also launched, the most comprehensive since the reign of Edward I, and the resultant fortifications were constructed at great expense to the Crown, apparently amounting to £376,477 including works at Calais.[134] Although this crisis point was reached in the early months of 1539, the situation had been brewing for much longer. England's security lay in the hostility which existed between France and the Empire, but towards the end of 1537 Henry observed with increasing alarm the signs of a prospective Franco-imperial reconciliation. On 16 June 1537 came the treaty of Bomy between France and the Netherlands, and in October an agreement between Francis and Charles to hold peace talks.[135] Between 15 May and 20 June 1538 these peace talks went ahead at Nice. Francis and Charles did not actually meet; the talks were mediated by the pope, who met both monarchs separately. Nevertheless, the ten-year treaty that was signed was further cemented by the eventual meeting of the two adversaries at Aigues-Mortes on 14 July 1538. It was during this meeting that Francis and Charles agreed to cooperate against the enemies of Christendom and pledged to bring heretics back into the fold.[136] Understandably, 'The truce of Nice was viewed by some, including Thomas Cromwell, as posing a massive threat to England.'[137] Significantly, this threat had been actively furthered by none other than the countess of Salisbury's son, Reginald Pole, who had been in attendance at the peace talks in Nice.

The reason Reginald and the pope were so actively involved in furthering the rapprochement between Francis and Charles, was because they knew that only by this could they hope to muster enough forces to destroy the enemies of the Church, which included Henry VIII. Both Reginald and the pope were committed to the idea of restoring papal authority to England. They realized that this might have to involve force, but believed it was better that the king 'and all his supporters should die rather than endanger the salvation of others'.[138] Reginald expressed such aims in a position paper to the pope, which Paul III duly included in the secret part of the bull appointing Reginald legate *a latere*. Finally issued on 31 March 1537 towards the end of the Pilgrimage of Grace, the bull also instructed Reginald to encourage the English rebels with a crusading indulgence.[139] Publicly Reginald's legation charged him to concentrate on obtaining 'peace with the princes beyond the mountains', the abolition of heresies and resistance against the Turk.[140] However, the English government was not blind to Reginald's real intentions. Although careful not to commit his plans to paper, Reginald instructed his servant Throckmorton to warn Henry of the dangers 'off those prynces to whose honour ytt ys iudgyd to apperteyne to defend tha lawes off the churche ageinst all other prynces or nations thatt wyll impugne them'.[141] Thomas Theobald, a protégé of Cranmer, informed his master that Reginald was disappointed that the pope was not taking more vigorous action against England, a sentiment remarked upon by Throckmorton himself. Furthermore, Francis I informed Henry that Reginald was coming with money to help the northern rebels.[142] Henry was fully aware that Reginald's mission also included the directive to exhort both Charles V and Francis I to take concerted action against England, and this is amply illustrated in the king's desperate attempts to have Reginald silenced. This, his agents were instructed, was to be achieved either by kidnapping or assassination. Reginald's secretary, Beccatelli, claimed that Henry had put a price of 50,000 crowns on his head and offered the estates of Flanders 10,000 foot soldiers with ten months' pay if they would hand Reginald over to him.[143] Compounding all of this was the prediction that had been circulating since 1512, and which could be interpreted in relation to Reginald, that after Wolsey's fall, Catherine's repudiation and 'much misery the land by another Red Cap be reconciled or else brought to utter destruction'.[144] In addition, other prophecies circulated concerning a deliverer coming from overseas and a battle of priests.[145] What is important about these prophecies is that the government actually took them seriously and investigations were launched which were supervised by Cromwell himself.[146] Therefore, by 1538 there was a crisis point in England. The government was genuinely afraid that there might be an invasion, with Reginald Pole playing a prominent role and possibly looking to find an entry point around the southern coast. Both the countess of Salisbury and the marquess of Exeter were considerable landowners in this region while Margaret had substantial areas of coastline under her control. If Henry could trust them to defend these areas for the Crown and maintain order within them, then their power and influence was a welcome necessity; but by 1538 could Henry trust them?

The Poles' track record with Henry VIII was not good. By 1538 relations between Henry and the head of the family had broken down to such an extent that the countess had withdrawn from court. Her behaviour over the previous two decades, which included her land disputes with Henry and support for Mary, had convinced the king that she was both disobedient and, like her perfidious son Reginald, ungrateful. Relations with Lord Montague and Geoffrey Pole were only marginally better. Geoffrey's indebtedness and reckless disregard of the king's wishes on several occasions had given Henry little reason to feel confident in him. Regarding Lord Montague, although he had always been careful not to provoke an open breach with the king, the two men simply never warmed to each other. From the evidence gathered against him in 1538, Montague's venomous personal attacks on the king revealed his true feelings. Whether or not Henry sensed this must always be open to question, but significantly Montague was never invited to enter the inner sanctum of the privy chamber and repeatedly lost out in the elections to the Order of the Garter, failing on no less than twelve occasions from 1518 to 1536.[147] Although he served as a justice of the peace, Montague enjoyed no real political role. He held no important household or governmental office, his presence at court being merely ceremonial, and this cannot be due to any ineptness on his part. Furthermore, Montague had been implicated in the duke of Buckingham's treason and had enjoyed a close friendship with Lord Bergavenny. Imprisoned over his involvement in the Buckingham affair, Bergavenny had also been prosecuted for illegal retaining in 1516.[148] Indeed, in 1525 during the collection of the Amicable Grant, the dukes of Norfolk and Suffolk wrote to Henry concerning the unrest over the exaction, warning: 'If this business spread, lords Burgayne and Stafford should be looked to. Do not know but what they might do well, but God knows what ill spirits might put in their minds.'[149] Furthermore, the brothers were not quite the innocents some historians would have us believe.

Lord Montague and his brother Geoffrey had definitely committed treason by keeping the imperial ambassador, Chapuys, informed of what was going on at court. In 1534 Montague had apprised Chapuys of the progress of the proposed interview between England and Germany.[150] In the same year Geoffrey, who had to be dissuaded by Chapuys from visiting him quite so frequently, implored the ambassador to encourage Charles V to invade England, explaining 'how very easy the conquest of this kingdom would be, and that the inhabitants are only waiting for a signal'.[151] In 1536, while dining with Chapuys and complaining of the bad state of the realm, Montague eagerly kept the ambassador up to date with the latest instalment on the state of the Boleyn marriage.[152] Either he or Geoffrey might also have kept Chapuys informed about the progress of the Pilgrimage of Grace. These bulletins could have been crucial, for, if Chapuys had learned that the Pilgrims had started to gain the advantage, it might just have been enough to persuade Charles V to act. Certainly, 'one of the principal gentlemen in the King's army' incorrectly told Chapuys that one of the Pilgrims' demands required that 'the property of the Duke of Buckingham and others, which has been taken by the King and his ministers, may be restored to the lawful heirs'.[153] The Misses Dodds feel that this suggests the informant might have been one of the Poles, as the northern rebels had no great interest in the duke of Buckingham's heir. They believe the Poles may have drawn up their own list of grievances and shown them to Chapuys before sending them north to Aske.[154] This seems unlikely as the risk of interception would have been far too great and the Poles had no known connection to Aske. A more reasonable explanation is that the Poles could have discussed these demands either with Lord Hussey, who had once served as Mary's lord chamberlain while Margaret had been her governess, or with Lord Darcy before his return to the north in 1536. Both Lord Hussey and Lord Darcy had had treasonous communications with Chapuys as early as 1534 when Darcy invited the emperor to invade England. Indeed, he wished to obtain licence to go home to Templehurst in Yorkshire so that 'With the assistance of your majesty he would raise the banner of the Crucifix together with yours'.[155] Moreover, after his departure and before the Pilgrimage had broken out, the Poles could easily have sent verbal messages to Darcy via the lawyer, Thomas Grice. Grice had served Darcy since 1492,[156] he was also, by 1528, the clerk of Margaret's court at Cottingham.[157] Searching through Darcy's correspondence, Cromwell's protégé Richard Pollard commented that Grice 'was a great doer among the commons in the insurrection'.[158] What is important is that Henry did suspect, and, as we have seen, quite rightly, that information was being betrayed to Chapuys. In January 1539 the ambassador informed Charles V that Cromwell had claimed the marquess 'and his accomplices' had had intelligence with Chapuys:

> for it had been found several times that your Majesty was informed beforehand of their intentions; and also they must have had intelligence with some other ambassadors or agents of your Majesty and with cardinal Pole, and it could not but be that their intrigues were known.[159]

Furthermore, as early as September 1533 Chapuys wrote to the emperor in support of Reginald's claim to the throne of England, informing him two months later of the illegitimacy of Henry VIII's mother, declared during the reign of Richard III.[160] It is disquieting that Chapuys knew about this since Henry VII had taken every step to ensure no copies of the statute remained. Nevertheless, in 1535 Chapuys made it quite clear to Cromwell that he knew all about the statute's contents, no doubt further fuelling suspicion as to his source of information.[161]

By 1538 Henry could not be confident that the Poles were wholehearted supporters of his government and the religious changes which had been introduced during the 1530s. He knew that they supported Mary and suspected that they had been passing information to the imperial ambassador. As the investigations of 1538 gained momentum, evidence was produced further proving all these suspicions and more. The head of the family, who had already proved herself resistant to the king's wishes, had her finger very firmly on the pulse of local religious feeling through unscrupulous means and used this to block the furtherance of religious changes in Hampshire. In addition, her sons had been in communication with their brother, a known traitor, through whom secrets of the realm had been betrayed to a hostile foreign power. In addition, this family was powerful, with vulnerable areas of the southern coast under the countess of Salisbury's control, and considerable resources and potential supporters in England and abroad. The marquess of Exeter was one of the most influential and popular figures in the region who had no difficulty in 'arraining some thousands to oppose the Yorkshire rebels'[162] during the Pilgrimage of Grace. The close friendship between Exeter and Lord Montague made the marquess a natural ally and, combined, their forces would be considerable, something of which Henry VIII was only too well aware. If we add to this the unnerving international situation of 1538 which threatened foreign invasion actively supported by Reginald Pole, then the result is nothing short of explosive. In fact it would have been surprising in light of this situation if the Pole family and Exeter had not been arrested.

Henry's understandable concern is further illustrated by his determination to maintain control over Margaret's lands and those of the marquess of Exeter following their arrests. Although in need of funds for the provision of defensive measures, apart from Warblington, Henry made no immediate grants of Margaret's southern manors. It was not until 1540 that the first grant occurred, that of a lease of part of the demesne land of Stokenham to Nicholas Upton.[163] Although a grant had been made of one of Exeter's Buckinghamshire manors in May 1539,[164] it was not until October 1539 that the first of his southern manors was granted, when John, Lord Russell, a staunchly loyal royal servant, received 'Caryfytzpayn' in Somerset.[165] The following year Prince Edward was granted certain of Exeter's manors in Cornwall in recompense for Wallingford, which was to be detached from the Duchy of Cornwall, while Margaret's steward of Pyworthy, Sir Thomas

Denys, received another of Exeter's possessions, the hundred of Budlegh in Devon.[166] In 1541 several more of Margaret's Devon and Somerset manors were granted to Henry's fifth queen, Catherine Howard, as were a selection of Exeter's manors in Cornwall, Devon, Dorset, Hampshire and Somerset,[167] and in 1545 Oliver Frankelyn, having proved himself in royal service, was granted his late mistress's manor of Clyst St Mary, Devon.[168] Obviously, the men appointed as chief stewards of these two estates were men on whom the king felt he could rely. Sir William Fitzwilliam, the man who had exercised such diligence in the prosecution of the Poles, was appointed chief steward of all Margaret's possessions in England, Wales and the marches following her attainder. It was to carry out this office that he had the privilege of being granted Warblington at the same time in July 1539.[169] Richard Pollard, Cromwell's protégé, who had also played a considerable role in the investigations of 1538, was chosen to exercise the office of chief steward of all Exeter's lands in March 1539.[170] In July of the same year John, Lord Russell, a man Henry was building up to fill the power vacuum left in the south by Exeter's fall, received several of the marquess's offices in Cornwall, Devon and Somerset.[171] Höllger attributes Margaret's downfall entirely to Henry's thirst for revenge,[172] and while this can be advanced as a convincing motive for her execution, regarding her arrest there is clearly more involved than just this. By 1538 Henry felt he was no longer able to trust her and, with the added threat of invasion, needed to take control of her extensive estates. Unlike Gertrude, marchioness of Exeter, Margaret was the head of her family, she alone held the estates, and therefore it was her arrest and attainder that was needed to allow the Crown to absorb them. Ironically, her privileged position had ultimately contributed to her downfall.

Muriel St Clare Byrne has described the fall of the Poles and Courtenays as 'one of the most violent and merciless political coups of the reign'.[173] What is in fact surprising is that it was not more of a bloodbath than it was. The Poles and Courtenays were not the only ones mentioned in the evidence of 1538, and many more escaped than were executed. Of the thirteen arrested in 1538, nine suffered punishment: seven were executed and two imprisoned. However, twelve further individuals were implicated who were all spared punitive action against them. John Stokesley, bishop of London, was also rector of Brightstone, Isle of Wight,[174] three-quarters of which manor was held by Margaret. He was also a known friend of Sir Geoffrey Pole.[175] In addition to the allegation of a scandalous affair with Anne Colte, abbess of Wherwell,[176] he had proved a troublesome figure during the 1530s. Although a supporter of the divorce, he opposed any kind of doctrinal change, and this brought him into conflict with the king and Cromwell. In 1535 a 'preaching war' broke out at St Paul's Cross between the preachers of Cranmer, Latimer and Cromwell, and those of Stokesley: 'At least twelve of Stokesley's chosen preachers came before the authorities for open resistance to the new ways and royal policies'.[177] In 1538 Cromwell was preparing to question John Dove of the Calais Chapter House about a letter Stokesley had written to Lord Lisle which ended with the possibly treasonous wish 'that all should not perish there as it is lost here.'[178] In the same year Praemunire charges were initiated against him, but having confessed he was pardoned.[179] During one of his examinations, Geoffrey Pole testified that Stokesley had complained to him that Cromwell and the bishop of Rochester had appointed heretics to preach at St Paul's Cross,[180] but despite this Stokesley escaped unscathed although Cromwell had had a perfect opportunity to rid himself of an enemy.

Cromwell was given a similar opportunity regarding Sir William Paulet. Comptroller of the king's household, steward of Winchester diocese and one of the most influential men in the locality, he had worked satisfactorily with Cromwell in the past, actively participating in the dissolution of the monasteries and the furtherance of the Reformation in Hampshire.[181] Unfortunately, Sir William's loose-tongued younger brother George revealed the Paulet family's true opinions of the lord privy seal in a series of insulting remarks that found their way back to Cromwell. As a result, George was committed to the Tower in May 1538, prompting Sir William to dash off a letter to Cromwell pleading for his release and promising that 'from hensfurth he will no more offend you nor oder noble man with word or ded'.[182] Although George was eventually released and was serving on the commission of the peace of 9 July 1538,[183] at the same time as this embarrassing incident, Paulet was implicated in the Helyar affair. According to Hugh Holland's evidence, he had brought replies from Helyar to several individuals including Paulet. In addition, Paulet had tried to prevent the sequestration of Helyar's goods, and this was also corroborated by the informer Peter.[184]

Nevertheless, Paulet survived and took every opportunity to demonstrate his loyalty to Henry VIII, becoming involved in the interrogation of Geoffrey Pole. George, earl of Huntingdon also realized he was in a dangerous position in 1538. Geoffrey Pole claimed that both Huntingdon and Montague, communing together, had complained about what was done in Parliament and said that only knaves and heretics agreed with what was done there out of fear.[185] As a result, Huntingdon fell abjectly under the tutelage of Cromwell. By March 1539 Cromwell was beginning to exact payment for his services by 'requesting' the reversion of the rape of Hastings. Huntingdon promised to do all he could to gratify Cromwell, 'for I shall never forget the good counsel you gave me between Mortlake and Wandsworth as you rode towards London before Christmas'.[186]

Mrs Roper and Mrs Clement, the daughter and foster daughter of Sir Thomas More, were also compromised by Geoffrey Pole, having apparently complained about the dissolution of the monasteries.[187] John Babham, the steward of Margaret's household and her surveyor, knew that Holland had spoken with Throckmorton,[188] while Morgan Wells himself admitted that he had intended to kill Peter Meotes or anyone else sent to assassinate Reginald.[189] Nevertheless, none of these appear to have suffered any investigation; in fact Babham continued to sit as a JP for Buckinghamshire. Despite evidence which suggested that John Gunter and Richard Cotton respectively tried to protect both Geoffrey and his mother, they also escaped the débâcle. Gunter received no more than a severe telling-off from Southampton, while Cotton was eventually granted the manor of Warblington in 1551. William Friend, schoolmaster of Chichester Prebendal school, and William Langley, subdeacon and vicar of St Peter's the Great, Chichester, with whom Geoffrey claimed to have discussed a change of the world, also lived to preach another day.[190]

This brings us finally to Thomas West, ninth Baron Delaware, who of all the other survivors came closest to losing his head. Based at Halnaker in Sussex, he was an associate of both the Poles and Lord Lisle and his name was put forward along with Lord Montague's to stand proxy for Lisle in the Lords in 1536.[191] He was on friendly terms with both Pole brothers, who were accustomed to visiting him at Halnaker. In the evidence gathered against the Poles, Delaware had been compromised for his conservative religious beliefs and his familiarity with the marquess of Exeter.[192] After ordering an investigation, Henry VIII received a letter from the Lords of the council reporting that they could find 'as yet no sufficient ground to commit him to the Tower' and begged pardon 'for not proceeding more summarily, as it would touch the King's honour if he were imprisoned on a weak ground'.[193] However, on 2 December, the day of Montague's trial, Delaware was sent to the Tower.[194] On 15 December William Ernley, a JP of Sussex and a colleague of both Delaware and Geoffrey Pole, wrote to John Hyberdyn, Cromwell's servant, reporting the sayings of a priest, Sir Simon Fowler. According to Fowler, the reason Delaware was sent to the Tower was because 'he wold not be ye foreman of ye quest to my lord Montagew'.[195] Perhaps Delaware had shown some reluctance to sit on the panel of peers, but, whatever the truth, by 21 December 1538 Husee was able to inform Lisle that Delaware had been discharged.[196] However, the recognizances required of him were substantial, £3,000 'for his personal appearance before the King and Council when called on, within a year of date'.[197] In addition, he had to relinquish Halnaker to the Crown, receiving in exchange the nunnery of Wherwell, Hampshire.[198]

Some of the above must have been on tenterhooks during the winter of 1538 and felt their heads loose on their shoulders. Certainly, the evidence would have allowed for the troublesome Stokesley's removal, and John Babham's, while the government could have made life difficult for Thomas More's daughters. Yet it chose not to, restricting itself to those Henry considered to be the most dangerous and those, like Collins, Croftes and Holland, who had committed blatant treason. The government probably believed, and quite rightly, that the executions would provide sufficient warning, and one only has to note the behaviour of men like Sir William Paulet and Sir Thomas Denys, who fell over themselves to prove their loyalty to the king, to see how successful that warning was. Moreover, Höllger has suggested that the reason Delaware obtained a pardon was because 'the Government wanted to avoid unrest among the nobility',[199] and this is probably true. If Henry had hauled in everyone against whom evidence pointed, he might have provoked the very disturbances he was trying to prevent. The resultant shift in the local power distribution would also have caused uncertainty, a consequence which would have gone against Henry's attempts to create stability and a united front in the face of a prospective invasion. What is clear is that the débâcle of 1538 was not as bloodthirsty as some historians have made out; certainly many more individuals could have gone to the block had Henry so chosen.

In light of the above evidence is it possible to justify the destruction of these two great houses? Despite the unsettled international situation of 1538, with hindsight we know that England was never in any danger of invasion. Neither Charles V nor Francis I had any intention of answering Reginald's call to arms, while the pope himself failed to give Reginald any practical or material assistance. The ease with which the families were removed, the lack of protest or outcry, also reveals that they probably would not have enjoyed the support their extensive contacts suggested. Moreover, should an invading force have landed, English xenophobia would undoubtedly have worked in Henry's favour, while a question mark must for ever hang over the families' actions in that instance. However, Henry could not have known that England was not in any danger from invasion, or that the families' support network was not as strong as it appeared. Indeed, at Margaret's removal to Cowdray Fitzwilliam felt it necessary to instruct several carefully chosen individuals,

> who be all gentlemen and neighbours there with other the kings servants and faithful subjects to have vigilant eye to the same, that if any stirring or misorder chance or befall, the same by their good means, powers and discretions may be stayed and put in quietness.[200]

The evidence of Lord Montague's and Geoffrey Pole's disaffection was overwhelming, while the countess of Salisbury's antipathy to the religious changes of the 1530s was well known. Among the five wealthiest peers in the country, her lands lay predominantly in the south and along the coast, areas vulnerable to invasion, while both her sons were competent military leaders. Close by lay the huge Courtenay estate headed by the marquess of Exeter, a close ally of the Poles. Indeed, the 1530s, as John Guy explains, was a time when 'not since Bosworth had the need for radical decisions and confidentiality in the Council been so pronounced',[201] yet the marquess had apparently kept Montague informed of everything. When the first signs of treason started to emerge with Holland's arrest, Exeter was given the chance to talk, for Henry was astute enough to know that through his closeness to Montague, he would be privy to the Poles' activities. Exeter's decision to put his friendship for Montague above his devotion to the king meant that Henry could no longer feel confident of his loyalty. Henry VIII demanded unconditional allegiance from his subjects as a means of guaranteeing the security of his throne; nothing less was acceptable to him. Individuals whose loyalty was conditional upon the king behaving in a manner which *they* considered to be acceptable were, quite simply, a security risk. The evidence presented above has not sought to prove that the Pole and Courtenay families were definitely conspiring against the Crown, or that they ever posed a serious danger to Henry: it has attempted to show that they possessed the inclination and a real potential to do so. Combined with the tense situation of 1538 and Reginald Pole's openly treasonous behaviour abroad, Henry VIII could not have taken any other course of action than the action he took in 1538. It was clear that the families had both the propensity and the capability to threaten the security of his throne, and it is not surprising that they died for it.

Epilogue

❧

*'God in His high grace pardon her soul, for certainly she was a
most virtuous and honourable lady.'*[1]

Although Henry's actions against the Pole family in 1538 are
understandable, Margaret was more the innocent bystander her
brother had been in 1499. None of the testimonies had incriminated her, and the worst of which she could be accused was
preventing members of her household and tenants from having the
Bible in English. Nevertheless, as it was too much of a risk to leave
the Salisbury lands under her control, she was imprisoned, but not
executed. Her attainder, passed through Parliament in May 1539,[2]
accused her and Hugh Vaughan of her manor of Welsh Bicknor,
Monmouth, of having 'trayterously confederate themselfes to and
withe the saide false and abhomynable trayters henrye poole late
lorde montacute and Reignold poole sonnes unto the saide countes
knowinge them to be false trayters and co[mm]en Enemyes unto
your maiestie and this your realme'. In addition to their being
further accused of having traitorously aided, maintained, abetted
and comforted Montague and Reginald in their 'false and horrible
treasons', the act also declared that Margaret and Vaughan had
'comytted and p[er]petrated div[er]se and sundrie other detestable
and abhomynable treasons to the moste fearfull p[er]il and
daunger of the destruction of your most royall p[er]son and to the
utter losse disherison and desolacon of thys your Realme'.[3] Due to
the lack of evidence against Margaret, the government was not
able to detail these sundry other detestable and abominable
treasons. In the document which proclaims itself to be 'A summary
declaration of the faith, uses and observations in England', an
explanation of the recent executions was given: 'The King never

caused any man to be put to death by absolute authority, but by ordinary process. No one has been condemned but by twelve of his peers, and no lord without the sentence of 24 lords at least.'[4] Whilst this is true regarding Montague and the others executed in December 1538, it cannot be said about the condemnation of Margaret and the marchioness of Exeter or the continued imprisonment of Margaret's grandson Henry Pole and Gertrude's son Edward Courtenay. They were accorded no trial, while nothing at all was put forward against the two children, who were not even included in the act of attainder, so that clearly the Crown had no legal pretext for keeping them prisoners.[5] The fate of Margaret and her fellow prisoners continued to attract comment abroad. Marillac made sure that Francis I and the court were kept informed[6] while Aguilar dashed off a report to Charles V on 20 July. Reginald took advantage of the situation to announce dramatically to Cardinal Contarini that Margaret had been condemned, not to death, but 'to eternal life'. Nevertheless, Reginald's genuine outrage, enhanced by the emperor's inactivity, is clear; not only had this 'western Turk' condemned his mother, 'a woman of seventy', but also Montague's son, 'the remaining hope of our race'. This tyranny, which began with priests and then extended to nobles, has now 'come to women and innocent children'.[7]

The countess of Salisbury's incarceration began at Cowdray, Fitzwilliam's residence. The tragedy and horror of 1538 had seen the execution of her beloved eldest son, left her youngest son a broken man and led to the ruin of her house. Despite the devastation she must have felt at these events, Margaret remained staunch in the defence of her innocence which still managed to perturb the brutish Fitzwilliam. Although he had appointed a gentleman to do 'nothing but attend on her', Margaret was bitterly upset that neither Fitzwilliam nor his wife would speak with her on their return to Cowdray. Having forced himself to visit her on 14 March 1539, Fitzwilliam told her, in no uncertain terms, that neither he nor his wife would speak to her while ' "that arrant whoreson traitor, her son the Cardinal, went abouts from prince to prince" to work trouble to the King and realm'. Margaret immediately replied 'with a wonderful sorrowful countenance' that, although Reginald was 'an ill man to behave so to the King who had been so good to him, yet he was no whoreson, for she was both a good woman and true'.

She declared that she wished Reginald was in heaven or that 'she could bring him to the King's presence, and she hoped the King would not impute his heinous offence to her'. At this, Fitzwilliam abruptly left and later wrote sullenly to Cromwell: 'I had no further talk with her, nor will I while I am here. I beg you to rid me of her company, for she is both chargeable and troubleth my mind.'[8] By 20 March Cromwell had promised to help, for on that date Fitzwilliam wrote: 'My wife is proud to hear that your lordship will help to deliver her of the lady of Sarum.' In fact, so agitated had his wife become about Margaret's presence in their household that Fitzwilliam had been forced to take her with him while he carried out his royal duties, 'for in nowise would she tarry behind me, the said lady being in my house'.[9]

Margaret was eventually removed to the Tower by no later than 20 November 1539,[10] and in 1540 she, along with her grandson Henry Pole, was specifically exempted from the king's general pardon.[11] What must have been extremely galling for Margaret was the release and pardon of the marchioness of Exeter on 21 December 1539.[12] Gertrude had been more seriously implicated in the evidence than Margaret and had certainly committed treason.[13] In February 1540, Gertrude received £100 'by way of his grace's reward'[14] and on 22 March she was granted an annuity of £163 15s 11d out of her late husband's lands in Devon and Essex.[15] Just why she was treated so generously we can never be sure. Whether it is in order to cast a sinister light upon her reward is impossible to say, but if she had been induced to provide any useful evidence against Margaret it would have been shouted from the rooftops by the government. Therefore, in this instance it does appear that Henry's quest for revenge, combined with his personal dislike of Margaret, played a part. Such a distinct difference between the way Margaret and her grandson were treated compared with Gertrude and her son sent a clear message to Reginald: they were being persecuted because they were his relatives. Thus Marillac wrote to Francis I in July 1540 that Edward Courtenay 'is more at large than he was, and has a preceptor to teach him lessons; a thing which is not done towards the little nephew of Cardinal Pole, who is poorly and strictly kept and not desired to know anything'.[16]

While Gertrude walked to freedom in December 1539, Margaret remained within the walls of the Tower where she was to end her days just as her father and brother had done before her.

Nevertheless, Henry VIII did ensure that the prisoners were well provided for, paying £13 6s 8d a month for the diets of Margaret and the two children. Moreover, Margaret was allowed a waiting woman to attend upon her who was paid 18d a week.[17] The cold eventually gave Margaret cause to complain, and in the autumn of 1539 Thomas Phillips informed Cromwell that 'the Lady Sallysbery maketh great moan for that she wanteth necessary apparel both for to change and also to keep her warm'.[18] It is not known whether Margaret's request was immediately granted, but in March 1541 her tailor Scutte, who also served the queen, was paid £11 16s 4d as reimbursement 'for certain apparel by him bought and made for Margaret Poole, late countess of Salisbury'.[19] On the first of that month the king ordered a number of warm and well-appointed garments and footwear for her including:

> a nyght gowne furred, a kyrtel of worsted, and a peticote furred, a nother gowne of the facon of a nyght gowne of saye lyned with saten of Cypres and faced with saten, a bonet and a frontlet, four payer of hose, four payer of shoys and one payer of slipps.[20]

The presence of four pairs of shoes in the order might suggest that she was allowed some little freedom to walk about. Again, in April 1541 a further 66s 8d was spent on necessaries for her.[21]

In March 1541 Henry VIII had spent a considerable sum on Margaret's new clothes, yet she was to die only two months after the order was placed. This would suggest that the decision to execute her was a spontaneous rather than a premeditated one. On 8 January John Babham, late steward of Margaret's household, was examined before the Privy Council. Unfortunately, no more details are given, but just over a week later, on 17 January, Sir Thomas Wyatt was arrested under suspicion of having had 'intelligence with the King's traitor Pole'.[22] On 23 February Jerome Ragland and his wife Anne were also examined 'touching the burning of certain letters after the apprehension of lord Montague',[23] but no action appears to have been taken against them. At about the same time, Sir John Wallop was arrested concerning letters he had written to Richard Pate. Pate had been the English ambassador at the imperial court before defecting to the pope who, in July 1541, appointed him to the bishopric of Worcester.[24] Wallop was brought before the council some time before March 1541, and on 5 March Babham was examined once again.[25] On the first day of the same month Margaret's new clothes had been ordered, so at this point it seems that the arrests of Wyatt and Wallop had not prompted Henry to take any action against Margaret. However, the examinations of Babham on 8 January and 5 March, and of the Raglands on 23 February tend to suggest that the government was searching for further evidence of contacts between the two ambassadors and Reginald. Moreover, the identities of those questioned suggest that they were also investigating the possibility of Margaret's involvement. Babham had been her steward and had enjoyed a close relationship with the family, while Anne Ragland had been one of her waiting ladies. On 22 March, the plans for a rising in the north had been discovered and arrests were already taking place.[26] Before the middle of May convictions were under way and on 20 May some of the northern rebels were confined in the Tower awaiting interrogation.[27] The full extent of the rising's potential would now be known. According to Chapuys, there were between forty and fifty conspirators involved, 'nearly twelve of whom were gentlemen, men of substance and mature age, or priests holding benefices from the English Church', complete with 'their ordinary servants and retainers to the number of upwards of 300'.[28] Indeed, Chapuys considered that this rising posed more of a danger than the Pilgrimage of Grace 'because the people's indignation against the King has risen to a higher pitch since then, owing to the cruelties and exactions that followed the rebellion in the North'. The time of year was also more favourable to warfare while the opportunity allowed 'for men to assemble together in arms, for there was to be a great fair at Pontfret [Pontefract] – the town in which the last rising took place'.[29] The time was propitious for a rising as Henry had just sent troops to France, while the Scots were massing on the border in preparation for renewed border raids. Indeed, the rebels had hoped to gain the support of the king of Scotland in addition to as many people as possible, and then planned to 'denounce, and declare openly against, the King's bad government and tyranny . . . and slay all those who should raise in defence of the commonwealth'.[30] Although twenty-five conspirators were captured, Marillac implied that most escaped.[31]

One of those gentlemen implicated in this latest rising possessed the dreaded surname of Neville; Sir John Neville of Chevet, high sheriff of Yorkshire in 1519, 1524 and 1528.[32] Henry would not have forgotten that Margaret was a Neville, a granddaughter of 'the kingmaker' himself, while the large involvement of priests may have reminded him once again of the prophecy that 'ther shallbe a battell of prelates and that the Kynge shalbe distroyed and ther shalbe never no kynges in Ynglond'.[33] There was also the prediction that 'thar is a religious man alyve in an ilond and he is called the ded man and he shall come and kepe a parlament at the Towr and it shalbe called the parlament of peace'.[34] Of course, Reginald was still at large, and it appears that he might have been trying to organize his mother's escape from the Tower. In a letter to the bishop of Lavaur, which unfortunately bears no date, Reginald wrote:

> As to what you write of my affairs, both what was lovingly planned for my mother's release and about that friend of ours who procured this, who afterwards on the shameless demand made by the enemy's letters was kept in custody, although you relate that he has since been liberated.[35]

In *Letters and Papers* the identity of this 'friend' is explained as Gregory Botulph, one-time chaplain to Lord Lisle, whose defection to the pope brought about Lisle's fall. Certainly, Botulph was imprisoned at Diest at the instigation of the English ambassador in 1540, and in June of that year Reginald informed Cardinal Cervini that he was going to write to the nuncio in the hope of obtaining Botulph's release.[36] Unfortunately, we have no more evidence than this and cannot even be sure if Henry was aware of any rescue attempt. Nevertheless, it seems that there was sufficient accumulation of incidents to prompt Henry to take the final step. First came the arrests of his ambassadors concerning their possible involvement with his nemesis, Reginald Pole; then another rising in the North prompted by animosity to the Royal Supremacy; and, finally, Henry may have become aware of Reginald's plans to rescue his mother. Margaret's execution would foil Reginald's plan to rescue her, hurt him just that little bit more and serve as a punishment for the northerners whose devotion to the old faith would have resulted in the death of Cardinal Pole's mother. Furthermore, Marillac reported on 29 May that he had heard from a good source that 'before St Johns tide, they reckon to empty the

Tower of the prisoners now there for treason'.[37] A month later, on 30 June, he confirmed that before departing on his northern progress Henry gave orders 'for the Tower to be cleared of prisoners, and, as he lately began by the execution of the countess of Salisbury . . . such progress has since been made that in eight days all will be despatched, either by condemnation or absolution'.[38]

The only extant contemporary accounts of Margaret's execution, which took place on 27 May 1541, are from Marillac, the French ambassador,[39] and Chapuys, the imperial ambassador,[40] whose reports diverge over the number of people who witnessed it. According to Marillac, Margaret was 'beheaded in a corner of the Tower, in presence of so few people that until evening the truth was still doubted', while Chapuys claimed that 150 people, including the lord mayor of London, were present. The fact that so few accounts survive and the news was slow to spread may suggest that Marillac was correct. Although he was the first to find out, sending off a report only two days later, it was two weeks before Chapuys was able to send his report to the queen of Hungary. On 22 June Francesco Contarini, Venetian ambassador with the emperor, could only write to the Signory that it was said Margaret had been executed from a letter he had seen written at Antwerp on 13 June, and it was not until 27 June that he could confirm it.[41] That her execution was something of a spur-of-the-moment decision is revealed by the lack of a proper scaffold, only a small block being provided. The entire execution seems to have been rushed, with the main concern being to get it over with as quickly as possible; Chapuys felt constrained to describe it as 'very strange'. However, the covert manner in which it was conducted was probably to ensure that the spectacle of an elderly lady's execution was avoided; indeed Marillac commented: 'those here are afraid to put to death publicly those whom they execute in secret.' Both ambassadors were shocked and at a loss to explain the necessity of her execution. Marillac found it hard to believe, 'as she had been long prisoner, was of noble lineage, above 80 years old, and had been punished by the loss of one son and banishment of the other, and the total ruin of her house'. Chapuys wrote in disgust that 'there was no need or haste to bring so ignominious a death upon her, considering that as she was then nearly ninety years old, she could not in the ordinary course of nature live long'. She was in fact sixty-seven years old, three months from her sixty-eighth birthday.

Margaret was not told she was to die until the morning of her execution, and she reacted, as she did at the time of her arrest, with shock: 'she found the thing very strange, not knowing of what crime she was accused, nor how she had been sentenced.' Nevertheless, with characteristic courage Margaret immediately composed herself, and at seven o'clock in the morning walked out to the small block which had been placed in a space in front of the Tower. Here she spoke, commending her soul to God and asking those present to pray for the king, queen, Prince Edward and Princess Mary. Her devotion to Mary had not diminished during their years of separation and the sufferings Margaret had undergone partly on her behalf. Of all the royal family, it was to Mary that she wished to be especially commended, sending her blessing and begging for hers in return. Margaret was not allowed to continue and prolong the scene; 'she was told to make haste and place her neck on the block, which she did.' Henry VIII did not even have the good grace to accord her a professional executioner. As the usual headsman had been sent north to deal with the executions of the northern rebels, Margaret was left to suffer at the hands of 'a wretched and blundering youth . . . who literally hacked her head and shoulders to pieces in the most pitiful manner'.[42] Margaret's body was laid to rest, not in her magnificent chantry in Christchurch Priory, but in the chapel of St Peter ad Vincula at the Tower, where the remains of her son, Lord Montague, also lay. On 11 November 1876, during restoration work on the chancel, Margaret's remains were discovered lying close to those of Lady Rochford, who had gone to the block with Queen Catherine Howard nine months later.[43] In 1886, 354 years after her death, Margaret was among fifty-four martys beatified by Pope Leo XIII in recognition of the fact that they had not hesitated 'to lay down their lives by the shedding of their blood' for the dignity of the Holy See 'and for the truth of the orthodox Faith'.[44] Reginald Pole might have shouted his devotion to the Holy See the loudest from the safety of Europe, but it was Margaret who was beatified as Blessed Margaret Pole, the only member of her family ever to be so honoured.

Margaret Pole had been restored to the earldom of Salisbury in 1512, yet a mere twenty-seven years later the earldom was forfeit to the Crown under her attainder, and everything she had worked so hard to achieve was destroyed. Her residences, her lands and her title were all taken from her; her eldest son and 'chief stay of his family', Lord Montague, had been executed as a traitor, and his young son mysteriously followed him to the grave some years later. The downfall of the Pole family might be viewed by some as a failure on Margaret's part: failure to maintain her family's position, failure to keep her sons more firmly under control, failure to act as politics and common sense dictated rather than in accordance with her conscience. But Margaret, like her sons, had convictions and beliefs, and she was prepared to risk her position and, ultimately, her life for those beliefs. Throughout the course of her life Margaret Pole remained true to herself, true to those individuals she cared about and true to her principles; can this really be considered a failure? She was a steadfast friend and, as countess of Salisbury, enjoyed well-deserved loyalty and diligent service from those in her employ. Again can this be considered a failure? In so many aspects of her life Margaret was a success, but unfortunately this success could not negate the consequences of her one serious deficiency: failing to be a consistently grateful and unconditionally submissive subject of Henry VIII. It was, not surprisingly, this one failure which brought her to the block.

Reginald's reaction to his mother's death was characteristically dramatic and somewhat stage-managed. After announcing to his 'thunder-struck' secretary that he was now the proud son of a martyr, he disappeared into his closet for about an hour 'and then came out as cheerful as before'.[45] With Mary's accession to the throne in 1553 Reginald was finally able to return to England. On 16 August 1557 Richard Pate, bishop of Worcester, wrote to the queen that Reginald 'is ordained . . . to complete his mother's handiwork of godly education in your youth'.[46] Indeed, Reginald did become one of the queen's closest and most trusted advisers, and in 1556 he was consecrated archbishop of Canterbury. He died aged fifty-eight in November 1558, shortly after Queen Mary herself, with a 'most tranquil and placid transit, which appeared a slumber'.[47] There is no record of Mary's reaction to Margaret's death, but her treatment of Margaret's relatives after her accession does give us some clue to her feelings. Her kindness to Lord Montague's daughters reveals that she had not forgotten her former governess, although at times it might have appeared so, nor the devotion of the Pole family to her cause. Catherine, countess of Huntingdon, Lord Montague's eldest daughter, and Lady Winifred, his younger daughter, were both restored in blood and honours by act of Parliament in 1554–5, and also received several manors which had once belonged to their grandmother.[48] Significantly, the grants were made 'in consideration of the service to the queen in her tender age of the said countess of Salisbury', in addition to the service of the two sisters and their respective husbands. Moreover, the manors were granted to Montague's daughters and their heirs, not the heirs of their husbands, and in default of issue, to the remaining heirs of the countess of Salisbury. Ursula and her husband, Lord Stafford, also fared well during Mary's reign. Stafford did not fail to take advantage of his late mother-in-law's past relationship with the queen to plead his cause. Writing to Queen Mary three months after her accession, he reminded her that his wife's family 'chose death rather than consent to your disinheritance in your tender years'.[49] Nevertheless, he was a genuine supporter of Mary and received as his rewards the chamberlainship of the Exchequer and reversion of the custody of the herbage and pannage in various hays of the royal forest of Cannock.[50] More importantly, he received Thornbury and other Gloucestershire lands that had belonged to his father, the duke of Buckingham,[51] and Margaret's daughter at last became mistress of Thornbury. Warm relations existed between Ursula and her niece Catherine, countess of Huntingdon; they socialized together and visited each other often. In November 1555 Reginald wrote to Catherine that he was glad to hear of her arrival home 'and of my sister's arrival with you, which I doubt not will be to both your comforts in this absence of your husbands'. Again in August 1556, when Catherine was not feeling well, Reginald wrote that he was sorry to hear of her malady, but

> for the recovery whereof you use a good remedy, as I take it, to make that little journey unto my lady my sister, where I trust you shall find yourself better in body for your exercise and change of air and comforted in mind with that company, to whom I pray you make my most heartiest commendations.[52]

Ursula survived to a great age and did not die until 1570, outliving her husband and all her siblings.[53] Six years later, her niece Catherine died aged about fifty-nine. She had lived a widow for sixteen years and, like her grandmother, had been responsible during her widowhood for the administration of extensive estates.[54] Margaret's grandson Henry Pole, Lord Montague's son, remained alive in the Tower following his grandmother's execution, but in 1542 the last payment for his diet was made.[55] After this no more was heard of him except that he was not alive in 1553 when Edward Courtenay, Gertrude's son, was released from the Tower by Mary, and no comment was made about his fate at that time. He may have died of natural causes or as a result of the rigours of his imprisonment for, as has been noted, he apparently suffered more harshly than Edward Courtenay. Certainly, his death was expected, Chapuys reporting that when Margaret's death had been decided upon, her grandson, 'who had occasionally permission to go about within the precincts of the Tower, was placed in close confinement, and it is supposed that he will soon follow his father and grandmother. May God help him!'[56]

Finally, we turn to Geoffrey Pole, whose life was spared, Chapuys believed, because the government hoped to learn something more from him. However, this would not explain his pardon, which was granted on 2 January 1539,[57] nor his subsequent freedom. The government perhaps hoped that Geoffrey's pardon would help to encourage others who, due to their own guilt, were too afraid to inform on their accomplices. In addition, his release, as opposed to his execution, might have been considered a greater humiliation for his family. Although he received occasional little marks of favour, Geoffrey was a broken man.[58] Writing pathetically to Cromwell in June 1539, he described himself as fatherless and motherless in an attempt to win Cromwell's sympathy and receive some 'comfort and help' for the sake of his children.[59] His plea must have worked, for in December Cromwell gave him £20.[60] In September 1540, without any provocation, Geoffrey sent for his former colleague John Gunter and berated him for telling Fitzwilliam the things he had been constrained to do in September 1538, believing it had made his situation worse. As the argument became heated, Geoffrey attacked Gunter, who sustained a head wound. Nevertheless, Fitzwilliam was loth to proceed against him, considering 'the ill and frantique furious nature of the unhappy man'. He was also unwilling to commit him to prison in case it should 'reduce him into his phrenzy or some other inconvenience'.

He was unable to obtain guarantors for him, for 'no man of wit will become his surety', but, knowing the friendship that had existed between Gunter and Geoffrey, Fitzwilliam believed that if the king was prepared to forget the matter Gunter would drop all charges.[61] However, Henry was not prepared to forget the matter, and on 9 September it was decided to commit Geoffrey to the Fleet.[62] Fortunately, following the pleadings of his wife, Constance, his sentence was revoked providing he came to an agreement with Gunter and stayed away from the court.[63] In April of the following year, a month before his mother's execution, Geoffrey was again in trouble, this time for assaulting the parson of Racton, John Mychaill.[64] He also prompted his chaplain, Robert Sandwich, to accuse Mychaill of traitorous words, which resulted in Mychaill's imprisonment until it was discovered that he had been accused only as a result of malice.[65] In May 1543, Geoffrey and Constance were granted the manor of 'Grandysomes' in Kent, possibly one of Margaret's former properties, with the issues from September 1537, but the following year Geoffrey alienated it to Sir Thomas Moyle.[66]

According to the anonymous writer of *The Chronicle of King Henry VIII,* Geoffrey 'went about for two years like one terror-stricken' before, unable to bear it any longer, he fled to Rome in 1548 where he threw himself at Reginald's feet and begged for forgiveness. The Misses Dodds feel that Reginald should have asked Geoffrey for forgiveness also, since his behaviour, they believe, had brought Geoffrey to his terrible predicament. Of course Reginald did not, but he did send his brother to the bishop of Liège, who treated him honourably.[67] His unbalanced state of mind must have blinded him to the fact that, by these actions, he had once again placed his family in extreme danger, but fortunately no action was taken against them. During the reign of Edward VI he tried to obtain leave to return to England but was unsuccessful, and in 1552 he sent a letter to his wife 'whom he pined to see after 4 years'.[68] With Mary's accession, Geoffrey was finally able to return to England, where he arrived before September 1553, but his sufferings were not over. Edward Courtenay, newly released from the Tower, held Geoffrey responsible for the death of his father and the countess of Salisbury and threatened to kill him. So seriously did the government take this that they lodged Geoffrey in a house and placed him under guard for his own protection.[69] Although included in the general pardon of 1554, Geoffrey Pole was to receive little else from Mary.[70] With ten children to support, five sons and five daughters,[71] Geoffrey and his family struggled on in poverty, although, according to Priuli, Reginald 'never failed to succour them as paupers' and stipulated that part of his property should be distributed to them after his death.[72] Geoffrey Pole's life had effectively ended on 9 December 1538 as surely as if his head had fallen with his brother's. Never more was he to enjoy peace of mind or be free of the nightmares his conscience would not let him forget. He was shunned and despised; the Misses Dodds have described Geoffrey's degradation as 'the worst insult to humanity'.[73] Indeed, when Geoffrey closed his eyes for the last time in November 1558, a few days before his brother Reginald, it was said that he made a 'very pious and catholic end'.[74] This is understandable, for with the sure knowledge of death was the anticipation of final relief.

Appendix I Genealogical Tree of

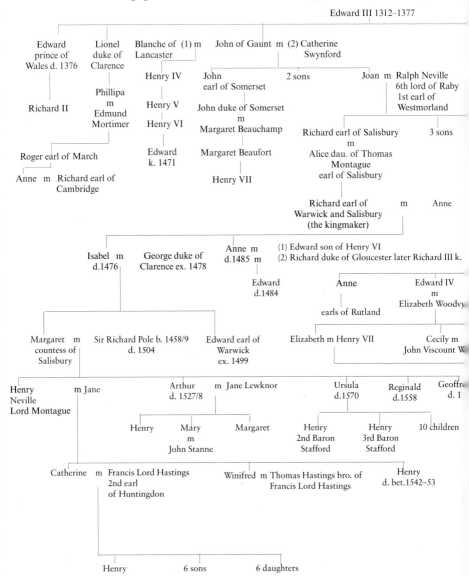

Margaret Pole, Countess of Salisbury

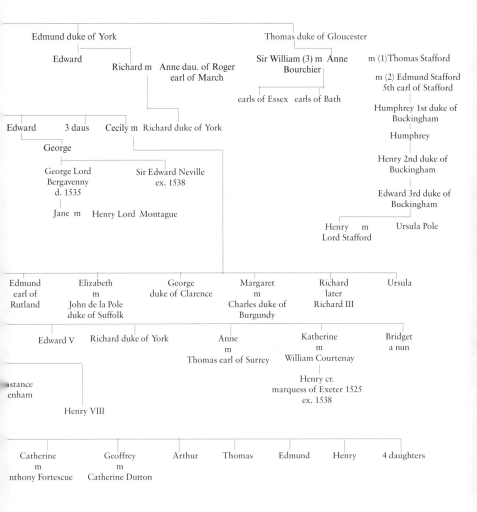

Appendix II Map of the Lands of the Countess of Salisbury in 1538

1. Aldbrough	10. Properties in	19. Clyst St	31. Hunton	Basset	50. Warblington
2. Aston	St Nicholas	Mary	32. Nth and Sth	40. Pyworthy	51. Ware
Clinton	Parish	20. Cogan	Kelsey	41. Ringwood	52. Welsh
inc. Aston	11. Catmerhall	21. Coleridge	33. Lambourn	42. Shipton	Bicknor
Chevery and	12. Catterick	22. Crayford	34. Lantyan	(Montague)	53. Willmington
Dundridge	13. Chalton	23. Crookham	35. Llanfair	43. Somerton	54. Wilton
3. Aylesbury	14. Chedzoy	24. Dartford	36. Llangyfiw	44. Stokenham	55. Wonford
4. Binstead	with	25. Donyatt	37. Newton	45. Stone	56. Yarlington
5. Bourne	Canteloes	26. Dunpole	38. Newton	46. Sutton at	57. Yealmpton
6. Bretts	15. Chesterfield	27. Earlstoke	Montague	Hone	
7. Brightstone	16. Chistlehurst	28. Easton	(Blackmoor	47. Swainstone	
8. Bushey	17. Christchurch	29. Fulnetby	Manor)	48. Swyre	
9. Caistor	18. Clavering	30. Girsby	39. Northweald	49. Tefont Evias	

I have been unable to locate Marden Borne and Chambeleyns Marshe in Sussex and Hang West Frendles in Yorkshire.

Appendix III
The Lands of the Countess of Salisbury in 1538 and their Descent[1]

England and Calais

Berkshire
Crookham	R
Lambourn	R

Buckinghamshire
Aston Clinton	R
Aston Chevery	A
Aylesbury	R
Dundridge[2]	R

Cornwall
Lantyan	R

Derbyshire
Chesterfield[3]	R

Devon
Clyst St Mary	R
Coleridge Hundred	R
Pyworthy	R
Stokenham	R
Wonford	R
Yealmpton	R

Dorset
Canford	L
Newton Montague (Blackmoor Manor)	R
Swyre	R

Essex
Bretts in West Ham	R
Catmerhall[4]	R
Clavering	R
Northeweald Basset	R

Hampshire and the Isle of Wight
Chalton	B
Christchurch	R
Hunton	R
Ringwood	R
Warblington	R
Binstead, IOW[5]	R
Brightstone/Brixton, IOW	R
Swainstone, IOW	R

Herefordshire
Dinmore	W
Kinnersley	W

Hertfordshire
Bushey	R
Ware	R

Kent
Chistlehurst[6]	U
Crayford	U
Dartford and Wilmington	R
Stone	U
Sutton at Hone	U

Lincoln
Coppices: Eselounde, Alanhill, Horowhill, Popeland and elsewhere in the lordship

of Bourne U

Lordship of Caister, incl. Nth
  and Sth Kelsey, Fulnetby and
  Girsby C

London

Le Herber[7] R

Middlesex

The Wyke[8] R

Northampton

Easton near Stamford R

Somerset

Charlton L
Chedzoy with Canteloes R
Donyatt R
Dunpole R
Henstridge L
Shipton Montague R
Somerton R
Yarlington R

Suffolk

Newton Hall R

Sussex

Lands in Marden Borne and
  Chambeleyns Marshe[9] D

Wiltshire

Alderbury L
Amesbury L
Crombridge L
Earlstoke R
Tefont Evias[10] R
Trowbridge L
Wilton R
Winterbourne L

Yorkshire

Aldbrough E
Cottingham F
Catterick E
Hang West Frendles E

Calais

Properties in St Nicholas
  Parish[11] R

Wales

Glamorgan

Cogan[12] R

Monmouth

Llanfair (Llanfair Discoed) U
Langyfiw U
Welsh Bicknor R

Fee Farms

Buckingham

Aylesbury: £60 from Thomas
  Boleyn, earl of Wiltshire R

Dorset

Lullworth: £20 from the abbot
  of Binden R

Hampshire

Pedilton: £20 from the prior of
  Christchurch R

Huntingdon

£50 from the abbey and
  convent of Ramsey R

Somerset		Yorkshire	
Axbridge, Cheddar and Congresbury: £54 from the Bishop of Bath and Wells	R	Christhall: £13 6s 8d from the Abbey and Convent	U

Key

A Purchased in 1532 from Sir John Gage[13]

B Purchased in 1532 from the earl of Shrewsbury[14]

C Margaret was apparently granted the lordship of Caister, formerly parcel of the Duchy of Lancaster, in 1518/19[15]

D Purchased in 1533 and 1534[16]

E Granted to Margaret in 1522/23,[17] formerly parcel of the Lordship of Richmond

F The fourth part of the lordship was granted to Margaret in 1516/17[18]

L Initially included in the restoration of 1512, by 1518 it had been repossessed by the Crown

R Restored to Margaret in 1512

U It is unclear how this manor came into Margaret's possession

W Delabere lands held by Margaret in wardship from 1521 to 1529

Notes

§

1 Ancestry and Marriage, 1473–1504

[1] T. Hearne, *Joannis Lelandi Antiquarii de Rebus Britannicis Collectanea* (6 vols, London, 1770), vol. 4, p. 225; BL, Egerton MS 985, f. 19.

[2] C. Ross (intro.), *The Rous Roll* by John Rous (Gloucester, 1980), no. 61.

[3] W. Dugdale, *Monasticon Anglicanum* (6 vols, London, 1846), vol. 2, p. 64.

[4] D. MacGibbon, *Elizabeth Woodville* (London, 1938), p. 51.

[5] *Collection of Ordinances and Regulations for the Government of the Royal Household,* printed for the Society of Antiquaries by John Nichols (London, 1790), pp. 99, 166, 100–1, 89, 91.

[6] A *cupbearer* served ale and wine; a *sewer* is a Middle English term for waiter; *carvers,* who were required to carve the meat at table, were specially trained and procedures were drawn up regarding each animal. *Amener* refers to an almoner, who was usually a cleric and responsible for the collection and distribution of alms from the household. K. Mertes, *The English Noble Household 1250–1600* (Oxford, 1988), pp. 40, 50.

[7] PRO, SP1/139, f. 79.

[8] Dugdale, *Monasticon Anglicanum*, vol. 2, p. 64. I shall, in future, refer to Edward as the earl of Warwick.

[9] On 13 March 1475 Clarence made changes to the descent of six manors he held in his own right which would allow inheritance by a female. It was for these manors that he subsequently gained a licence to enfeoff, although the exact terms of the enfeoffment are not known. 14 Edward IV, cap. 20 in J. Strachey et al. (eds), *Rotuli Parliamentorum, 1278–1504* (6 vols, London, 1767–83), vol. 6, p. 126; *CPR, 1467–77*, p. 517.

[10] Dugdale, *Monasticon Anglicanum*, vol. 1, pp. 64–5.

[11] M. Hicks, *False, Fleeting, Perjur'd Clarence* (Bangor, 1992), p. 114.

[12] Ross, *The Rous Roll*, no. 59.

[13] Hicks, *False, Fleeting, Perjur'd Clarence*, p. 181.

[14] P. M. Kendall, *Warwick the Kingmaker* (London, 1957), pp. 259–60.

[15] Hicks, *False, Fleeting, Perjur'd Clarence*, p. 114.

[16] Ibid., pp. 116–27, 153.

[17] J. Gairdner (ed.), (intro., R. Virgoe), *The Paston Letters* (1 vol., Gloucester, 1983), vol. 5, no. 730.

[18] PRO, E.404/77/2, pencil no. 47.

[19] PRO, E.404/77/3, pencil no. 66.

[20] *CPR*, 1476–85, p. 212.

[21] M. Hicks, 'Descent, partition and extinction: the Warwick inheritance', in M. Hicks, *Richard III and his Rivals: Magnates and their Motives in the Wars of the Roses* (London, 1991), p. 331.

[22] C. A. J. Armstrong (trans.), *The Usurpation of Richard the Third* by Dominic Mancini (Gloucester, 1989), p. 89.

[23] M. Levine, *Tudor Dynastic Problems 1460–1571* (London, 1973), p. 137.

[24] 17 Edward IV, in Strachey, *Rotuli Parliamentorum*, vol. 6, p. 194.

[25] Levine, *Tudor Dynastic Problems*, p. 138.

[26] For this description of Sheriff Hutton see R. W. Howarth, *Some Notes on the Castle at Sheriff Hutton* (Bangor, 1993).

[27] On 24 July 1484 a set of regulations were to take effect regarding the household set up in the north to house the earl of Warwick, the earl of Lincoln and those 'persons as shallbe in the northe as the kinges household'.

> Item My lord of Lincoln and my lord Morley to be at oon brekefast. the Children togeder at oon brekefast. suche as be present of the Counsaille at oon brekefast. Item that noo lyveres of brede wyne nor ale be had but such as be mesurable and convenyent and that noo potte of lyverey excede mesure of a potelle. but oonly to my lord and the Children etc. Item that noo boyes be in household but suche as be admytted by the Counsaille etc.

The first two items reveal that there was more than one child in the household, the third item suggests the presence of a female child. We know that Elizabeth of York joined Warwick at Sheriff Hutton, but at Christmas 1484 she danced at Richard's court in Westminster Hall and probably did not arrive at Sheriff Hutton until 1485. Therefore, she could not have been the female they were trying to seclude from male company in July 1484. Also, at eighteen years of age she could hardly be described as a child. Consequently, these items probably indicate the presence of Margaret. It is true that 'the Children' may refer to other noble boys brought in to share Warwick's education as was common practice or, as P. W. Hammond has suggested, the two illegitimate children of Richard III, John of Gloucester and Katherine Plantagenet. Whilst these explanations are likely, it is still almost certain that Margaret was there. For the 1484 regulations see R. Horrox and P. W. Hammond (eds), *British Library Harleian Manuscript 433* (4 vols, London, 1982), vol. 3, p. 114, f. 269. For Richard III's illegitimate children see P. W. Hammond, 'The illegitimate children of Richard III', in J. Petre (ed.), *Richard III: Crown and People* (London, 1985).

[28] R. Horrox, *Richard III: A Study of Service* (Cambridge, 1991), p. 215.

[29] A. Raine (ed.), *York Civic Records* (1), Yorkshire Archaeological Society, 98 (1938), p. 116.

[30] A. Hanham, 'John Rous's account of the reign of Richard III', in A. Hanham, *Richard III and his Early Historians 1483–1535* (Oxford, 1975), p. 123.

[31] Horrox, *Richard III: A Study of Service*, p. 299.

[32] Lincoln's position is suggested by his appointment as lieutenant of Ireland and head of the Council of the North.

[33] J. R. Lander, 'The treason and death of the duke of Clarence', in J. R. Lander, *Crown and Nobility 1450–1509* (London, 1976), pp. 242–66.

[34] Levine, *Tudor Dynastic Problems*, p. 134.

[35] In 1397 Richard II legitimized the Beauforts born out of wedlock to John of Gaunt and his mistress Catherine Swynford in a patent which was then ratified by Parliament. In 1407 Henry IV confirmed the patent but added a clause barring the Beauforts from the succession to the crown. This clause was not ratified by Parliament and so might not prevail against the legal superiority of Richard II's parliamentary ratified patent. See M. Levine, *Tudor Dynastic Problems*, p. 16.

[36] K. Pickthorn, *Early Tudor Government: Henry VII* (2 vols, Cambridge, 1934), vol. 1, p. 2.

[37] D. Hay (ed. and trans.), *The Anglica Historia of Polydore Vergil A.D. 1485–1537*, Camden Society, third series, 74 (1910), p. 3.

[38] A. Goodman and A. Mackay, 'A Castilian report on English affairs, 1486', *EHR*, 88 (1973), 93, 95, 97.

[39] C. S. L. Davies, 'Bishop John Morton, the Holy See, and the accession of Henry VII', *EHR*, 102 (1987), 27.

[40] D. Loades, *Politics and the Nation 1450–1660* (London, 1988), p. 97, n. 18.

[41] PRO, E.404/79, nos. 45 or 337. A warrant of 24 February 1486 ordered payment of £200 to Margaret Beaufort because she 'had the keeping and guiding of the ladies daughters of king Edward the IIII th, and also of the young lords the duke of Buckingham the earls of Warwick and Westmoreland to her great charges'. Although Margaret's name is absent from the list it is inconceivable that she would have been omitted from such a gathering. It is therefore a probable oversight on the part of the clerk writing the warrant.

[42] Indeed, the imperial ambassador Chapuys made much of this fact on more than one occasion in the 1530s. *L&P*, VI, no. 1528; VIII, no. 750; *CSP*, Spain, 1509–1603 (20 vols, London, 1866–1954), vol. V (i), no. 109.

[43] Levine, *Tudor Dynastic Problems*, p. 398.

[44] BL, Add. MSS 6113, f. 77b; Hearne, *Joannis Lelandi Antiquarii*, vol. 4, p. 206.

[45] Hearne, *Joannis Lelandi Antiquarii*, vol. 4, p. 225; BL, Egerton MS 985, f. 19.

[46] *The Complete Peerage* states that she 'probably' married in 1491, but no later than 1494, while Michael Jones and Malcolm Underwood, who discuss her marriage as part of their study of Margaret Beaufort, give 1494 as the date. G. E. Cokayne, *The Complete Peerage of England, Scotland, Ireland and Great Britain* (12 vols, London, 1841), vol. 11, pp. 399–400; M. Jones and M. Underwood, *The King's Mother* (Cambridge, 1992), p. 82.

[47] PRO, C.66/620, m. 19; C.82/393; *L&P*, I (ii), no. 2137 (5).

[48] For a discussion of this document see P. W. Hammond, 'The coronation of Elizabeth of York', *The Ricardian*, 6, 83 (1983), 270–2.

[49] J. R. Lander, *Government and Community: England 1450–1509* (London, 1988), p. 339.

[50] PRO, E.404/79, no. 26 or 182. Anne, countess of Warwick was the widow of Richard Neville, earl of Warwick (the kingmaker). As she was never accused of or indicted for treason, her estates and jointure should not have been affected by her husband's treason. Therefore, in order to allow the dukes of Clarence and Gloucester to enjoy the lands their wives would eventually inherit, the countess of Warwick had been declared legally dead by Edward IV.

[51] Loades, *Politics and the Nation*, p. 99.

[52] Regarding Edward IV's other daughters, in 1487 Anne was twelve, Katherine eight and Bridget seven.

[53] BL, Egerton MS 2219; BL, C. Yarnold, *A Collection for Buck's History of*

Richard III, ff. 137–137b; A. F. Pollard, *The Reign of Henry VII from Contemporary Sources* (3 vols, London, 1913), vol. 1, p. 152.

⁵⁴ Shakespeare, *King Richard the Third*, IV.iii.

⁵⁵ PRO, E.36/247, f. 35.

⁵⁶ M. Hicks, *False, Fleeting, Perjur'd Clarence*, p. 164.

⁵⁷ For a full discussion of Richard Pole's life and career and the role of Henry VII's half-blood family in his regime see H. Pierce, 'The king's cousin: the life, career and Welsh connection of Sir Richard Pole, 1458–1504', *WHR*, 19, 2 (1998), 187–225.

⁵⁸ For Geoffrey Pole's life and career see R. S. Thomas, 'Geoffrey Pole: a Lancastrian servant in Wales', *National Library of Wales Journal*, 17 (1971–2), 277–86.

⁵⁹ A. H. Plaisted, *The Manor and Parish Records of Medmenham Buckinghamshire* (London, 1925), pp. 45–53; Thomas, 'Geoffrey Pole: a Lancastrian servant', pp. 282–3. Geoffrey bequeathed Stoke Mandeville to his younger son Henry, who died unmarried shortly after his father.

⁶⁰ Jones and Underwood, *The King's Mother*, p. 31.

⁶¹ *CPR*, 1485–94, pp. 481–2, 5, 78.

⁶² R. A. Griffiths, *King and Country: England and Wales in the Fifteenth Century* (London, 1991), p. 67; J. B. Smith, 'Crown and community in the Principality of north Wales in the reign of Henry Tudor', *WHR*, 3, 2 (1966), 160.

⁶³ Hearne, *Joannis Lelandi Antiquarii*, vol. 4, pp. 210, 214–15; BL, Cotton MS Julius B. XII, f. 29; BL, Add. MSS 38,133, f. 127b.

⁶⁴ *CCR*, 1399–1509 (18 vols, London, 1927–63), 1485–1500, no. 255.

⁶⁵ For this celebration she was cried by the heralds 'Largesse de noble Princesse la Seur, de la Reyne nostre Soveraigne Dame, et Countesse de Wellys'. At the same time 'my Lorde Wells gave for him and my Lady his wiff xxs'. Hearne, *Joannis Lelandi Antiquarii*, vol. 4, 235; BL, Egerton MS 985 Plut.541. E, f. 27b in which he gives 26s 8d.

⁶⁶ BL, Add. MSS 38,133, f. 132b; J. G. Nichols (ed.), *Collectanea Topographica et Genealogica* (London, 1834), p. 21.

⁶⁷ BL, Egerton MS 985, ff. 16–16b, 19, 23b; Hearne, *Joannis Lelandi Antiquarii*, vol. 4, pp. 221–3, 225, 230.

⁶⁸ H. Pierce, 'The life, career and political significance of Margaret Pole, countess of Salisbury, 1473–1541' (unpublished Ph.D. thesis, University of Wales, Bangor, 1997), 63–4; H. M. Colvin (ed.), *The History of the King's Works*, vol. 2: *The Middle Ages* (London, 1963), p. 978.

⁶⁹ PRO, SP1/105, f. 66; *L&P*, XI, no. 93.

⁷⁰ During repairs in 1834, two receptacles for coffins were found below the floor. C. D. Bell, *Notices of the Historic Persons Buried in the Chapel of St Peter ad Vincula in the Tower of London* (London, 1877), p. 122.

⁷¹ A celure and tester was a canopy for a four-poster bed, either suspended from the posts of the bed or suspended from the ceiling. PRO, SP1/139, ff. 72, 81, 82.

⁷² Plaisted, *The Manor and Parish Records of Medmenham*, pp. 72, 97–8.

⁷³ PRO, E.36/247, f. 35.

⁷⁴ Pierce, 'The king's cousin', pp. 220–1.

⁷⁵ CP5/1/22/127, no. 14; CCR, 1485–1500, p. 273; Plaisted, *The Manor and Parish Records of Medmenham*, pp. 373–6. According to the *VCH*, the manor was back within the Brudenell family by the seventeenth century, whilst Joan Wake states that Sir Robert Brudenell leased out a field at Stoke Mandeville in 1491. W.

Page, *VCH, Buckinghamshire*, vol. 2, p. 361; J. Wake, *The Brudenells of Deene* (London, 1954), p. 27.

[76] Hearne, *Joannis Lelandi Antiquarii*, vol. 4, pp. 241, 245.

[77] BL, Add. MSS 7099, f. 20.

[78] Although Arthur had enjoyed an establishment of his own long before this which was certainly becoming formalized by 1490, no extant evidence suggests that Richard was appointed before 1493. *CPR, 1485–94*, p. 441. For Arthur's household, see PRO, E.101/412/20, nos. 18, 16; *CPR, 1485–94*, p. 312.

[79] D. Starkey et al. (eds), *The English Court from the Wars of the Roses to the Civil War* (London, 1992), pp. 4, 33–4.

[80] C. A. J. Skeel, 'Wales under Henry VII', in R. W. Seton-Watson (ed.), *Tudor Studies Presented to A. F. Pollard* (London, 1924), p. 9.

[81] D. Lewis, 'The court of the president and Council of Wales and the marches from 1478–1575', *Y Cymmrodor*, 12 (1897), 21.

[82] H. Owen and J. B. Blakeway, *A History of Shrewsbury* (2 vols, London, 1825), vol. 1, pp. 261–3.

[83] *CPR, 1485–94*, pp. 439, 453; P. Williams, *The Council in the Marches of Wales under Elizabeth I* (Cardiff, 1958), p. 10.

[84] J. Anstis (ed.), *The Register of the Most Noble Order of the Garter* (2 vols, London, 1724), vol. 1, p. 240.

[85] R. A. Griffiths, 'Richard duke of York and the royal household in Wales, 1449–50', *WHR*, 8 (1976), 22.

[86] PRO, SC6/HenVII/1592.

[87] Smith, 'Crown and community', pp. 159, 160.

[88] H. Thomas, *A History of Wales, 1485–1660* (Cardiff, 1972), p. 25.

[89] PRO, SC6/HenVII/1552.

[90] Smith, 'Crown and community', p. 161, n. 75.

[91] SC6/HenVII/1595; S. B. Chrimes, *Henry VII* (London, 1972), p. 55.

[92] P. Worthington, 'Royal government in the counties palatine of Lancashire and Chester 1450–1509' (unpublished Ph.D. thesis, University of Wales, Swansea, 1991), 59–60.

[93] *CPR, 1494–1509*, pp. 30–1, 646–8, 652–3, 666.

[94] PRO, E.404/80, pencil no. 160.

[95] PRO, E.101/72/4, 1109.

[96] *Excerpta Historica*, p. 104.

[97] BL, Add. MSS 7099, f. 27.

[98] *CPR, 1494–1509*, p. 67.

[99] Chrimes, *Henry VII*, p. 140.

[100] The duke of Buckingham, the earls of Derby, Suffolk, Northumberland and Shrewsbury, Lords Denham, Brooke and Daubeney, Sir Charles Somerset, Sir Edward Poynings and Sir Gilbert Talbot. Anstis, *The Register of the Most Noble Order of the Garter*, pp. 237–9.

[101] Hearne, *Joannis Lelandi Antiquarii*, vol. 4, p. 292.

[102] B. Pye (trans.), *The Life of Cardinal Reginald Pole by Lodovico Beccatelli* (London, 1766), p. 13.

[103] A. Strickland, *The Lives of the Queens of England* (8 vols, London, 1851–2), vol. 2, pp. 70, 77; G. Mattingly, *Catherine of Aragon* (London, 1944), p. 29; J. Gairdner, *History of the Life and Reign of Richard the Third* (Cambridge, 1898), p. 207; M. Bennet, *Lambert Simnel and the Battle of Stoke* (Gloucester, 1987), p. 33; J. A. Williamson, *The Tudor Age* (New York, 1982), p. 59.

[104] H. Ellis (ed.), *Hall's Chronicle* (London, 1809), p. 490.

[105] 5 Henry VIII, cap. 12, in A. Luders et al., *Statutes of the Realm* (11 vols, London, 1810–28), vol. 3, p. 100.

[106] Hay, *Polydore Vergil*, p. 19.

[107] Many grants involving Warwick's lands were made during this period which specifically state that they were made due to his minority.

[108] Apparently, in May of that year Henry VII allowed Warwick to witness a document in Warwickshire. I. Arthurson, *The Perkin Warbeck Conspiracy* (Stroud, 1994), p. 6.

[109] Ibid., pp. 207–10.

[110] Hay, *Polydore Vergil*, p. 119.

[111] Ellis, *Hall's Chronicle*, p. 491.

[112] J. Gairdner (ed.), *Letters Illustrative of the Reigns of Richard III and Henry VII* (2 vols, London, 1861–3), vol. 1, pp. 113–14.

[113] Pollard, *The Reign of Henry VII from Contemporary Sources*, vol. 1, pp. 206–8; F. H. Crossley and M. H. Ridgway, 'Screens, lofts and stalls situated in Wales and Monmouthshire', *Archaeologia Cambrensis*, 110–11 (1961–2), 64.

[114] A. H. Thomas and I. D. Thornley (eds), *The Great Chronicle of London* (London, 1938), pp. 291–2; *Excerpta Historica*, p. 123, cited in Arthurson, *The Perkin Warbeck Conspiracy*, p. 215.

[115] PRO, LC2/1, f. 10.

[116] Hearne, *Joannis Lelandi Antiquarii*, vol. 5, p. 373.

[117] *The 37th Annual Report of the Deputy Keeper of the Public Records Office*, pt. 2 (London, 1876), Appendix 2, pp. 144, 593.

[118] His Inquisition Post Mortem, *virtute officii*, drawn up on 29 January 1505 states that he died '20 December last' thus 20 December 1504. However, on 20 October 1504 Margaret and Sir Charles Somerset apparently borrowed £40 for Richard's burial, while on 17 November Richard was replaced as one of the guarantors for Lord Mountjoy, keeper of Hammes Castle. Therefore, the evidence would suggest that the date mentioned in the Inquisition Post Mortem is inaccurate and that Richard died towards the end of October 1504. *Calendar of the Inquisitions Post Mortem, 1485–1509* (3 vols, London, 1898–1955), 1505–9, no. 876; BL, Add. MSS 59899, ff. 168, 69b; *CCR*, 1500–9, no. 428.

[119] *CSP, Sp.*, 1534–5 (i), no. 80, 235.

2 Widowhood and Restoration, 1504–1519

[1] William Lord Mountjoy to Erasmus in 1509. E. Emerton, *Desiderius Erasmus of Rotterdam* (London, 1899), p. 181.

[2] B. Rowland (trans. and intro.), *Medieval Woman's Guide to Health: The First English Gynaecological Handbook* (Kent, OH, 1981), pp. 139, xv.

[3] R. Morisyne, *An Invective ayenste the Great and Detestable Vice, Treason, wherein the Secrete Practises, and Traterous Workynges of theym, that Suffrid of late are Disclosed* (London, 1539; reprinted New York, 1972). Unfortunately there are no folio numbers in this text.

[4] PRO, SC6/Hen.VIII/219.

[5] *L&P*, XI, no. 92.

[6] BL, Add. MSS 59899, f. 168.

[7] Ibid.

[8] BL, Add. MSS 7099, f. 80. This gift is inaccurately placed under the year 1503.

[9] D. I. Grummitt, 'The economic and social history of Calais and the Pale under English rule between 1485 and 1558' (unpublished Ph.D. thesis, London University, 1997). I am very grateful to Dr Steven Gunn for drawing my attention to Dr Grummitt's redating of this conversation.

[10] Gairdner, *Letters and Papers Illustrative of the Reigns of Richard III and Henry VII*, vol. 1, p. 233.

[11] Mattingly, *Catherine of Aragon*, p. 95.

[12] *L&P*, I (i), p. 1442.

[13] Ibid., no. 81, p. 41; PRO, LC9, f. 134.

[14] Margaret and the countesses received twelve yards, the baronesses ten yards, knights' wives ten yards and the rest seven yards. PRO, LC9, f. 134.

[15] PRO, C.82/338, 400, bundle 1; *L&P*, I (i), no. 158 (19).

[16] *L&P*, I (i), nos. 234, 609, 774, 957, 1192.

[17] *L&P*, I (ii), p. 1455; no. 2055 (35).

[18] For Tuchet's restoration see H. Miller, *Henry VIII and the English Nobility* (Oxford, 1989), pp. 209–10.

[19] Reginald to the protector of England, 1549. *CSP*, Venetian, 1534–1554, pp. 246–7, no. 575.

[20] Reginald to the protector of England, 1549. Ibid., pp. 257–8.

[21] Reginald to the cardinal archbishop of Burgos, 1 August 1541. Ibid., no. 272.

[22] Other restorations included Thomas Grey, marquess of Dorset for whom letters patent of general pardon were issued on 26 August 1509 for him to sue for, and in November 1512 the attainder against James Tuchet, Lord Audley was repealed, enabling his son John to succeed to the barony. Miller, *Henry VIII and the English Nobility*, pp. 7–9.

[23] D. M. Loades, *The Tudor Court* (Bangor, 1992), p. 138; D. R. Starkey, 'Rivals in power: the Tudors and the nobility', in D. R. Starkey (ed.), *Rivals in Power* (London, 1990), p. 10.

[24] Miller, *Henry VIII and the English Nobility*, p. 8; *L&P*, I (i), no. 158 (20).

[25] Loades, *The Tudor Court*, p. 47.

[26] Miller, *Henry VIII and the English Nobility*, pp. 195–6.

[27] Cokayne, *Complete Peerage*, vol. 11, pp. 253–5.

[28] 5 Hen VIII, cap. 12 in Luders, *Statutes of the Realm*, vol. 3, 100–2.

[29] *L&P*, I (ii), no. 1924.

[30] Ibid.; PRO, E.36/215, f. 676; *L&P*, I (ii), p. 1486.

[31] PRO, E.314/79, no. 305. The act of restoration was enrolled on the patent roll in October 1513 but Margaret claimed that by 'dyvers progacons' she did not actually enter the manors until 20 January 1515. 5 Hen, VIII, cap. 12, in Luders, *Statutes of the Realm*, vol. 3, p. 101; *L&P*, I (ii), no. 2422 (11); PRO, E.314/18. This is probably a mistake as Parliament did not meet in 1515 until February. In 1514, however, the parliamentary session did run from January to March. J. Loach, *Parliament under the Tudors* (Oxford, 1991), p. x. Moreover, the Parliament roll for the fifth year of Henry VIII includes Margaret's petition for restitution, the second prorogation beginning on 20 January, the date mentioned by Margaret, with Parliament sitting from 23 January to 4 March. *L&P*, I (ii), no. 2590. Hence, she most likely formally entered her manors in January 1514.

[32] Her properties in Calais comprised 'V tenements sometyme a mansion and a great court V tenements and two sellars' in St Nicholas's parish. PRO, E.315/371, f.

73. I am grateful to Dr David I. Grummitt for providing me with this information from his unpublished Ph.D. thesis, 'The economic and social history of Calais and Pale' (London University, 1997).

[33] In Monmouth she held Llanfair (Llanfair Discoed) near Caerwent and land at Llangyfiw near Usk, seven miles away. The smaller manor of Welsh Bicknor was near Symonds Yat. M. Gray, 'The dispersal of Crown property in Monmouthshire 1500–1603' (unpublished Ph.D. thesis, University of Wales, Cardiff, 1984), 132–3, courtesy of Gwent Record Office. In Kent she held Chesylhurst, Crayford, Stone and Sutton at Hone, and in Lincoln she held four coppices in the lordship of Bourne. PRO, SC6/Hen.VIII/6875.

[34] PRO, SC6/Hen.VIII/6875.

[35] *L&P*, IV (ii), no. 2972.

[36] PRO, SC6/Hen.VIII/6875.

[37] T. Wright, *The History and Topography of the County of Essex* (London, 1831), p. 195.

[38] PRO, SP1/30, no. 122.

[39] PRO, E.101/490/12, ff. 1, 2, 203. On both these occasions Margaret issued payments whilst at Bisham towards the construction of her new residence at Warblington, and on 7 July and 20 September 1518 she issued two further payments from Bisham for the same purpose. Unfortunately, this extensive document contains no folio numbers; therefore, for ease of reference, the folio numbers are my own.

[40] W. Page and P. H. Ditchfield (eds), *VCH, Berkshire*, vol. 3 (reprinted London, 1972), pp. 139–40.

[41] E. Powell (ed.), *The Travels and Life of Sir Thomas Hoby, Kt., of Bisham Abbey, Written by Himself. 1547–1564* (Camden Miscellany, third series, 4 (London, 1902), pp. xviii, xii.

[42] In November 1543 the king was in residence at Bisham from where he issued two grants on 30 November and three grants on 1 December. *L&P*, XVIII (ii), no. 529 (4, 29, 3, 11, 31). The Privy Council also met there in December 1543. Ibid., no. 450.

[43] Ibid., XVI, no. 947, (31); XVII, no. 881 (18); H. B. Wheatley (intro.), *Stowe's Survey of London* (London, 1956), p. 207; T. Pennant, *Some Account of London* (London, 1790), p. 309.

[44] Wheatley, *Stowe's Survey of London*, pp. 80–1.

[45] M. D. Lobel, *The British Atlas of Historic Towns*, vol. 3: *The City of London from Prehistoric Times to c. 1520* (Oxford, 1989), p. 73, Map 3.

[46] PRO, SC12/11/34, nos. 3, 4.

[47] Ibid., no. 2.

[48] Although a residence of some kind may have pre-dated Margaret's building, her extensive renovations between 1517 and 1518 may be said to have virtually rebuilt any existing structure. Indeed, in the building accounts of 1517–18 the castle is described as 'the newe byldyng upon the manor of Warblyngton'. PRO, E.101/490/12, f. 202.

[49] M. Howard, 'Power and the early Tudor courtier's house', *History Today*, 37 5 (1987), 46.

[50] PRO, E.101/490/12, ff. 48, 49, 60, 206.

[51] Warblington Castle was dismantled during the Civil War.

[52] This information originates from a survey carried out upon Warblington in 1632 by William Luffe, general surveyor to Richard Cotton Esq., lord of the manor. PCRO/906A, courtesy of Portsmouth Record Office.

[53] PRO, SP1/139, ff. 72–84.

[54] Portsmouth Record Office, PCRO/906A.

[55] PRO, E.101/490/12, f. 202.

[56] PRO, SP1/139, f. 78.

[57] The portrait believed to be of Margaret Pole, countess of Salisbury, is at present in the National Portrait Gallery, no. 2607. The panel is of oak, and tree-ring dating suggests that it was felled in 1482; thus the most likely period of use is believed to have been between 1515 and 1525. Roy Strong has discussed the portrait in his catalogue: *Tudor and Jacobean Portraits* (London, 1969), pp. 271–3. He notes that the portrait was first recorded in 1785 as *The Countess at Barrington Hall* and believes that it might have been a Barrington lady of that date who was 'dressed up' as the countess, upon whose lineage the family prided itself. Initially it did appear that the ermine spots on the outer part of the headdress had been painted over the original craquelure, which indicates that these were later additions along with the ermine spots on the outer sleeves. However, when the picture was finally cleaned in 1973 the ermine spots did not disappear; neither did the barrel bracelet or the 'W' suspended from the sitter's fingers, which suggests that they may have been original after all. The barrel will refer to the duke of Clarence and the 'W' to Warwick. Therefore, the results of the cleaning point once more to the portrait being an authentic likeness of Margaret, countess of Salisbury. I am grateful to the National Portrait Gallery Archives for this information.

[58] PRO, SP1/139, ff. 83–4.

[59] For the definitions of offices see Mertes, *The English Noble Household*, pp. 39, 34, 22.

[60] PRO, SP1/139, f. 84.

[61] PRO, SC6/Hen VIII/6875. For eighty-six days from September to December 1538 household expenses, including servants' wages, amounted to £237 12s 6d. Although £72 3s 4d of this constituted rewards given to servants by order of the king, under normal circumstances expenses would probably have been in the region of £150–£170 which, at a rough estimation, could have amounted to between £700–£900 a year.

[62] PRO, SP1/139, ff. 72, 72b, 73b, 74, 76, 76b, 77, 82.

[63] *L&P*, IV (i), no. 2343; IV (ii), no. 2407.

[64] PRO, SP1/139, ff. 72b, 79b, 80, 80b, 82.

[65] *L&P*, XIII (ii), nos. 804, 955.

[66] W. Page (ed.), *VCH, Hampshire and the Isle of Wight* (London, 1912), vol. 5, p. 103; *L&P*, XIV (ii), no. 627.

[67] The other godmother was the duchess of Norfolk, while Wolsey stood as godfather. *L&P*, II (i), no. 1573.

[68] PRO, E.36/216, f. 58.

[69] Reginald to Granvelle, 11 April 1539. Papiers d'État et Audience, 128, ff. 241–5, cited in C. Höllger, 'Reginald Pole and the legations of 1537 and 1539: diplomatic and polemical responses to the break with Rome' (unpublished Ph.D. thesis, University of Oxford, 1989), 225.

[70] PRO, C.82/490; *L&P*, III (i), no. 805. In this grant of 1520 Margaret is described as Mary's governess. For Elizabeth Denton and Margaret Brian see Loades, *Mary Tudor: A Life*, pp. 28–9.

[71] Loades, *Mary Tudor: A Life*, p. 29.

[72] BL, Cotton MS Vitellius C, f. 24, cited in Strickland, *Lives of the Queens of England*, vol. 3, pp. 312–13.

[73] For instance, see Loades, *Mary Tudor: A Life*, pp. 61, 81.

[74] M. Dowling, *Humanism in the Age of Henry VIII* (London, 1986), p. 146.

[75] W. Schenk, *Reginald Pole Cardinal of England* (London, 1950), p. 5.

[76] *L&P*, V, no. 985; N. Simmonds, *Warblington Church* (Havant, 1979), p. 9; L. Stephen and S. Lee (eds), *DNB* (63 vols, London, 1885–1900), vol. 25, p. 381.

[77] He wrote to Cromwell in their defence following the arrival of Reginald's *De Unitate* in 1536 explaining that Lord Montague, 'hys most dere brother, who by hys acte ys depryvyd of a grete comfort of hys lyfe', and in his will bequeathed £4 to 'the veray honnerable and my singulier good lorde, my lorde Montague . . . to bie hym a hagg'. BL, Cotton MS Cleopatra E. VI, f. 384; *L&P*, XI, no. 157; W. G. Zeeveld, *Foundations of Tudor Policy* (London, 1969), p. 228.

[78] J. A. Gee, *The Life and Works of Thomas Lupset* (Oxford, 1928), pp. 171, 111.

[79] *L&P*, XIV (i), no. 181 (iv).

[80] Schenk, *Reginald Pole Cardinal of England*, p. 5.

[81] PRO, C.82/393; C.66/620, m. 19; *L&P*, I (ii), no. 2137.

[82] PRO, SC6/Hen VIII/219.

[83] J. J. Scarisbrick, *Henry VIII* (London, 1988), p. 38.

[84] *L&P*, I (ii), no. 2480 (27).

[85] C. Cruickshank, *Henry VIII and the Invasion of France* (Gloucester, 1990), p. 90.

[86] Ibid., p. 135.

[87] *L&P*, I (ii), no. 2301.

[88] For instance, on 8 February 1530 she was described as 'Countess of Salisbury and Lady of Montague' in her appointment of Oliver Frankelyn as her receiver-general. PRO, E.312/8. See also Miller, *Henry VIII and the English Nobility*, p. 9.

[89] In addition to Henry Pole, three other sons of earls were summoned to the Lords during the reign of Henry VIII: Lord Rochford, son of the earl of Wiltshire in 1532/3; Lord Maltravers, son of the earl of Arundel in 1533/4; and Lord Talbot, son of the earl of Shrewsbury in 1533/4. *Complete Peerage*, vol. 1, Appendix G, p. 490.

[90] Ibid., p. 78. William, earl of Salisbury's great-grandson Thomas was restored as earl of Salisbury and Lord Montague in 1421 following his father's attainder. His only child was Alice, countess of Salisbury and Baroness Montague in her own right, mother of 'the kingmaker', Henry Pole's great-grandfather.

[91] *L&P*, II (ii), p. 3357. I shall, in future, refer to Henry Pole as Lord Montague.

[92] Ibid., no. 2736, p. 874.

[93] A. Young, *Tudor and Jacobean Tournaments* (London, 1987), p. 67.

[94] *L&P*, II (ii), p. 1510.

[95] The King's Spears performed military and ceremonial functions and consisted of gentlemen and sons of noblemen under the captaincy of the earl of Essex. B. A. Murphy, *Bastard Prince: Henry VIII's Lost Son* (Stroud, 2001), p. 19.

[96] D. Starkey, 'The Tiltyard: the jousts of July 1517', in D. Starkey (ed.), *Henry VIII: A European Court in England* (London, 1991), p. 40.

[97] *L&P*, III (i), p. 313, no. 869.

[98] Ibid., II (ii), no. 4409. The other gentlemen appointed were Sir Edward Neville, Nicholas Carewe, Francis Bryan, Henry Norris and William Coffin. For the inception of the office see D. R. Starkey, 'The development of the privy chamber, 1485–1547' (unpublished Ph.D. thesis, University of Cambridge, 1973), 97–106.

[99] PRO, E.36/216, f. 17; *L&P*, II (ii), p. 1479.

[100] Starkey, 'The development of the privy chamber', p. 95.

[101] Schenk, *Reginald Pole Cardinal of England*, p. 7.

[102] 'First a gown of fine tawney velvet containing fourteen yards. Item seven yards of cloth of gold for edging and lining of the same gown. Item a gown of fine black velvet containing fourteen yards. Item seven yards of crimson satin for edging and lining of the same gown. Item four ells of black sarcenet. Item a roll of fine bokeram. Item a kirtle of black satten containing seven yards with lining and edging to the same. Item a kirtle of russet damask containing seven yards with lining and edging to the same.' BL, Add. MSS 18826, f. 38.

[103] BL, Cotton MS Vitellius B. XVIII, f. 75; *L&P*, II (i), no. 167.

[104] *L&P*, III (i), p. 499, no. 1285. In 1532 their eldest daughter, Catherine, married Francis, Lord Hastings. Although twelve was the minimum age of cohabitation for a female, Reginald had persuaded his family that Catherine should reach a more marriageable age before her nuptials took place. Princess Mary was not considered marriageable until the age of fourteen or fifteen, whilst Margaret Pole and Margaret Tudor both married at fourteen. Hence, if Catherine married at fourteen in 1532, she must have been born in 1518 which would date her parents' marriage to no later than about 1517. F. Bickley (ed.), *HMC*, Reports 78, Hastings (ii) (1930), pp. 5–6.

[105] *Complete Peerage*, vol. 1, p. 31. He was sixteen years or older at his mother's death in 1485.

[106] It is not clear how many sisters Jane had, but that she had sisters is shown by the articles of marriage negotiated between Margaret and Lord Bergavenny, where Jane is described as 'one of the daughters and heirs' of Lord Bergavenny. PRO, E.314/79, no. 300.

[107] Miller, *Henry VIII and the English Nobility*, p. 139.

[108] PRO, E.314/79.

[109] PRO, SP1/140, f. 64; E.314/79, nos. 300, 303.

[110] PRO, E.314/79, no. 300.

[111] In 1519 Jane's first husband died. E. Cobby, *The Lewknors of Sussex* (Cranleigh, 1991), p. 15. On 24 October 1522 Arthur made reference to his father-in-law in a letter. *L&P*, III (ii), no. 2636.

[112] In her father's Inquisition Post Mortem of 1543, Jane was described as 'aged 40 and more'. F. W. T. Attree (trans.), *Sussex Inquisitions Post Mortem 1485–1649*, Sussex Record Society, 14 (Lewes, 1912), p. 142.

[113] Cobby, *The Lewknors of Sussex*, p. 14. She was twelve years old in 1470.

[114] Ibid. Jane had one daughter, Anne, by her first marriage but, if she were to have a son by Arthur, his claim would supersede Anne's.

[115] W. Bugden, 'The divorce of Sir William Barentyne, 1540', *Sussex Notes and Queries*, 9 (1942–3), 168.

[116] J. Cornwall, 'Sussex wealth and society in the reign of Henry VIII', *SAC*, 114 (1976), 11.

[117] Ibid.

[118] In July 1525 Constance Pole's name appeared on the household list of Princess Mary. BL, Harl. MS 6807, f. 3; *DNB*, vol. 46, p. 23.

[119] The *DNB* claims that Constance was the elder daughter. Certainly, in her father's will her one bequest precedes that of her sister Katherine, and, although Katherine and her husband, Edmund Mervyn, are the main beneficiaries of the will, this probably has more to do with Pakenham's affection for Mervyn and disenchantment with Geoffrey than Katherine's age. It seems probable, therefore,

that Constance was the elder sister. PRO, Prob.11/22 (36 Porch).

[120]He held Lordington in Sussex which also included the manor of Whiteway, the moiety of Gatcombe manor on the Isle of Wight, and the moiety of Westover or Calbourne manor, part of the manor of Gatcombe. L. F. Saltzman (ed.), *VCH, Sussex*, vol. 4 (London, 1973), p. 116; W. Page (ed.), *VCH, Hampshire and the Isle of Wight*, vol. 5 (London, 1912), pp. 249, 219.

[121]L. C. Loyd and D. M. Stenton (eds), *Sir Christopher Hatton's Book of Seals Presented to F. M. Stenton* (Oxford, 1950), pp. 15–16, no. 21.

[122]B. J. Harris, *Edward Stafford, Third Duke of Buckingham, 1478–1521* (Stanford, CA, 1986), p. 104.

[123]*L&P*, II (i), no. 1893. The reason for Buckingham's refusal is not clear due to mutilation of the letter. The sentence 'she must leve the more barly monny yerres' provides the only clue. 'Barly' might mean frugally, perhaps he was suggesting that Margaret would not be able to pay the dowry he required.

[124]C. Rawcliffe, *The Staffords, Earls of Stafford and Dukes of Buckingham 1394–1521* (Cambridge, 1978), p. 136.

[125]Ibid.

[126]*HMC*, Report 7, 1879 (reprinted 1979), p. 584. 'Certain lands' refers to lands the ownership of which was under dispute between Margaret and the king. See below, ch. 4.

[127]*HMC*, Report 7, 1879, p. 584.

[128]Rawcliffe, *The Staffords, Earls of Stafford and Dukes of Buckingham*, p. 136; Harris, *Edward Stafford, Third Duke of Buckingham*, p. 55.

[129]Dugdale states that 'it appears' Margaret settled several manors, which are listed, on the couple and their heirs. W. Dugdale, *The Baronage of England*, vol. 1, (London, 1675), p. 170.

[130]The manors in question were: Somerton, Chedzoy, Donyatt, Yarlington and Shipton Montague in Somerset; Stokenham, Yealmpton, Pyworthy, Wonford and Clyst St Mary in Devon. *HMC,* Report 78, Hastings, vol. 1 (1928), p. 308. Loyd and Stenton, *Sir Christopher Hatton's Book of Seals,* pp. 15–16. These manors were still in Margaret's possession in 1538.

[131]*HMC*, Report 7, 1879, p. 584.

[132]C. A. Sneyde (trans.), *A Relation or Rather a True Account of the Island of England*, Camden Society, old series, 37 (London, 1847), pp. 125–31. A *placard* was a separate accessory: it covered the gentleman's chest and could be very ornamental. J. Ashelford, *A Visual History of Costume: The Sixteenth Century* (London, 1993), p. 36.

3 *The Countess of Salisbury: A Female Magnate*

[1]Francis Boyle, Viscount Shannon, *Discourses and Essays* (1696), p. 107, cited in C. Carlton, 'The widow's tale: male myths and female reality in 16th and 17th century England', *Albion*, 10, 2 (1978), 126.

[2]Thomas Becon, *An Humble Supplication unto God,* published in 1554, cited in M. Levine, 'The place of women in Tudor government', in D. J. Guth and J. W. McKenna (eds), *Tudor Rule and Revolution: Essays for G. R. Elton from his American Friends* (Cambridge, 1982), p. 111.

[3]S. H. Rigby, *English Society in the Later Middle Ages* (London, 1995), p. 248.

[4]Ibid., pp. 249, 248.

[5] In 1532 Anne Boleyn was created marquess of Pembroke, the male title denoting that Anne held this newly created peerage title in her own right. E. Ives, *Anne Boleyn* (Oxford, 1988), p. 198, n. 51.

[6] If Sir Richard Pole had been living the situation would have been very different. Her estates and the income from them would have been controlled by him, and she would not have been able to bequeath or alienate any part of them without his permission.

[7] B. J. Harris, 'The view from my lady's chamber: new perspectives on the early Tudor monarchy', *Huntington Library Quarterly*, 60, 3 (1998) 217, 229.

[8] F. Pollock and F. W. Maitland, *The History of English Law*, ed. S. F. C. Milsom, vol. 1 (2 vols, Cambridge, 1968), p. 482.

[9] R. E. Archer, 'Rich old ladies: the problem of late medieval dowagers', in A. J. Pollard (ed.), *Property and Politics: Essays in Later Medieval English History* (Gloucester, 1984), pp. 23–4.

[10] J. Ward, *English Noblewomen in the Later Middle Ages* (London, 1992), p. 269; P. Hogrefe, *Tudor Women: Commoners and Queens* (Ames, 1975), p. 32; S. Shahar, *The Fourth Estate: A History of Women in the Middle Ages* (London, 1991), p. 149.

[11] Jones and Underwood, *The King's Mother*, pp. 98–9, 88–9.

[12] Harris 'The view from my lady's chamber', p. 223.

[13] BL, Harl. MS 6807, f. 3. There is some confusion regarding Katherine Poole due to similarity of names. According to David Loades this lady was the Katherine Pole who had been Mary's nurse in 1520 and who was married to Leonard Pole, a gentleman usher of the king's chamber. However, on 18 August 1525 another list of these ladies was drawn up together with their individual allowance of black velvet. Katherine Poole is missing altogether and in her place, third on the list, is a Mistress Katherine Mountecue. Therefore it is likely that Katherine Pole and Katherine Mountecue are the same lady, the countess of Salisbury's granddaughter and Lord Montague's daughter. D. M. Loades, *Mary Tudor: A Life* (Oxford, 1989), pp. 40, 29; PRO, E.101/419/16, f. 117.

[14] For his appointment as Mary's controller see Loades, *Mary Tudor: A Life,* p. 41. In a letter written to his 'cosyen Gyfford', in which he states that he is the steward of Margaret's lordship of Pyworthy, he signs as plain Thomas Denys. PRO, SP1/140, f. 66; *L&P,* XIII (ii), no. 1016. In *Letters and Papers* a date of 1523 is estimated for this letter. However, when he was appointed as the princess's comptroller in 1526, Denys had been knighted; therefore his association with Margaret pre-dated his appointment as Mary's comptroller.

[15] Loades, *Mary Tudor: A Life*, p. 40.

[16] *LL* (6 vols, London, 1981), vol. 2, p. 77, no. 145; p. 28, no. 113.

[17] Ibid., p. 63, no. 136.

[18] Ibid., p. 77, no. 145.

[19] S. T. Bindoff (ed.), *The History of Parliament: The House of Commons 1509–1558,* vol. 3 (3 vols, London, 1982), 116; S. Quail, *Spirit of Portsmouth* (Portsmouth, 1989). I am grateful to Diana M. Gregg of the Portsmouth City Record Office for drawing my attention to this work; PRO, SP1/142, f. 194; *L&P*, XIV (i), no. 181; J. P. Collier (ed.), *The Trevelyan Papers prior to A.D. 1558*, (3 vols, Camden Society, old series, 67 (London, 1857), vol. 1, p. 159.

[20] B. J. Harris, 'Women and politics in early Tudor England', *Historical Journal*, 33 (1990), 262.

[21] PRO, SP1/139, f. 83.

[22] *LL*, vol. 2, p. 217.

[23] In 1538 they were among those named to a commission of sewers for Sussex. *L&P*, XIII (i), no. 1519 (17).

[24] An Inquisition Post Mortem, PRO, Court of Wards, no. 100/2, survives for him, 27 Henry VIII. *LL*, vol. 1, p. 488.

[25] E. W. Ives, *The Common Lawyers of Pre-Reformation England* (Cambridge, 1983), p. 372.

[26] Margaret was the daughter of Bergavenny's second marriage.

[27] PRO, SP1/139, f. 79; *L&P*, XIII (ii), no. 818 (2).

[28] Harris, 'Women and politics in early Tudor England', p. 265.

[29] PRO, SP1/142, f. 194.

[30] BL, Cart. Harl. MS 43, f. 9; Harl. Ch. 43, f. 8; PRO, SP1/142, f. 194.

[31] PRO, E.36/225, f. 42; *L&P*, IV (i), no. 1792, p. 795.

[32] *LL*, vol. 4, p. 107, no. 863.

[33] PRO, SC12/11/34, no. 6.

[34] *L&P*, XIII (ii), no. 817.

[35] Ibid., VI, no. 1540.

[36] PRO, SP1/50, f. 4; *L&P*, IV, no. 654.

[37] *CSP*, Spain, 1534–1535, p. 235, no. 80.

[38] Harris, *Edward Stafford, Third Duke of Buckingham*, p. 61.

[39] *L&P*, III (i), no. 1285, p. 499.

[40] Ibid., pp. 498, 499.

[41] On 1 May 1521 he informed the Signory that two of Buckingham's nephews, the brothers of Reginald Pole, had been arrested with the duke. *CSP*, Venetian, 1520–1526, no. 204.

[42] PRO, SC6/Hen VIII/6875; PRO, SP1/139, f. 13; *L&P*, XIII (ii), no. 829 (2); no. 796; PRO, SP1/138, f. 220; *L&P*, XIII (ii), no. 804 (7).

[43] By 1519 Lord Bergavenny had married the duke of Buckingham's daughter, Mary. Harris, *Edward Stafford, Third Duke of Buckingham*, pp. 60–1.

[44] PRO, SP1/138, f. 33b; *L&P*, XIII (ii), no. 702.

[45] PRO, Prob. 11/25 (35 Hogen); *L&P*, V, no. 909 (36).

[46] PRO, Prob. 11/25 (35 Hogen).

[47] PRO, SP1/136, f. 16; *L&P*, XIII (ii), no. 695 (2).

[48] C. Cross, *The Puritan Earl: A Life of Henry Hastings Third Earl of Huntingdon 1536–1595* (London, 1966), pp. 5–6.

[49] *DNB*, vol. 25, p. 123.

[50] Ibid.

[51] Loades, *Mary Tudor: A Life*, p. 57.

[52] PRO, SP1/138, f. 211; *L&P*, XIII (ii), no. 803.

[53] PRO, SP1/138, f. 218b; *L&P*, XIII (ii), no. 804 (6).

[54] *LL*, vol. 2, p. 138, no. 174.

[55] Ibid., vol. 3, p. 489, no. 769.

[56] PRO, Prob. 11/22 (36 Porch).

[57] Geoffrey's presence at an Inn of Court is testified to by his mother in 1538. PRO, SP1/138, f. 245b; *L&P*, XIII (ii), no. 818 (15).

[58] Also see Bindoff (ed.), *The History of Parliament: The House of Commons*, vol. 3, p. 116.

[59] PRO, Req. 2/2/182.

[60] *L&P*, XVI, no. 74; Bindoff (ed.), *The History of Parliament: The House of Commons*, vol. 3, p. 117.

[61] PRO. Prob. 11/52 (28 Lyon).

[62] Mervyn was admitted to the Middle Temple in 1506 and was reader there in 1523 and 1530. He became king's sergeant in 1539, served on numerous royal commissions, and his career continued into the reign of Queen Mary. J. Hutchinson, *A Catalogue of Notable Middle Templars* (London, 1902), p. 161; PRO, CP25/2, bundle 37/245, f. 66; PRO, SP1/142, f. 194.

[63] This document is very difficult to read. The original appears to read Ciatton or Cratton, which is probably Trotton, Sir Roger Lewknor's seat. PRO, SP1/26, f. 123; *L&P*, XIII (ii), no. 2636.

[64] In a petition drawn up by his brother-in-law, Edmund Mervyn, in 1531 Geoffrey Pole claimed that upon his enclosure of Lysley Wood, which he legally held, several armed tenants of the earl of Arundel, at his instigation, had pulled down and destroyed the hedge. Those accused, while admitting that Geoffrey was legally seised of the wood which lay within the larger wood held by Arundel, claimed that they, and also the tenants of the duke of Norfolk, enjoyed the right to graze the wood according to the custom of the manor, and therefore Geoffrey had no right to enclose it. Geoffrey's petition, they declared, was merely formed to hurt them and slander the earl. PRO, Stac 2/19/306; PRO, Stac 2/19/377.

[65] *L&P*, VI, no. 589.

[66] PRO, E.179/69/2; *L&P*, IV (ii), no. 2972.

[67] PRO, SC6/Hen VIII/6875.

[68] *LL*, vol. 1, p. 172, no. 1; p. 330, no. xxxi.

[69] BL, Add. MSS 39404, A, no. 3, f. 25.

[70] PRO, SP1/175, ff. 81–2; *L&P*, XVIII (i), no. 67 (5, 6).

[71] F. Ward, 'The divorce of Sir William Barentyne', *SAC*, 68 (1927), 279.

[72] Cobby, *The Lewknors of Sussex*, p. 16.

[73] It stated that, as Jane had been married to two husbands and had had issue by both of them, she could not take such vows. Also, the vows had been taken before the bishop of a foreign diocese, St Asaph, without authorization of the bishop of the diocese and had been 'forced upon her by Henry Pole, then Lord Montague . . . when she was in extreme grief for the death of her husband Sir Arthur and one of her children'. *L&P*, XVIII, no. 67 (5).

[74] *LL*, vol. 1, pp. 179, 195.

[75] Ibid., p. 492, no. 19.

[76] Ibid., vol. 2, p. 138, no. 174a; ibid., vol. 1, p. 492, no. 19; ibid., vol. 3, p. 489, no. 769.

[77] Ibid., vol. 2, pp. 44–5, no. 126.

[78] Ibid., vol. 4, p. 140, no. 876.

[79] Ibid., vol. 2, p. 131, no. 172.

[80] Ibid., vol. 4, p. 378, no. 1001; pp. 247–8; ibid., vol. 3, p. 489, no. 769.

[81] John Husee, Leonard Smyth and Diggory Grenville. Ibid., vol. 2, pp. 519, 520, 522, 527, 532, nos. 412, 413, 415, 419, 421; ibid., vol. 4, p. 32, no. 836.

[82] Ibid., vol. 3, p. 387, no. 705.

[83] Ibid., vol. 5, p. 513, no. 1436.

[84] Exeter was between four and six years younger than Montague.

[85] PRO, SP1/139, f. 14b; *L&P*, XIII (ii), no. 827 (1).

[86] *L&P*, XIII (ii), no. 802.

[87] Ibid., no. 779.

[88] PRO, SP1/138, f. 34; *L&P*, XIII (ii), no. 702.

[89] *CSP*, Venetian, 1534–1554, no. 806.

[90] PRO, SP1/138, f. 222; *L&P*, XIII (ii), no. 772.

[91] *L&P*, VIII, no. 802; ibid., XIX, no. 1068 (37).

[92] *CAD*, XI, A. 3223; R. W. Hoyle, 'Henry Percy, sixth earl of Northumberland, and the fall of the House of Percy, 1527–1537', in G. W. Bernard (ed.), *The Tudor Nobility* (Manchester, 1992), pp. 184–6; PRO, E.150/928.

[93] PRO, SP1/138, ff. 222b, 34b; *L&P*, XIII (ii), nos. 702, 772.

[94] *L&P*, IV (ii), no. 68; N. H. Nicolas, *Testamenta Vetusta* (London, 1826), p. 633. Humphrey Tyrell was probably the Essex gentleman who was a gentleman usher of the king in 1526. *L&P*, IV (i), no. 1939, p. 868; *Valor Ecclesiasticus* (6 vols, London, 1810–34), vol. 2, p. 439.

[95] PRO, SP1/138, f. 212; *L&P*, XIII (ii), no. 803. John Stokesley granted him the keeping of a park and lent him money.

[96] Shahar, *The Fourth Estate*, p. 12. Had Margaret been a man, Montague could still have been summoned to the Lords, at the king's discretion, as Lord Montague, but he would have attended with his father. *Journals of the House of Lords*, vol. 1, *1509–1577* (London, 1846), pp. 58–9.

[97] PRO, SP1/140, f. 66; *L&P*, XIII (ii), no. 1016.

[98] PRO, SP1/106, f. 273–4; *L&P*, XI, no. 556; *L&P*, XI, no. 580.

[99] Although Margaret Beaufort's position had sparked a debate about the ability of a woman who was *femme sole* to be appointed a justice of the peace by royal commission, this never appears to have actually happened in the sixteenth century.

[100] R. H. Fritze, 'Faith and faction: religious changes, national politics, and the development of local factionalism in Hampshire, 1485–1570' (unpublished Ph.D. thesis, University of Cambridge, 1981), 4.

[101] *L&P*, IV (ii), no. 5083 (12); ibid., V, no. 166 (15).

[102] PRO, E.36/215, f. 676.

[103] PRO, E.40/1362; *L&P*, XIII (i), no. 294.

[104] PRO, SP1/139, f. 131 (lower f. number); *L&P*, XIII (ii), no. 855 (2); PRO, SC6/Hen VIII/6875.

[105] PRO, SC12/11/34, no. 6; PRO, SP1/139, f. 30; *L&P*, XIII (ii), nos. 829, 779.

[106] *L&P*, XI, no. 719; ibid., XII (i), no. 182; ibid., IV (iii), App. 89; *LL*, vol. 1, pp. 163, 182.

[107] Pye, *The Life of Cardinal Reginald Pole*, p. 157.

[108] BL, Cotton MS Appendix L, f. 79; *L&P*, XIII (ii), no. 855.

[109] BL, Harl. MS 3881, f. 31.

[110] *L&P*, IV (ii), no. 3029; ibid., V, no. 198.

[111] PRO, SP1/18, f. 275; *L&P*, III (i), no. 411.

[112] PRO, C.1/761/28.

[113] PRO, C.1/401/11.

[114] PRO, Stac 2/18/167; Stac 2/29/112.

[115] PRO, Stac 2/22/377.

[116] PRO, SP1/138, no. 249.

[117] PRO, SC6/Hen VIII/ 6875.

[118] *CAD*, V, A. 12129.

[119] PRO, SC6/Hen VIII/6875.

[120] PRO, C82/490, no. 58. In his will Sir Richard Delabere specified that should his eldest son, Thomas, die without heirs then the Delabere lands should pass to his second son, Sevacar, and his heirs. Elizabeth was Sevacar's only surviving child and thus heiress to the Delabere lands. PRO, Prob.11/18 (2 Holder).

[121] C. J. Robinson, *A History of the Castles of Herefordshire* (London, 1869), p.

90.

[122] Hertford CO Records, no. 6454. Courtesy of Dr Kathryn Thompson, Hertfordshire County Record Office.

[123] PRO, CP25/2/43/299, f. 27.

[124] PRO, CP25/2/37/245, f. 66; *L&P*, V, no. 909 (21).

[125] PRO, SP1/30, ff. 118–22.

[126] PRO, E.36/155, f. 34.

[127] PRO, SC6/Hen VIII/6875.

[128] This has been calculated using the ministers' accounts, PRO, SC6/Hen VIII/6874, 6875. The manors were: Aston Clinton in Buckinghamshire, Lantyan in Cornwall, Clyst St Mary, Coleridge Hundred, Pyworthy, Stokenham, Wonford, Yealmpton in Devon, Newton Montague in Dorset, Christchurch, Ringwood in Hampshire, Easton in Northamptonshire, Chedzoy with Canteloes, Donyatt, Dunpole, Shipton Montague, Somerton, Yarlington in Somerset, Earlstoke in Wiltshire.

[129] *L&P*, XIV (i), no. 181 (iv).

[130] S. J. Gunn, *Charles Brandon, Duke of Suffolk c. 1484–1545* (Oxford, 1988), pp. 137–9; Hoyle, 'Henry Percy, sixth earl of Northumberland, and the fall of the House of Percy', pp. 193–4; Harris, *Edward Stafford, Third Duke of Buckingham*, pp. 101–3.

[131] Harris, *Edward Stafford, Third Duke of Buckingham*, pp. 105, 138.

[132] Hertford County Office Records, no. 6454.

[133] H. L. Lyster Denny, *Memorials of an Ancient House: A History of the Family of Lister or Lyster* (Edinburgh, 1913), p. 258; Ives, *The Common Lawyers of Pre-Reformation England*, p. 98.

[134] In 1546 he was made chief justice of the king's bench and master of the wards. Lyster Denny, *Memorials of an Ancient House*, p. 258.

[135] PRO, E.36/155; *L&P*, I (i), nos. 132 (48), 381 (39); *L&P*, XX, no. 773 (I), p. 425.

[136] PRO, SP1/139, f. 83; PRO, SC6/Hen VIII/6875.

[137] C. W. Boase (ed.), *Register of the University of Oxford*, I (1449–1463, 1505–1571) (Oxford, 1885), p. 90.

[138] *L&P*, XVI, no. 779 (8).

[139] PRO, SC6/Hen VIII/6875. Another Middle Templar, Lewis Fortescue was admitted in 1519 and by 1536 was autumnal reader. On commissions of the peace for Devon five months before Margaret's arrest, he was appointed, along with three other professional lawyers, to the Council of the West in 1539. *Register of Admissions to the Honourable Society of the Middle Temple, Fifteenth Century–1944*, vol. 1 (London, 1944), p. 10; J. A. Youings, 'The Council of the West', *TRHS*, fifth series, 10 (1959), 53.

[140] PRO, SC6/Hen VIII/6875; *Records of the Honourable Society of Lincoln's Inn*, vol. 1: *Admissions 1420–1799* (London, 1896), p. 24; *DNB*, vol. 52, p. 359; *L&P*, III (ii), no. 391. Skewes had married Exeter's aunt by 1509 when he was appointed executor of the will of Edward Courtenay, earl of Devon, Exeter's grandfather. PRO, Prob. 11/16 (15 Bennett).

[141] SP1/139, f. 83; *L&P*, XX (ii), no. 266; PRO, Prob. 11/34 (26 Bucke); Ward 7/6/34; *L&P*, I (i), no. 707; PRO, SC6/Hen VIII/1593; 6874, ff. 3, 3b, 4; PRO, SP1/30, ff. 118–22; *L&P*, IV, no. 100. In a receipt issued by William Wintringham in the nineteenth year of Henry VIII's reign, Frankelyn is described as 'receyvour Generall of my lady of Salysburyes lands'. PRO, SP1/46, f. 12; *L&P*, IV, no. 3730. For the formalization of Frankelyn's appointment see PRO, E.312/8; *L&P*, XVII, no. 1251

(15); no. 71 (12); no. 880; PRO, SC6/Hen VIII/6867.

[142] PRO, SC6/Hen VIII/6875.

[143] *Register of Admissions, the Middle Temple*, vol. 1 (London, 1944), p. 11. He sat on commissions of the peace, of gaol delivery, of oyer and terminer, and of sewers. S. Leadam (ed.), *Select Cases in the Court of Requests 1497–1569*, Selden Society, vol. 12 (London, 1898), p. lxiii.

[144] *L&P*, XIV (i), no. 181 (ii); PRO, SC6/Hen VIII/6875.

[145] *L&P*, I (i), no. 1123 (26).

[146] PRO, Stac 2/18/167; *L&P*, XIV (i), no. 181 (ii); *LL*, vol. 4, p. 56; *Records of the Honourable Society of Lincoln's Inn*, p. 37; PRO, SC6/Hen VIII/6875.

[147] PRO, E.101/490/12, f. 3; Harris, *Edward Stafford, Third Duke of Buckingham*, p. 224.

[148] P. Gwyn, *The King's Cardinal* (London, 1990), p. 199; *L&P*, IV (ii), no. 3087; *L&P*, V, p. 314; *L&P*, XIV (I), no. 181 (ii). An Inquisition Post Mortem exists for a Thomas Hackluyt of Herefordshire for 1516/17. Although it cannot be our Thomas Hackluyt, it could very well be a relative. Chancery series, 2/30/121, Exchequer series, 2/418/3, reference in *Index of Inquisitions Preserved in the Public Record Office, Henry VIII–Philip and Mary*, Lists and Indexes, vol. 23 (New York, 1963), p. 110.

[149] *L&P*, XIV (i), no. 181 (ii); Gwyn, *King's Cardinal*, pp. 585, 615; *DNB*, vol. 25, p. 407.

[150] BL, Lansdowne MS, 203; *L&P*, XI, no. 1219; *L&P*, XIV (i), no. 181 (ii); *DNB*, vol. 25, p. 407.

[151] A. C. Chibnall (ed.), 'The certificate for musters for Buckinghamshire in 1522', *Buckinghamshire Record Society*, vol. 17 (1973), p. 66; Loyd and Stenton (eds.), *Sir Christopher Hatton's Book of Seals*, pp. 15–16.

[152] *CAD*, vol. 5, A. 13349.

[153] *DNB*, vol. 52, p. 359.

[154] *DNB*, vol. 25, p. 407: Gwyn, *The King's Cardinal*, pp. 585, 615; Loades, *Mary Tudor: A Life*, p. 41; *L&P*, II (i), no. 2481.

[155] PRO, SC6/Hen VIII/6875.

[156] Rawcliffe, *The Staffords, Earls of Stafford and Dukes of Buckingham*, p. 89; PRO, SP1/142, f. 194; PRO, SP1/139, f. 83; *L&P*, XIV (i), no. 181 (iv). The countess had apparently discharged this debt by 1538.

[157] Shahar, *The Fourth Estate*, p. 11.

[158] PRO, SC6/Hen VIII/6874, f. 4b.

[159] PRO, SC6/Hen VIII/6875.

[160] PRO, SC6/Hen VIII/1833.

[161] Ibid., first receipt.

[162] Jane was the daughter of Sir Ralph Shirley, one of the knights of the body to Henry VII. Lyster Denny, *Memorials of an Ancient House*, p. 260.

[163] PRO, E.101/518/42.

[164] Harris, *Edward Stafford, Third Duke of Buckingham*, pp. 100, 143, 188.

[165] PRO, SP1/142, f. 194; *L&P*, XIV, no. 181 (iii); PRO, Prob. 11/32 (8 Populwell).

[166] He received £10 a year as receiver-general and £4 as feodary, 13s 8d a year for his custody of the wood at Cottingham, £6 20s as bailiff of Ware, £4 13s 4d as bailiff of Clavering and £6 13s 4d a year as keeper of Donyatt Park. In addition, by 1538 he was also receiving 74s 2d, £4 13s 4d and 53s 4d for offices on the manors of Yarlington, Stokenham and the hundred of Christchurch, respectively. PRO, E.312/8; PRO, SC6/Hen VIII/6875; *L&P*, XIV (i), no. 181 (ii). For his annuity see

PRO, SP1/132, f. 194; SP1/139, f. 83.

[167] The earliest surviving complete set of ministers' accounts for Margaret's lands begins in 1518. Using these and those ministers' accounts of 1538 we can attempt to discover how long her estate officers remained in her employ. PRO, SC6/Hen VIII/6874; 6875.

[168] PRO, SP1/18, f. 275; *L&P*, XIV (i), no. 181 (ii); PRO, SP1/139, 11, f. 83b; PRO, SP1/142, f. 194.

[169] *L&P*, I (i), no. 82, p. 41; ibid., IV (iii), no. 6121.

[170] Ibid., I (i), no. 218 (9).

[171] PRO, SP1/46, f. 12; *L&P*, IX, no. 3730.

4 *The Beginning of the End, 1519–1538*

[1] R. Horrox (ed.), *Fifteenth Century Attitudes: Perceptions of Society in Late Medieval England* (Cambridge, 1994), p. 8.

[2] Starkey, *The English Court: from the Wars of the Roses to the Civil War*, pp. 103–4; J. Guy, *Tudor England* (Oxford, 1990), pp. 96–7.

[3] G. Walker, 'The "expulsion of the minions" of 1519 reconsidered', *Historical Journal*, 32 (1989), 1–16.

[4] *L&P*, III (i), no. 704, p. 242; ibid., no. 999.

[5] Ibid., IV (i), no. 1939; W. Jerdan, *The Rutland Papers*, Camden Society, old series, 21 (London, 1842), 101.

[6] *L&P*, III (i), no. 198.

[7] Ibid., (ii), p. 1557.

[8] Harris, *Edward Stafford, Third Duke of Buckingham*, p. 209.

[9] *L&P*, III (i), no. 1268.

[10] Ibid., no. 1204.

[11] PRO, SP1/29, f. 296; *L&P*, III (ii), Appendix 24.

[12] *L&P*, III (i), no. 1293; *CSP*, Venetian, 1520–1526, no. 204.

[13] *CSP, Domestic*, 1509–1580, Henry VIII, vol. 1 (11 vols, 1862–1932) (i), nos. 14, 43.

[14] The confession of the duke's chancellor. *L&P*, III (i), no. 1284 (3).

[15] Ibid., p. 492, no. 1284.

[16] PRO, SP1/233, f. 222b; *L&P*, III, Addenda, no. 367; *L&P*, III (ii), no. 2288 (2).

[17] *L&P*, III (ii), nos. 3281, 3288, 3281; IV (i), nos. 214, 293; III (ii), p. 1464, no. 3516.

[18] *L&P*, III (i), p. 501, no. 1285.

[19] A. H. Anderson, 'Henry, Lord Stafford (1501–63) and the lordship of Caus', *WHR*, 6, 1 (1972), 1.

[20] Ibid.

[21] *L&P*, XII (i), no. 638.

[22] *Complete Peerage*, vol. 1, p. 33.

[23] *DNB*, vol. 40 (London, 1894), p. 257.

[24] PRO, E.179/69/16; *L&P*, IV (ii), no. 2972.

[25] Ward, 'The divorce of Sir William Barentyne', p. 281.

[26] Gwyn, *The King's Cardinal*, pp. 58, 440; Ives, *Anne Boleyn*, p. 120.

[27] *L&P*, XIII (ii), no. 1070. According to Fitzwilliam, who saw Margaret's wills in 1538 and stated: 'I looked only at the dates, the first dated anno 20 and the new

anno 30 in September last.'

[28] Cobby, *The Lewknors of Sussex*, pp. 14–15.

[29] Ibid., p. 16.

[30] Even the marriage of Margaret's granddaughter Catherine to Lord Hastings was not without its problems. Following the marriage Huntingdon's debts rose to such an extent that he sold and mortgaged part of Francis's inheritance contrary to the marriage agreement. This compounded his existing debts as he found himself owing Margaret a considerable sum for breaking the covenants. By 1538 his debts amounted to the immense sum of £9,466 4s 2d. Therefore, on 18 March 1538 he enfeoffed his son Francis and Lord Montague with several manors until those mortgaged lands were redeemed and Huntingdon's debts discharged.

[31] PRO, SP1/50, f. 4; *L&P*, IV (ii), no. 4654.

[32] *L&P*, III (ii), no. 3694.

[33] Based upon the various proofs of inheritance advanced by both Margaret and the king. PRO, E.36/155, ff. 3, 17–26; E.314/79, no. 305; SP1/7, f. 12; SP1/138, ff. 206, 208, and, for documents in Cromwell's possession, *L&P*, VI, no. 299.

[34] *L&P*, I (i), no. 1662 (58).

[35] Ibid., no. 447 (18); ibid., no. 1123 (26).

[36] PRO, SP1/50, f. 4; *L&P*, IV (ii), no. 4654. She was holding Ware in 1518 and 1538. PRO, SC6/Hen VIII/6874, 6875. In February 1538 she sold the Wyke to William Bower. PRO, E.40/136/2; *L&P*, XIII (i), no. 294.

[37] *HMC*, 7th Report, p. 584. This is the covenant made at the time of the marriage referred to in a further indenture of February 1519. Loyd and Stenton, *Sir Christopher Hatton's Book of Seals*, p. 15.

[38] PRO, SP1/7, f. 12. Margaret Beaufort's grandmother had inherited it as one of the co-heiresses of Thomas, earl of Kent.

[39] Jones and Underwood, *The King's Mother*, p. 102.

[40] PRO, SP1/102, f. 129. 'List of original ministers accounts preserved in the Public Record Office' (ii), *Lists and Indexes*, vol. 34 (Dublin, 1910), pp. 185, 190.

[41] PRO, SP1/138, f. 206.

[42] Amesbury, Canford, Charlton, Henstridge and Winterbourne.

[43] M. Hicks, 'The Neville earldom of Salisbury, 1429–71', in M. Hicks (ed.), *Richard III and his Rivals: Magnates and their Motives in the Wars of the Roses* (London, 1991), pp. 358–61.

[44] Jones and Underwood, *The King's Mother*, p. 103.

[45] PRO, E.36/155, f. 17.

[46] The statute did not go through Parliament until 1530–1, 22 Hen VIII, c. 17, in which Deeping and Canford were included. As Richmond definitely received Deeping in 1525, it is safe to assume that he was granted Canford at the same time. He had certainly taken possession by 21 July 1528, when there was a slight dispute between himself and his father over the appointment of Compton's replacement as steward. *Lists and Indexes*, vol. 34, p. 82; *L&P*, IV (ii), no. 4536. For the grant of Winterbourne, *Lists and Indexes*, vol. 34, p. 165; *L&P*, X, no. 1256 (5).

[47] PRO, E.314/79, no. 305.

[48] PRO, SP1/50, f. 4; *L&P*, IV (ii), no. 4654.

[49] PRO, E.504/2.

[50] PRO, E.111/131.

[51] BL, Cotton MS Titus. B. I, f. 486; *L&P*, V, no. 394.

[52] *L&P*, VI, no. 299 (ix, F).

[53] For this see Miller, *Henry VIII and the English Nobility*, pp. 219–20.

[54] Ibid., p. 220.

[55] For this see Gunn, *Charles Brandon, Duke of Suffolk*, pp. 135–6.

[56] Ibid., p. 136.

[57] *L&P*, VIII, no. 1130.

[58] Loades, *Mary Tudor: A Life*, p. 45.

[59] D. Knowles, *The Religious Orders in England*, vol. 3: *The Tudor Age*. (Cambridge, 1959), pp. 124–5; Loades, *Mary Tudor: A Life*, p. 45; *L&P*, IV (ii), no. 2407; W. R. B. Robinson, 'Princess Mary's itinerary in the marches of Wales 1525–1527: a provisional record', *Historical Research*, 71, 175 (1998), 233–52; *L&P*, IV (i), no. 1519.

[60] Loades, *Mary Tudor: A Life*, p. 45.

[61] R. J. Knecht, *Francis I* (Cambridge, 1988), p. 213.

[62] Loades, *Mary Tudor: A Life*, pp. 45, 49.

[63] Ibid., pp. 46–7.

[64] Ibid., pp. 60–2.

[65] Ibid., p. 61.

[66] During her period in Elizabeth's household she had, on one occasion, been dumped bodily into a litter as a result of her refusal to make the move with the rest of the household. On another occasion she had to be physically restrained from confronting the French ambassador. Loades, *Mary Tudor: A Life*, p. 82. Again in 1551, after a histrionic display before a deputation of the Privy Council, she continued to shout her defiance at them out of a window. *APC*, pp. 347–52. In 1557 Giovanni Michiel, the late Venetian Ambassador to England, described her as 'sudden and passionate' and affirmed that she was often subject 'to a very deep melancholy, much greater than that to which she is constitutionally liable, from menstruous retention and suffocation of the matrix'. This affliction, he continued, had plagued her for many years 'so that the remedy of tears and weeping, to which from childhood she has been accustomed, and still often used by her, is not sufficient'. *CSP*, Venetian, 1556–1557, pp. 1055–6, no. 884.

[67] Ives, *Anne Boleyn*, p. 167.

[68] Ibid., p. 198.

[69] Loades, *Mary Tudor: A Life*, p. 73.

[70] PRO, SP1/78, f. 160; *L&P*, VI, no. 1009.

[71] Ibid.

[72] Ibid.

[73] PRO, SP1/78, f. 194; *L&P*, VI, no. 1041.

[74] *L&P*, VI, no. 918.

[75] Although it must be remembered that she was never formally created princess of Wales.

[76] Loades, *Mary Tudor: A Life*, p. 73.

[77] Ives, *Anne Boleyn*, p. 246.

[78] *CSP*, Spain, 1531–1533, p. 882, no. 1161.

[79] Ibid.

[80] *L&P*, VIII, no. 263.

[81] Ibid.

[82] *L&P*, VIII, no. 263.

[83] *LL*, vol. 2, p. 45, no. 126.

[84] *CSP*, Spain, 1531–1533, p. 863, no. 1153.

[85] A. Denton Cheney, 'The holy maid of Kent', *TRHS*, new series, 18 (1904), 112; Mattingly, *Catherine of Aragon*, p. 299.

[86] Scarisbrick, *Henry VIII*, p. 322.

[87] *L&P*, VI, no. 1468.

[88] A. Neame, *The Holy Maid of Kent* (London, 1971), p. 174.

[89] Ibid., p. 178.

[90] John Fisher to Cromwell, 18 February 1534, cited ibid., p. 308.

[91] Neame, *The Holy Maid of Kent*, p. 223.

[92] The lord chancellor's introduction to the bill of attainder against Barton and her associates cited ibid., p. 304.

[93] Ibid., p. 139; Loades, *Mary Tudor: A Life*, p. 61.

[94] Neame, *The Holy Maid of Kent*, pp. 181, 180, 260.

[95] *L&P*, VI, no. 1382. Equally, however, this could be related to Margaret's refusal to surrender Mary's jewels and plate.

[96] J. S. Block, *Factional Politics and the English Reformation 1520–1540* (Woodbridge, 1993), pp. 41–2.

[97] PRO, SP1/92, f. 74; *L&P*, VIII, no. 596.

[98] PRO, SP1/88, f. 174; *L&P*, VII, Appendix 32.

[99] Loades, *Mary Tudor: A Life*, p. 93.

[100] Mattingly, *Catherine of Aragon*, pp. 344–6.

[101] Ives, *Anne Boleyn*, p. 355.

[102] Ibid., p. 400.

[103] *L&P*, X, no. 1212.

[104] Schenk, *Reginald Pole Cardinal of England*, p. 62.

[105] Ibid., p. 64.

[106] *L&P*, IX, no. 701.

[107] Schenk, *Reginald Pole Cardinal of England*, pp. 71–2.

[108] T. F. Mayer, *Reginald Pole Prince and Prophet* (Cambridge, 2000), pp. 19, 20, 21.

[109] Schenk, *Reginald Pole, Cardinal of England*, p. 72.

[110] *L&P*, XIII (ii), no. 818 (19). Unfortunately, at this point the original document has faded and become particularly difficult to read. PRO, SP1/138, f. 202.

[111] PRO, SP1/105, f. 66; *L&P*, XI, no. 93.

[112] PRO, SP1/106, ff. 168–9; *L&P*, XI, no. 451.

[113] Schenk, *Reginald Pole Cardinal of England*, p. 25.

[114] *L&P*, XII (i), no. 444. Thomas Mayer, however, suggests that this interview might never have taken place. Mayer, *Reginald Pole Prince and Prophet*, pp. 59–61.

[115] Loades, *Mary Tudor: A Life*, pp. 105–6.

[116] F. Madden, *The Privy Purse Expenses of Princess Mary* (London, 1831), pp. 9, 51. Two rewards to servants 'of my Lady of Salysbery' of 15s and 20s in January 1537 and January 1538 respectively.

[117] PRO, SP1/139, f. 77b. In 1538 her stables contained only four horses, while the fifth was with her 'cator'.

[118] T. F. Mayer, 'A fate worse than death: Reginald Pole and the Parisian theologians', *EHR*, 102 (1988), 884–5.

[119] *L&P*, V, no. 737.

[120] Ibid., IV (ii), no. 5083 (12); ibid., (iii), no. 5243 (26, 28).

[121] Ibid., (iii), no. 6044. W. Dugdale, *A Perfect Copy of the Nobility to the Great Councils and Parliaments of the Realm* (London, 1685), p. 496.

[122] W. A. Shaw, *The Knights of England* (London, 1906), p. 47. This states that Geoffrey was knighted after 3 November 1529. Indeed, on the commission of the peace in January 1529 he was not knighted, but by 13 May 1530 in his letter to Mr

Frynde Geoffrey had been knighted. *L&P*, IV (iii), no. 5243 (28); PRO, SP1/57, f. 101; *L&P*, IV (iii), no. 6384.
[123] *L&P*, IV (iii), no. 6513.
[124] Ibid., V, Appendix 33. Calais was a costly excursion for Montague, as he was instructed to bring twenty men with him. Ibid., VI, no. 562.
[125] Ibid., VI, no. 601.
[126] Ibid., VII, no. 55; Dugdale, *A Perfect Copy of the Nobility*, p. 497; *L&P*, VII, no. 391.
[127] Ibid., VIII, nos. 609, 974.
[128] Examination of Jerome Ragland, 1538. PRO, SP1/138, f. 35; *L&P*, XIII (ii), no. 702 (1).
[129] *L&P*, VIII, no. 974; *LL*, vol. 2, pp. 519, 520, no. 412.
[130] *L&P*, X, no. 834.
[131] Ibid., no. 580 (2).
[132] Ibid., XII (ii), nos. 911, 1060.
[133] Neame, *The Holy Maid of Kent*, p. 170.
[134] In 1532 a gilt salt with a cover, 20 oz. Lord Stafford's weighed only 17 oz., and the marchioness of Exeter's 14 oz. PRO, E.101/420/15, ff. 2, 3. In 1533, a gilt cruse glass, 'one of highest fashion', 19 oz. PRO, SP2/N (1), f. 1; *L&P*, VI, no. 32; *L&P*, IV (ii), no. 3748.
[135] *L&P*, XI, no. 523.
[136] *LL*, vol. 2, p. 404, no. 329.
[137] PRO, SP1/57, f.101; *L&P*, IV (iii), no. 6384.
[138] *L&P*, VII, no. 923.
[139] PRO, SP1/75, f. 171.
[140] *L&P*, VI, no. 562.
[141] Ibid., no. 841 (ii).
[142] Ibid., VII, no. 1498.
[143] Ibid., XII, no. 313. Gostwike was the treasurer of the First Fruit and Tenths. Bindoff, *History of Parliament: The House of Commons*, vol. 3, p. 116.
[144] 'Inventories of goods of the smaller monasteries and friaries in Sussex'. *SAC*, 44 (1901), 70.
[145] *L&P*, XII (i), no. 829.
[146] Ibid., no. 921.
[147] Examination of George Croftes, 1538. *L&P*, XIII (i), no. 828.
[148] Copy of the examination of George Croftes on 12 November, 1538. Ibid., no. 829 (1).
[149] An abstract of evidence against Lord Montague, 1538. Ibid., no. 955.
[150] PRO, E.40/1362; *L&P*, XIII (i), no. 294.

5 The Fall of the Pole Family, 1538

[1] Margaret to Lord Montague, September 1538. PRO, SP1/139, f. 131.
[2] Chapuys to Mendoza, 31 August 1538. *L&P*, XIII (ii), no. 232.
[3] Castillon to Cardinal du Bellay and Montmorency, 5 November 1538; Robert Warner to Lord Fitzwater, 21 November 1538. *L&P*, XIII (ii), nos. 752, 753, 884.
[4] Interrogation of Margaret, countess of Salisbury, 12, 13 November 1538; Fitzwilliam and Goodrich to Cromwell, 16 November 1538. PRO, SP1/138, ff. 243–246b; BL, Cotton MS Appendix L, f. 79; *L&P*, XIII (ii), nos. 818, 855.

[5] Sir Edward Neville was the younger brother of Lord Bergavenny, George Croftes was chancellor of Chichester Cathedral, John Collins was chaplain to Lord Montague and Hugh Holland, yeoman, was a servant of Geoffrey Pole.

[6] Richard Morisyne claimed that God would not even give Exeter 'a fayre daye to dye in'. Morisyne, *An Invective ayenste the Great and Detestable Vice, Treason.*

[7] Those arrested were Henry Courtenay, marquess of Exeter, his wife, Gertrude and son Edward; Lord Montague and his son Henry; Sir Geoffrey Pole; Margaret, countess of Salisbury; Sir Edward Neville; Thomas West; Lord Delaware; George Croftes; John Collins; Hugh Holland; and Thomas Standish, the countess of Salisbury's clerk of the kitchen. Gertrude, marchioness of Exeter, Lord Delaware and Geoffrey Pole were pardoned by Henry VIII, Edward Courtenay was pardoned by Mary I, Henry Pole (Lord Montague's son), disappeared from all records in 1542, and the fate of Thomas Standish is not known.

[8] Confession of Alice Patchet, 18 September 1538. PRO, SP1/136, f. 202b; *L&P*, XIII (ii), no. 392 (2, iii).

[9] M. H. and R. Dodds, *The Pilgrimage of Grace 1536–1537 and the Exeter Conspiracy 1538*, vol. 2 (2 vols, London, 1971). p. 304; Höllger, 'Reginald Pole and the legations of 1537 and 1539', pp. 85–6. Höllger believes it proved Holland intended to betray Geoffrey in order to save himself but at least had the decency to warn his master first!

[10] Geoffrey Pole testified that Lord Montague showed him 'att the Ruffle when hugh holland was taken thatt he hadd burnyd many lettres att his howse callyd bukmar'. Geoffrey Pole's fourth examination, 5 November 1538. PRO, SP1/138, f. 216b; *L&P*, XIII (ii), no. 804 (4). The wording of this indicates that Montague told Geoffrey at the time of Holland's arrest.

[11] Geoffrey Pole gave Collins a ring by way of a token which he showed to Geoffrey's wife, Constance, who took Collins to her husband's closet, where he burned five or six letters. Constance Pole's examination, 11 November 1538. *L&P*, XIII (ii), no. 796.

[12] PRO, SP1/138, f. 40; *L&P*, XIII (ii), nos. 702 (3), 796; SP1/139, f. 23; *L&P*, XIII, no. 828 (2); SP1/139, f. 30; *L&P*, XIII, no. 829 (2). Testimonies of Jerome Ragland, Constance Pole, Morgan Wells and John Collins respectively. Unfortunately, the original of John Collins's statement is now badly mutilated in this section.

[13] In August 1535 Tyndall was schoolmaster of the free school of Grantham in Lincolnshire. *L&P*, IX, no. 179 (x). For his attendance at Cardinal's College, Oxford see *L&P*, XII (ii), no. 817. Höllger mistakenly claims that Tyndall was in Margaret's service carrying out some kind of medical function. Höllger, 'Reginald Pole and the legations of 1537 and 1539', p. 111.

[14] *L&P*, IX, no. 740.

[15] Ibid., XII (ii), no. 848.

[16] Information against the countess of Salisbury by Gervase Tyndall. *L&P*, XIII (ii), no. 817. As the original of Tyndall's evidence is mutilated and the version in *L&P* is fully transcribed, I have used the latter.

[17] Southampton to Cromwell, 20 September 1538; answer of Laurence Taylor to the confession of Alice Patchet. PRO, SP1/136, ff. 204b, 203; *L&P*, XIII (ii), nos. 393, 392 (2, iv).

[18] Examination of Morgan Wells. PRO, SP1/139, f. 23; *L&P*, XIII (ii), no. 828 (2).

[19] Examination of John Collins, November. PRO, SP1/139, f. 30; *L&P*, XIII (ii), no. 829 (2).

[20] Fritze, 'Faith and faction', pp. 98–9, 100, 104–5, 133–7, 141–2.

[21] *L&P*, XIII (ii), no. 817; PRO, E.36/120, ff. 131–131b. The confession of Myghell Jamys made before John Cooke, commissary of the Admiralty in the county of Southampton, 11 March 1534.

[22] Information against the countess of Salisbury by Gervase Tyndall. *L&P*, XIII (ii), no. 817, f. 84b. According to what Richard Ayer told John Ansard.

[23] Ibid., f. 83. For which information Tyndall said he had good witness.

[24] Ibid., f. 84b. According to what Ayer told Ansard.

[25] Ibid.

[26] Ibid., f.83. Gathered by Tyndall from the whispering of Margaret's household.

[27] Ibid.

[28] Ibid., f. 83b.

[29] Ibid., f. 84.

[30] Ibid., f. 85.

[31] We know from this document that the informer was called Peter. Unfortunately, only the first two letters of his surname have survived, Wy. It is possible that his name was Peter Wythends, for in 1538 Margaret's laundress is described as 'Wythends wife'. Obviously, her husband was well known enough in the household for his full name not to be necessary. It might be stretching the evidence too far to make this assumption, but it is the only information we have relating to this informer's identity.

[32] This was most probably Richard Cotton who sat as a JP, for Hampshire 1538–55. He had connections with John Gunter, Geoffrey Pole's colleague, and Sir Oliver Wallop, constable of Margaret's castle at Christchurch. Gunter was one of the overseers of his will and Wallop was given £200 to hold as a marriage portion for his daughter. Fritze, 'Faith and faction', p. 375. In 1551 Cotton was granted the manor of Warblington and his son George succeeded to it in 1556. W. Page (ed.), *VCH, Hampshire and the Isle of Wight*, vol. 3 (London, 1908), 135.

[33] Information against the countess of Salisbury by Gervase Tyndall. *L&P*, XIII (ii), no. 817, f. 85.

[34] Ibid., f. 85b. Due to mutilation of the document it is unclear whether he actually made this last claim.

[35] Ibid.

[36] Ibid.

[37] Ibid., f. 84.

[38] Ibid.

[39] Ibid., f. 84b.

[40] Examination of Oliver Frankelyn, 20 November 1538. PRO, SP1/139, ff. 154–154b; *L&P*, XIII (ii), no. 875.

[41] Frankelyn makes clear in his evidence that the priest of Havant and one Wysedom told Geoffrey all that Tyndall had said, and this concerned Holland's conveyance of letters from Margaret and Geoffrey to John Helyar. His visit to Reginald is not mentioned, nor the sending of letters to the cardinal. PRO, SP1/139, f. 154.

[42] It is much more likely that Cromwell received Tyndall's evidence at this time than at the beginning of November as Höllger alleges. Höllger, 'Reginald Pole and the legations of 1537 and 1539', p. 111.

[43] *L&P*, V, no. 985.

[44] S. N. Simmonds, *Warblington Church* (Havant, 1979), p. 9.

[45] Ibid., pp. 13–14; T. F. Mayer, 'A diet for Henry VIII: the failure of Reginald Pole's 1537 legation', *Journal of British Studies*, 26 (1987), 316. By 1540 Helyar had become master of the English hospice in Rome through Reginald's patronage. Mayer, 'A diet for Henry VIII', p. 316.

[46] Mayer, 'A diet for Henry VIII', p. 316.

[47] Examination of Hugh Holland, 3 November 1538. PRO, SP1/138, f. 198; *L&P*, XIII (ii), no. 797. In his evidence Holland said three or four years ago. The letter written by Stephen Gardiner to Cromwell informing him of Helyar's flight was written on 26 July, but unfortunately no year is specified. PRO, SP1/88, f. 174; *L&P*, VII, Appendix 32.

[48] Examination of Hugh Holland, 3 November 1538. PRO, SP1/138, f. 198; *L&P*, XIII (ii), no. 797.

[49] Ibid. PRO, SP1/138, f. 198b.

[50] Ibid.

[51] Ibid.

[52] Ibid., ff. 199–199b. Helyar sent letters from Newhaven to Geoffrey by a Frenchman, Geoffrey sent Holland with letters to Helyar after his benefices were sequestrated, and Holland brought replies for which Geoffrey gave him 40s. In 1537 Helyar's brother-in-law was sent to see him by Geoffrey.

[53] Ibid., f. 199b.

[54] Ibid.

[55] Ibid., f. 200.

[56] Ibid., f. 200b.

[57] Ibid., f. 201.

[58] Ibid., f. 200b.

[59] Ibid. The reasons for Geoffrey's fears are not clear, but this may be a reference to Montague's reaction to his wife's death.

[60] Ibid., f. 202.

[61] Ibid.

[62] John Hutton to Cromwell, 26 May 1537. *L&P*, XII (i), no. 1293.

[63] Examination of Hugh Holland, 3 November 1538. PRO, SP1/138, ff. 202b–203; *L&P*, XIII (ii), no. 797 (ii).

[64] PRO, SP1/138, ff. 202b–203; *L&P*, XIII (ii), no. 797 (3).

[65] *LL*, vol. 5, p. 269; Bindoff, *The History of Parliament: The House of Commons*, vol. 3, p. 117.

[66] Sir Thomas Denys to Cromwell, examination of Gulphinus Abevan, 29 August 1538. *L&P*, XIII (ii), no. 267 (2). Abevan's motive may have been revenge. He apparently entered Geoffrey Pole's service and remained with him for seven months and three weeks; however, receiving 'nought for his labour', he left and tried unsuccessfully to become Lord Montague's chaplain. Montague, knowing Abevan to have been Reginald's chaplain, 'would not meddle with him'.

[67] Ibid., no. 267 (1).

[68] Confessions of John Wissedome and Joan Triselowe, 13 September 1538. PRO, SP1/136, ff. 202–3; *L&P*, XIII (ii), no. 392 (2, i–iv).

[69] Höllger criticizes the Misses Dodds for connecting this information with the evidence of Thomas Coke and Thomas Cheselett, taken before John Gunter on 8 May 1538, concerning the desire of certain of Margaret's servants to go and fight for the emperor or, failing that, to be retained by Reginald. *L&P*, XIII (ii), no. 592; Höllger, 'Reginald Pole and the legations of 1537 and 1539', p. 89, n. 21; Dodds and Dodds, *The Pilgrimage of Grace*, vol. 2, p. 308. However, the Doddses have

merely assumed that the band of men gossiped about in September 1538, that
Geoffrey was supposed to be sending to Reginald, were the men who, in May 1538,
had expressed the desire to go. Höllger also claims to have found no reference for
the rumour that Margaret would have been burnt if she had been younger, and that
if it existed it can certainly not be traced back to Laurence Taylor. However,
Johanne Sylkden plainly confessed she heard this rumour from her mother, Alice
Patchet, who had direct contact with Taylor, and had heard other snippets of
gossip from him including the tale of Holland's meeting with Geoffrey after his
arrest. Höllger, 'Reginald Pole and the legations of 1537 and 1539', p. 85.

[70] Fitzwilliam to Cromwell, 20 September 1538. PRO, SP1/136, f. 200; *L&P*, XIII
(ii), no. 392 (1).

[71] PRO, SP1/136, f. 200.

[72] Ibid., f. 200b.

[73] Ibid., f. 201.

[74] Two of the questions are phrased in a way that indicates that previous interrogations had taken place. In question 1 he is asked regarding Reginald's
proceedings, 'which he had said that he well liked'. First examination of Geoffrey
Pole, 26 October 1538. *L&P*, XIII (ii), no. 695 (1). Questions 46–9 concerned with
whom he had discussed wishing for a change of this world 'other than yow have
declaryd allredye'. *L&P*, XIII (ii), no. 695 (1); SP1/138, f. 14.

[75] *L&P*, XIII (ii), no. 695 (1); SP1/138, ff. 11b–12.

[76] Ibid., ff. 12–13.

[77] Ibid., ff. 16–16b; *L&P*, XIII (ii), no. 695 (2).

[78] Mr Friend was William Friend and Mr Langley, according to *L&P*, was
William Langley, subdeacon and vicar of St Peter's the Great, Chichester, in 1531.
L&P, XIII (ii), no. 695 (2)n.

[79] John Stokesley was the bishop of London, Mrs Roper refers to Margaret More,
Sir Thomas More's eldest daughter who had married William Roper, and Mrs
Clement to Margaret Gigs, More's foster daughter who had married John Clement.

[80] First examination of Geoffrey Pole, 26 October 1538. PRO, SP1/138, f. 16b;
L&P, XIII (ii), no. 695 (2).

[81] The anonymous author of the Spanish Chronicle certainly asserts this, stating
that Cromwell said to Geoffrey: 'if you do not tell the truth I will have you
tortured, but if you tell the truth I promise you to get the King to give you an ample
revenue to live upon.' M. A. S. Hume, *Chronicle of King Henry VIII of England*
(London, 1889), p. 132.

[82] First examination of Geoffrey Pole, 26 October, 1538. PRO, SP1/138, f. 16b;
L&P, XIII (ii), no. 695 (2).

[83] G. R. Elton, *Reform and Reformation* (London, 1977), p. 279.

[84] Examination of Constance Pole, 11 November, 1538. *L&P*, XIII (ii), no. 796.

[85] John Husee wrote to Lord Lisle on 28 October that Geoffrey 'was so in despair
that he would have murdered himself and, as it was told me, hurt himself sore'. *LL*,
vol. 5, pp. 266–7, no. 1259. According to Richard Morisyne, Geoffrey tried to stab
himself in the chest with a blunt knife which, although the wound bled, was not fatal.
Morisyne, *An Invective ayenste the Great and Detestable Vice, Treason*.

[86] Second examination of Geoffrey Pole. PRO, SP1/138, ff. 214b–215b; *L&P*,
XIII (ii), no. 804 (2).

[87] Ibid.

[88] *L&P*, XIII (ii), no. 743.

[89] Third examination of Geoffrey Pole, 3 November 1538. PRO, SP1/138, ff.

215b–216; *L&P*, XIII (ii), no. 804 (3).
⁹⁰ PRO, SP1/138, ff. 215b.
⁹¹ Ibid., ff. 215b–216.
⁹² Depositions of Sir Geoffrey Pole touching the lady marquis. PRO, SP1/138, f. 216; *L&P*, XIII, no. 831 (1, ii).
⁹³ Third examination of Geoffrey Pole, 3 November 1538. PRO, SP1/138; *L&P*, XIII, no. 804 (3).
⁹⁴ Examination of Morgan Wells. PRO, SP1/139, f. 23; *L&P*, XIII, no. 828 (2).
⁹⁵ Examination of Jerome Ragland, 28 October 1538. PRO, SP1/138, ff. 33–40; *L&P*, XIII (ii), no. 702.
⁹⁶ Ibid., PRO, SP1/138, f. 35; *L&P*, XIII (ii), no. 702 (1).
⁹⁷ Ibid., PRO, SP1/138, f. 36; *L&P*, XIII (ii), no. 702(2).
⁹⁸ Ibid., f. 36b.
⁹⁹ PRO, SP1/138, f. 219b; *L&P*, XIII, no. 804 (7): 'that the kyng shulde say one day to the lords, that he . . . goo from them one daye and where be yow then, and the said [lord M]ontacut at the same tyme said, if he wyll serve us so wee shall be happ[ily] rydd'.
¹⁰⁰Examination of Jerome Ragland, 28 October 1538. PRO, SP1/138, f. 37; *L&P*, XIII, no. 702 (2).
¹⁰¹PRO, SP1/138, f. 36.
¹⁰²Ibid., f. 33b; *L&P*, XIII, no. 702 (1).
¹⁰³Höllger, 'Reginald Pole and the legations of 1537 and 1539', p. 93.
¹⁰⁴Examination of Jerome Ragland, 28 October 1538. PRO, SP1/138, f. 36b; *L&P*, XIII (ii), no. 702 (2).
¹⁰⁵PRO, SP1/138, f. 37.
¹⁰⁶Ibid., f. 38.
¹⁰⁷Geoffrey Pole's fifth examination, 7 November 1538. PRO, SP1/138, f. 218; *L&P*, XIII, no. 804 (5).
¹⁰⁸PRO, SP1/138, f. 218; *L&P*, XIII, no. 804 (5).
¹⁰⁹Geoffrey Pole's sixth examination, 9 and 11 November 1538. PRO, SP1/138, f. 218b; *L&P*, XIII, no. 804 (6).
¹¹⁰Geoffrey Pole's seventh examination, 12 November 1538. PRO, SP1/138, f. 219b; *L&P*, XIII, no. 804 (7).
¹¹¹Geoffrey Pole's sixth examination, 9 and 11 November 1538. PRO, SP1/138, f. 218b; *L&P*, XIII, no. 804 (6).
¹¹²Geoffrey Pole's seventh examination, 12 November 1538. PRO, SP1/138, f. 219b; *L&P*, XIII, no. 804 (7). Höllger mistakenly interpreted this document to mean that the feelings of dislike between Montague and Henry VIII were mutual. Höllger, 'Reginald Pole and the legations of 1537 and 1539', p. 101.
¹¹³Geoffrey Pole's seventh examination, 12 November 1538. PRO, SP1/138, f. 219b; *L&P*, XIII (ii), no. 804 (7).
¹¹⁴PRO, SP1/138, f. 220; *L&P*, XIII (ii), no. 804 (7).
¹¹⁵Geoffrey Pole's sixth examination, 9 and 11 November 1538. PRO, SP1/138, f. 218; *L&P*, XIII, (ii) no. 804 (6).
¹¹⁶PRO, SP1/138, ff. 218, 219.
¹¹⁷Ibid., f. 218b.
¹¹⁸Ibid., f. 219.
¹¹⁹Geoffrey Pole's seventh examination, 12 November 1538. PRO, SP1/138, ff. 219–219b; *L&P*, XIII (ii), no. 804 (7).
¹²⁰PRO, SP1/138, ff. 220; *L&P*, XIII (ii), no. 804 (7).

[121] Ibid.

[122] Lord Montague's examination, 7 November 1538. PRO, SP1/138, ff. 222–222b; *L&P*, XIII (ii), no. 772.

[123] Constance Pole's examination, *L&P*, XIII, no. 796.

[124] PRO, SP1/138, f. 222; *L&P*, XIII (ii), no. 772. William Brent, one of Montague's most trusted servants who, with Jerome Ragland and Thomas Nanfant, continued to serve Montague during his imprisonment, elaborated credibly upon this claiming that Montague bemoaned in the Tower 'thatt he hadd rather lyve ther in prison than abroad in suspition and thatt he had lyvyd in prison all thes vj yeres ever sins he . . . his brother hath taken this way'. PRO, SP1/138, f. 17; *L&P*, XIII (ii), no. 827 (3).

[125] Lord Montague's examination, 7 November 1538. PRO, SP1/138, f. 222; *L&P*, XIII (ii), no. 772.

[126] PRO, SP1/138, f. 222; *L&P*, XIII (ii), no. 772. She then, as we know, told Geoffrey.

[127] F. Rose-Troup, *The Western Rebellion of 1549* (London, 1913), p. 33.

[128] PRO, SP1/138, f. 222; *L&P*, XIII (ii), no. 772.

[129] Ibid.

[130] Ibid.

[131] Like Ragland, Collins was another unwilling witness. He was devoted to his master, and the delivery of his evidence reveals his attempts to protect Montague. Initially claiming that after he had burned Geoffrey's letters Montague did not ask anything about it, he then claimed that on better remembrance he thought he did tell him. Obviously, Collins would not have forgotten something so crucial and probably only admitted it when convinced by his examiners that they already knew of Montague's involvement. Copy of John Collins's examination. PRO, SP1/139, f. 30b; *L&P*, XIII (ii), no. 829 (2).

[132] John Collins's examination, 14 November 1538. PRO, SP1/139, f. 14b; *L&P*, XIII (ii), no. 827 (1).

[133] Copy of John Collins's examination. PRO, SP1/139, f. 31; *L&P*, XIII (ii), no. 829 (2).

[134] Ibid., ff. 31b–32.

[135] Ibid., f. 32. Montague apparently complained: 'it wylbe a strange worlde saying words be made treason.'

[136] John Collins's examination, 14 November 1538. PRO, SP1/139, f. 14b; *L&P*, XIII (ii), no. 827 (1).

[137] PRO, SP1/139, f. 14b; *L&P*, XIII (ii), no. 827 (1).

[138] *L&P*, XIII (ii), no. 1017.

[139] Examination of George Croftes, 12 November 1538. PRO, SP1/138, f. 211; *L&P*, XIII (ii), no. 803.

[140] Second examination of George Croftes, 13 November 1538. *L&P*, XIII (ii), no. 822.

[141] Copy of George Croftes's second examination conducted on 13 November 1538. PRO, SP1/139, f. 27b; *L&P*, XIII (ii), no. 829 (II).

[142] Copy of George Croftes's second examination conducted on 13 November 1538. *L&P*, XIII (ii), no. 822.

[143] Ibid.

[144] He apparently told Geoffrey of a dream he had had in which Our Lady appeared to him and warned him that Geoffrey's leaving would be to the destruction of Geoffrey and his family. Copy of George Croftes's examination taken on 12 November 1538. PRO, SP1/138, f. 25b; *L&P*, XIII (ii), no. 829 (I).

[145] PRO, SP1/138, f. 25b; *L&P*, XIII (ii), no. 829 (I).

[146] Ibid.

[147] William, Lord Sandys.

[148] Copy of George Croftes's second examination conducted on 13 November 1538. PRO, SP1/139, f. 27b; *L&P*, XIII (ii), no. 829 (II).

[149] Sir Henry Owen's examination, 13 November 1538. *L&P*, XIII (ii), no. 821.

[150] Examination of Elizabeth Darrell, 6 November 1538. PRO, SP1/138, f. 160; *L&P*, XIII (ii), no. 766.

[151] Examination of Morgan Wells. PRO, SP1/139, f. 23; *L&P*, XIII (ii), no. 828 (2).

[152] Examination of George Tyrell, 8 November 1538. *L&P*, XIII (ii), no. 779.

[153] Examination of the marchioness of Exeter, 6 November 1538. PRO, SP1/138, f. 224; *L&P*, XIII (ii), no. 765.

[154] Second examination of the marchioness of Exeter, 9 November 1538. PRO, SP1/138, f. 224; *L&P*, XIII (ii), no. 765.

[155] Geoffrey Pole's fifth examination, 7 November 1538. PRO, SP1/138, f. 217; *L&P*, XIII (ii), no. 804 (5).

[156] PRO, SP1/138, f. 217b.

[157] Extracts from depositions of various witnesses concerning the marquess of Exeter. PRO, SP1/140, f. 9. *L&P*, XIII (ii), no. 962 gives the witnesses' names but not the extracts from their depositions.

[158] PRO, SP1/140, f. 9b.

[159] Geoffrey Pole's fifth examination, 7 November 1538. PRO, SP1/138, f. 217b; *L&P*, XIII (ii), no. 804 (5).

[160] PRO, SP1/140, f. 12.

[161] Evidence against the countess of Salisbury by Gervase Tyndall. *L&P*, XIII (ii), no. 817.

[162] Unfortunately, none of Exeter's depositions have survived.

[163] Questions for the marquis of Exeter. *L&P*, XIII (ii), no. 771 (iii, 4, 6).

[164] The first reference to the king's presence at Woking is a grant issued from there on 20 July. *L&P*, XIII (i), no. 1519 (72). It becomes clear from the 'King's Payments' that by Sunday 28 July the king was at Petworth, West Sussex. Ibid. (ii), no. 1280, f. 27b.

[165] In 1531 Exeter's servant, William Kendal, was arrested. He had apparently been retaining men on behalf of his master during a dispute between Exeter's father-in-law and Sir Anthony Willoughby. Rose-Troup, *The Western Rebellion of 1549*, p. 25. At the same time, some of Exeter's followers were also reported to have made such treasonous remarks as describing Exeter as heir apparent and promising that he 'shold wear the garland att the last'. These allegations appear again at this time under the title 'An abbreviation of th'old accusation against the lord Marquis of Exeter'. PRO, SP1/140, f. 10; *L&P*, XIII (ii), no. 961.

[166] PRO, SP1/139, f. 131. The second page is extremely faded and some words are still illegible even under ultraviolet light.

[167] George Tyrell's examination, 8 November, 1538. *L&P*, XIII (ii), no. 779.

[168] Oliver Frankelyn's examination, 20 November 1538. PRO, SP1/139, f. 154b; *L&P*, XIII (ii), no. 875 (i).

[169] The countess of Salisbury's examination, 12 and 13 November 1538. PRO, SP1/138, f. 246; *L&P*, XIII (ii), no. 818 (19).

[170] Fitzwilliam and Goodrich to Cromwell, 16 November 1538. BL, Cotton MS Appendix L, f. 79; *L&P*, XIII (ii), no. 855.

[171] BL, Cotton MS Appendix L, f. 77; *L&P*, XIII (ii), no. 855.

172 BL, Cotton MS Appendix L, f. 79; *L&P*, XIII (ii), no. 855.
173 The countess of Salisbury's examination, 12 and 13 November. PRO, SP1/138, f. 243; *L&P*, XIII (ii), no. 818 (1).
174 Copy of John Collins's examination. PRO, SP1/139, ff. 31b–32; *L&P*, XIII (ii), no. 829 (2).
175 The countess of Salisbury's examination, 12 and 13 November. PRO, SP1/138, ff. 243b, 245b; *L&P*, XIII (ii), no. 818 (6, 17).
176 PRO, SP1/138, f. 244b; *L&P*, XIII (ii), no. 818 (11).
177 PRO, SP1/138, f. 245; *L&P*, XIII (ii), no. 818 (12).
178 PRO, SP1/138, f. 245; *L&P*, XIII (ii), no. 818 (13).
179 PRO, SP1/138, f. 245; *L&P*, XIII (ii), no. 818 (14).
180 Fitzwilliam and Goodrich to Cromwell, 14 November 1538. BL, Cotton MS Appendix L, f. 77b; *L&P*, XIII (ii), no. 835.
181 The countess of Salisbury's examination, 12 and 13 November. PRO, SP1/138, f. 246; *L&P*, XIII (ii), no. 818 (19).
182 PRO, SP1/138, f. 243b; *L&P*, XIII (ii), no. 818 (5).
183 PRO, SP1/138, f. 245b.
184 Fitzwilliam and Goodrich to Cromwell, 14 November 1538. BL, Cotton MS Appendix L, ff. 77–77b; *L&P*, XIII (ii), no. 835.
185 BL, Cotton MS Appendix L, f. 77b.
186 *DKR*, 3, Appendix 2, p. 256, m. 20; p. 251, m. 24; p. 253, m. 32; *L&P*, XIII (ii), nos. 979 (16); 986 (7), (15).
187 W. D. Hamilton (ed.), *A Chronicle of England during the Reigns of the Tudors from AD 1485–1559*, Camden Society, new series 20 (2 vols, 1877), vol. 1, p. 92. The executions as recorded by Charles Wriothesley, Windsor Herald.
188 *L&P*, XIV (i), nos. 191 (3), 37.

6 Assessment

1 Cromwell to Sir Thomas Wyatt, 28 November 1538. *L&P*, XIII (ii), no. 924.
2 *L&P*, XIII (ii), no. 1036.
3 Ibid., no. 1124.
4 Ibid., no. 884.
5 Chapuys to Don Diego de Mendoza. *CSP*, Spain, 1538–1542, p. 31, no. 7.
6 *L&P*, XIV (i), no. 37.
7 Ibid., XIII (ii), no. 753.
8 Ibid., no. 1292.
9 *CSP*, Venetian, 1534–1554, no. 199.
10 PRO, SP1/138, f. 215; *L&P*, XIII (ii), no. 804 (2).
11 *L&P*, XIV (i), no. 37.
12 Ibid., nos. 233, 280.
13 Dodds and Dodds, *The Pilgrimage of Grace*.
14 Ibid., vol. 1, p. 338.
15 Ibid., vol. 2, p. 278.
16 Ibid.
17 Miller, *Henry VIII and the English Nobility*, p. 68.
18 Youings, 'The Council of the West', p. 45.
19 Levine, *Tudor Dynastic Problems*, p. 71; Harris, *Edward Stafford, Third Duke of Buckingham*, p. 206.

[20] Neame, *The Holy Maid of Kent*, p. 104.

[21] R. B. Merriman, *The Life and Letters of Thomas Cromwell* (2 vols, Oxford, 1968), vol. 1, p. 208.

[22] Montague apparently considered that Henry VIII 'wolde be out of his wyttes one daye, for when he came to his chamber he wolde loke Angarly and after fall to fyghting'. Geoffrey Pole's seventh examination. PRO, SP1/133, f. 219b; *L&P*, XIII (ii), no. 804 (7).

[23] A. S. MacNalty, *Henry VIII: A Difficult Patient* (London, 1952), p. 183.

[24] Elton, *Reform and Reformation*, p. 280.

[25] Mayer, 'A diet for Henry VIII', p. 305; Bernard, *The Tudor Nobility*, pp. 29, 13.

[26] Höllger, 'Reginald Pole and the legations of 1537 and 1539', pp. 124, 125, 109.

[27] *DKR*, 3, p. 254, m. 13.

[28] Höllger, 'Reginald Pole and the legations of 1537 and 1539', pp. 105–6.

[29] *L&P*, XIII (ii), nos 830 (iii, 1), 765, 830 (iv, 1), 831.

[30] Ibid., 830 (iv, 3) and 831.

[31] Dodds and Dodds, *The Pilgrimage of Grace*, vol. 2, p. 311.

[32] J. Bellamy, *The Tudor Law of Treason* (London, 1979), pp. 10–11.

[33] Ibid., p. 11.

[34] Ibid., p. 32.

[35] Ibid., p. 11.

[36] From the evidence of Geoffrey Pole's third and fifth examinations and the evidence of Jerome Ragland.

[37] From Geoffrey Pole's third examination and the evidence of John Collins.

[38] From the fourth and fifth examinations of Geoffrey Pole and the evidence of Jerome Ragland and John Collins.

[39] *DKR*, 3, p. 255, mm. 27, 26.

[40] Geoffrey Pole confessed this (*L&P*, XIII (ii), no. 695 (2)) and claimed Exeter said this. PRO, SP1/140, f. 9; *L&P*, XIII (ii), no. 962.

[41] Bellamy, *The Tudor Law of Treason*, p. 9.

[42] From Geoffrey Pole's fifth examination.

[43] *DKR*, 3, p. 255, mm. 27, 26.

[44] I. D. Thornley, 'The treason legislation of Henry VIII (1531–1534)', *TRHS*, third series, 11 (1917), 104. The Misses Dodds, however, do not accept that expressing joy at the prospect of the king's death suggests a wish for it. Dodds and Dodds, *The Pilgrimage of Grace*, vol. 2, p. 311.

[45] From Geoffrey Pole's seventh examination and the evidence of Jerome Ragland.

[46] Geoffrey Pole's seventh examination.

[47] John Collins's examination. *L&P*, XIII (ii), no. 830 (ii, 10).

[48] John Collins, ibid., nos. 827 (1), 830 (ii, 4).

[49] Geoffrey Pole's fifth examination.

[50] Geoffrey Pole, PRO, SP1/140, f. 9, nos. 1, 962.

[51] Geoffrey Pole, ibid., f. 9.

[52] Geoffrey Pole's fifth examination and ibid., f. 9, no. 3.

[53] Geoffrey Pole, ibid., nos. 32, 33; ff. 11b–12.

[54] Although Exeter did not personally threaten the king, any attack upon the king's ministers was a challenge to his right to choose his own officers and an encouragement of disorder and disobedience which could be harmful to the king.

[55] Geoffrey Pole's seventh examination. *L&P*, XIII (ii), no. 830 (iii, 1).

[56] *DKR*, 3, p. 252, m. 19.

[57] Ibid., p. 254, m. 13.

[58] The evidence of George Croftes.

[59] Geoffrey Pole confessed to this, while Holland, Croftes and Collins all testified to it.

[60] Croftes's evidence.

[61] Collins's evidence.

[62] Morisyne, *An Invective ayenste the Great and Detestable Vice, Treason.*

[63] Constance reported Geoffrey's frenzied condition to Lord Montague, while John Husee had heard of Geoffrey's first suicide attempt two days after the incident.

[64] Following his conviction he made a statement declaring his innocence; he affirmed that 'I never ded nor syde the thyng that scholde be conttrary to me ellegens nor harde no oddar, as Gode schalle joge me at my dethe, but that I have reherssyd, wyche cleres ny none conssyens'. *L&P*, XIII (ii), no. 987.

[65] G. R. Elton (ed. and intro.), *The Tudor Constitution* (Cambridge, 1968), p. 80.

[66] *DKR*, 3, p. 257; Miller, *Henry VIII and the English Nobility*, p. 66.

[67] He had stood surety for Sir Richard Pole in 1504 and shared the same great-grandmother.

[68] Mayer, 'A diet for Henry VIII', p. 324, n. 115.

[69] Unfortunately, as the date of the marriage is not known it is not certain whether it was Andrew or William, Lord Windsor. W. B. Bannerman (ed.), *The Visitations of the County of Sussex, made and taken in the years 1530* (Harleian Society, 53 (London, 1905), p. 89.

[70] *DKR*, 3, p. 257.

[71] Ibid., p. 254.

[72] Höllger, 'Reginald Pole and the legations of 1537 and 1539', pp. 100, 104–5.

[73] Ibid., pp. 214–15.

[74] Ibid., p. 215.

[75] *L&P*, XIII (ii), no. 753.

[76] Höllger, 'Reginald Pole and the legations of 1537 and 1539', p. 84.

[77] BL, Cotton MS Appendix L, f. 71; *L&P*, XIII (ii), no. 825.

[78] PRO, SP1/138, ff. 217, 227; *L&P*, XIII (ii), no. 804 (4); IV, no. 2.

[79] See Appendix I.

[80] Ibid.

[81] M. L. Bush, 'The Tudors and the royal race', *History*, 55 (1970), 37–48; D. Starkey, *The Reign of Henry VIII: Personalities and Politics* (London, 1991), p. 43.

[82] Descended from Anne, countess of Stafford, granddaughter of Edward III by her third marriage to Sir William Bourchier, count of Eu. In 1536 John Bourchier was created earl of Bath.

[83] Buckingham, Montague, Exeter and the earl of Surrey. Bush, 'The Tudors and the royal race', p. 40.

[84] PRO, SP1/138, f. 34; *L&P*, XIII (ii), no. 702 (2).

[85] PRO, SP1/139, f. 14b; *L&P*, XIII (ii), no. 827 (1).

[86] The only other candidate Chapuys advanced as a husband for Mary was Montague's son Henry in 1536. *CSP, Spain, 1536–1538*, p. 199, no. 72.

[87] *L&P*, VIII, no. 263.

[88] It is most likely that this tunic was forged by Cromwell. Warblington was searched thoroughly at Margaret's arrest in November, as were her coffers. It is hard to believe that this tunic did not come to light until six months later.

[89] In the words of John Worth:

by the one side of the coat there was the King's Grace his arms of England, that is, the lions without the flower de luce and about the whole arms was made pansies for Pole and marigolds for my Lady Mary. This was about the coat-armour. And betwixt the marigold and the pansy was made a tree to rise in the midst; and on the tree a coat of purple hanging on a bough, in tokening of the coat of Christ; and on the other side of the coat all the Passion of Christ.

Worth clearly interpreted this to mean that 'Pole intended to have married my Lady Mary and betwixt them both should again arise the old doctrine of Christ'. *LL*, vol. 4, no. 1419.

[90] Dodds and Dodds, *The Pilgrimage of Grace*, vol. 1, pp. 355–7.

[91] Loades, *Mary Tudor: A Life*, p. 120.

[92] Ibid.

[93] MacNalty, *Henry VIII: A Difficult Patient*, p. 103.

[94] Mayer, *Reginald Pole Prince and Prophet*, p. 28.

[95] Mayer, 'A diet for Henry VIII', p. 313.

[96] Ibid., p. 325.

[97] PRO, SP1/136, f. 205.

[98] He had been a companion of Henry VIII from the age of ten, and from then on rose steadily in favour. By 1538 he held the offices of chancellor of the Duchy of Lancaster, lord high admiral and treasurer of the king's household, and on 18 October 1537 was raised to the peerage as earl of Southampton. *DNB*, vol. 19 (London, 1889), pp. 230–2.

[99] He wrote to the king in order to try and prevent Geoffrey being sentenced to a spell in the Fleet prison after his attack on John Gunter.

[100] *L&P*, XIV (i), no. 520.

[101] PRO, SP1/138, f. 34b; *L&P*, XIII (ii), no. 702. Wyatt enjoyed twenty-five days' leave from the imperial court in the summer of 1538 and was in England from 24 May to 20 June. He may have told Darell about the poison during this visit.

[102] K. Muir, *Life and Letters of Sir Thomas Wyatt* (Liverpool, 1963), p. 83.

[103] P. Thomson, *Sir Thomas Wyatt and his Background* (London, 1964), p. 63.

[104] Ibid., p. 71.

[105] *CSP*, Domestic, Henry VIII, vol. VIII, p. 415, n. 1.

[106] *DNB*, vol. 59, pp. 152–5.

[107] *L&P*, XII (i), no. 705.

[108] *CSP*, Spain, 1538–1542, no. 155. Although the charges are not specific, it appears that his treasons were manifest in certain letters he had written to Richard Pate. During his examination before the king and Privy Council these letters were presented to him, at which 'he cryed for mercy, knowleaging his offences' but declared that 'the same never passed upon any yvel mynde or malicious purpose, but only upon wilfulnes and ultraquidance'. A. J. Slavin, 'Cromwell, Cranmer and Lord Lisle: a study in the politics of reform', *Albion*, 9 (1977), 319. Fortunately for Wallop, Henry accepted that he was genuinely repentant and, like Wyatt, he was eventually pardoned.

[109] Slavin, 'Cromwell, Cranmer and Lord Lisle', p. 319.

[110] Ibid., p. 323.

[111] *LL*, vol. 6, p. 118.

[112] Fritze, 'Faith and faction', p. 81.

[113] Fritze describes the 1530s as a period of deteriorating health for Sandys. However, he also states that Sandys feigned ill health as an excuse to stay away

from court. Ibid., pp. 82, 117.

[114] Ibid., p. 81.

[115] Ibid., p. 117.

[116] Slavin, 'Cromwell, Cranmer and Lord Lisle', p. 324.

[117] PRO, SP1/139, f. 27b; *L&P*, XIII (ii), no. 829.

[118] Youings, 'The Council of the West', pp. 46, 48.

[119] A. Fletcher, *Tudor Rebellions* (London, 1990), p. 53; Youings, 'The Council of the West', p. 46.

[120] *L&P*, XII (ii), no. 476 (83). In 1546 John Worseley was granted the reversion of Swainstone following the expiration of Standishe's tenure.

[121] Page, *VCH, Hampshire and the Isle of Wight*, vol. 5, p. 89.

[122] B. L. Beer, *Rebellion and Riot: Popular Disorder in England during the Reign of Edward VI* (Kent, OH, 1982), p. 44.

[123] Appointed on 25 May 1523. *L&P*, XIII (ii), no. 1002. The minister's accounts of 1539 and 1540–1 reveal that Exeter held thirteen manors in Cornwall and seven manors in Devon. *Lists and Indexes*, vol. 34, p. 283.

[124] Fritze, 'Faith and faction', p. 132.

[125] Ibid., pp. 147–9.

[126] *L&P*, IV (i), no. 823.

[127] This rising was in protest against the tax Henry VII was attempting to levy in order to defend the northern marches.

[128] J. Cornwall, *Revolt of the Peasantry 1549* (London, 1977), p. 42.

[129] Ibid.

[130] Youings, 'The Council of the West', p. 45.

[131] Ibid., p. 49.

[132] Ibid.

[133] Williamson, *The Tudor Age*, p. 161.

[134] Guy, *Tudor England*, p. 184.

[135] D. Potter, 'Foreign policy', in D. MacCulloch (ed.), *The Reign of Henry VIII: Politics, Policy and Piety* (London, 1995), p. 117.

[136] Knecht, *Francis I*, p. 292.

[137] Potter, 'Foreign policy', p. 120.

[138] T. F. Mayer, 'If martyrs are to be exchanged with martyrs: the kidnappings of William Tyndale and Reginald Pole', *Archiv fur Reformationsgeschichte*, 81 (1990), 296.

[139] Ibid.

[140] Ibid., p. 295.

[141] Mayer, 'A diet for Henry VIII', p. 312.

[142] Merriman, *The Life and Letters of Thomas Cromwell*, vol. 1, p. 205.

[143] Pye, *The Life of Cardinal Reginald Pole*, pp. 47–8.

[144] S. L. Jansen, *Political Protest and Prophecy under Henry VIII* (Woodbridge, 1991), p. 26.

[145] Ibid., p. 34.

[146] Ibid., p. 57.

[147] The closest he came to gaining entry was in 1531 when, with Lord Delawarre, he received eight votes, the highest number for the barons. On this occasion Montague was pipped at the post by the earl of Northumberland with nine votes. Anstis, *The Register of the Most Noble Order of the Garter*, vol. 1, pp. 386–8.

[148] Harris, *Edward Stafford, Third Duke of Buckingham*, p. 177.

[149] *L&P*, IV (i), no. 1319.

[150]Ibid., VII, no. 957.

[151]*CSP*, Spain, 1534–1535, p. 325, no. 109.

[152]*CSP*, Spain, 1536–1538, no. 43. Also present were Henry Grey, marquess of Dorset, the dowager countess of Kildare, probably Dorset's sister Lady Elizabeth Grey, and several others not named.

[153]*L&P*, XI, no. 1143.

[154]Dodds and Dodds, *The Pilgrimage of Grace*, vol. 1, p. 332.

[155]*L&P*, VII, 467, no. 1206.

[156]Ives, *The Common Lawyers of Pre-Reformation England*, p. 13.

[157]*L&P*, IV (ii), no. 4653.

[158]Ives, *The Common Lawyers of Pre-Reformation England*, p. 15.

[159]*L&P*, XIV (i), no. 37.

[160]*L&P*, IV (i), no. 1164; ibid., VI, no. 1528.

[161]Ibid., VIII, no. 750.

[162]BL, Harl. MS 2194, f. 18b.

[163]*L&P*, XV, no. 611 (12).

[164]Ibid., XIV (i), no. 1056 (21, 22).

[165]Ibid., (ii), no. 435 (17).

[166]Ibid., XV, no. 498, cap. 34; ibid., no. 282 (39).

[167]Ibid., XVI, no. 503 (25), p. 241.

[168]Ibid., XV, item 282 (39).

[169]Ibid., XIV (i), no. 113 (18).

[170]Ibid., no. 651 (15).

[171]Ibid., no. 1354 (12).

[172]Höllger, 'Reginald Pole and the legations of 1537 and 1539', p. 123.

[173]*LL*, vol. 5, p. 322.

[174]Fritze, 'Faith and faction', p. 106.

[175]*L&P*, XIII (ii), no. 803.

[176]Fritze, 'Faith and faction', p. 106.

[177]S. Brigden, 'Popular disturbance and the fall of Thomas Cromwell and the reformers, 1539–1540', *Historical Journal*, 24 (1981), 259.

[178]*L&P*, XIII (ii), no. 248; Slavin, 'Cromwell, Cranmer and Lord Lisle', p. 332.

[179]*DNB*, vol. 54, p. 404.

[180]*L&P*, XIII (i), no. 695 (2).

[181]Fritze, 'Faith and faction', p. 152.

[182]Ibid., p. 155.

[183]Ibid., p. 156.

[184]PRO, SP1/138, f. 199b; *L&P*, XIII (ii), no. 797. Information against the countess of Salisbury by Gervase Tyndall. *L&P*, XIII (ii), no. 817, f. 85b.

[185]PRO, SP1/138, f. 218b; *L&P*, XIII (ii), no. 804 (6).

[186]*L&P*, XIV (i), no. 513. Huntingdon was unable to gratify Cromwell immediately because he had settled his inheritance upon his son Francis and Lord Montague, with bonds of £5,000 to maintain the same until his debts were paid. Consequently, after Montague's arrest and attainder the bonds stood to the king's use and Huntingdon was powerless to act unless the king discharged him of them.

[187]*L&P*, XIII (ii), no. 695 (2).

[188]Examination of Hugh Holland, 3 November 1538. PRO, SP1/138, ff. 202b–203; *L&P*, XIII (ii), no. 797 (3).

[189]Examination of Morgan Wells. PRO, SP1/139, f. 23; *L&P*, XIII (ii), no. 828 (2).

190 *L&P*, XIII (ii), no. 695 (2).
191 *LL*, vol. 3, p. 387, no. 705.
192 PRO, SP1/139, ff. 27b, 28b; *L&P*, XIII (ii), no. 829 (II, III).
193 *L&P*, XIII (ii), 968.
194 *LL*, vol. 5, p. 320, no. 1299.
195 *L&P*, XIII (ii), no. 1062.
196 *LL*, vol. 5, p. 343, no. 1316.
197 *L&P*, XIII (ii), no. 1117. Standing surety for the recognizance were the dukes of Norfolk and Suffolk, the earl of Sussex, Sir John Dudley, Sir Owen West, Sir William Gownynge, George Blunt and John Guldyfford.
198 Harris, 'Women and politics in early Tudor England', p. 273; *DNB*, vol. 60, p. 343.
199 Höllger, 'Reginald Pole and the legations of 1537 and 1539', p. 110.
200 BL, Cotton MS Appendix L, f. 78; *L&P*, XIII (ii), no. 835.
201 Guy, *Tudor England*, p. 160.

Epilogue

1 Chapuys to the queen of Hungary, 10 June 1541. *CSP*, Spain, 1538–1542, p. 332, no. 166.
2 John Worth to Lord Lisle. *LL*, vol. 5, p. 481, no. 1419.
3 PRO, C.65/147, m. 22.
4 *L&P*, XIV (i), no. 402.
5 The government did try to find that pretext, however, when they questioned John Collins regarding any involvement of Montague's son in the burning of Geoffrey's letters at Lordington. See above, ch. 5.
6 *L&P*, XIV (i), nos. 988, 989, 1091.
7 Ibid., (ii), no. 212.
8 Ibid., XIV (i), no. 520.
9 Ibid., no. 573.
10 Ibid., (ii), no. 554.
11 Ibid., XV, no. 498 (II, cap. 49), p. 217.
12 Ibid., XIV (ii), no. 780 (32).
13 In November 1535 Gertrude sent to Chapuys begging him to inform Charles V of Henry VIII's threats against Catherine and Mary, praying Charles 'to have pity upon the ladies, and for the honour of God and the bond of kin to find a remedy'. In order to impress the urgency of the situation Gertrude then came in person to Chapuys, the perilous position she knew she was in illustrated by her use of a disguise. Ibid., IX, nos. 776, 861.
14 BL, Arundel MS 97, f. 116b.
15 *L&P*, XV, no. 436.
16 Ibid., XVI, no. 1011.
17 BL, Arundel MS 97, f. 186.
18 *L&P*, XIII (ii), no. 1176. Although there is no date on the document, the marchioness is included as a prisoner while one of her waiting ladies is described as having been with her a whole year.
19 Ibid., XVI, no. 1489, f. 185b.
20 H. Nicolas (ed.), *Proceedings and Ordinances of the Privy Council of*

England, vol. 7: 32–3 Henry VIII (London, 1837), p. 147.

[21] BL, Arundel MS 97, f. 186.

[22] *L&P*, VI, no. 641.

[23] Ibid., no. 557.

[24] *DNB*, vol. 44 (London, 1895), p. 11.

[25] *L&P*, XVI, no. 596.

[26] A. G. Dickens, 'Sedition and conspiracy in Yorkshire during the later years of Henry VIII', *Yorkshire Archaeological Journal*, 34 (1939), 393.

[27] Ibid., 394.

[28] *CSP*, Spain, 1538–1542, p. 321, no. 158.

[29] Ibid.

[30] Ibid.

[31] Dickens, 'Sedition and conspiracy in Yorkshire', p. 385.

[32] Ibid.

[33] Jansen, *Political Protest and Prophecy under Henry VIII*, p. 33.

[34] Ibid.

[35] *L&P*, XVI, no. 403.

[36] Ibid., XV, no. 1017.

[37] Ibid., XV, no. 868.

[38] Ibid., no. 941. In June another of the Poles' kinsmen, Lord Leonard Grey, son of Eleanor St John and Thomas, marquess of Dorset, went to the block for aiding and abetting the escape of his nephew Gerald, eleventh earl of Kildare. It was with Reginald that the young earl of Kildare subsequently found refuge, and the cardinal arranged his education and settled an annuity of 300 crowns upon him. B. FitzGerald, *The Geraldines: An Experiment in Irish Government 1169–1601* (London, 1951), pp. 241–2. Among the accusations against Grey was that he employed the services of a page who had been in Lord Montague's service for four or five years, and used him as a messenger during his treasonous intrigues. Moreover, in 1538, as deputy of Ireland, he reputedly left all the king's artillery in Galway ready to be put at the disposal of the pope or the Spaniards should they invade 'as a report was that cardinal Pole with an army would land about that time'. *L&P*, XV, no. 830, pp. 398, 399; ibid., XVI, no. 304 (iii).

[39] *L&P*, XVI, no. 868.

[40] *CSP*, Spain, 1538–1542, no. 166.

[41] *CSP*, Venetian, 1534–1554, nos. 265, 267.

[42] There is a story originating from 'a person of great quality' who told Lord Herbert of Cherbury that Margaret refused to lay her head on the block declaring:

> So should Traitors do, and I am none: neither did it serve that the Executioner told her it was the fashion; so turning her grey head every which way, shee bid him, if he would have her head, to get it as he could: So that he was constrained to fetch it off slovenly.

Life and Reign of King Henry VIII (1649), p. 468, cited in *Complete Peerage*, vol. 11, p. 402. As the editor of the peerage correctly notes, this tale was probably a later invention to explain Margaret's appalling end.

[43] Bell, *Notices of the Historic Persons Buried in the Chapel of St Peter ad Vincula*, p. 24. Queen Catherine Howard's remains, due to her youth and the presence of lime in the interments, had completely disintegrated.

[44] Due to the veneration paid through the centuries to sixty-three martyrs who had suffered during the reigns of Henry VIII and Elizabeth I, Pope Leo XIII judged

that veneration to constitute 'a legitimate and immemorial cult'. Such a judgement was equivalent to papal approval of 'the fact of martyrdom', and sixty-three martyrs were beatified, fifty-four on 29 December 1886 and nine on 13 May 1895. *The Catholic Martyrs of England and Wales* (Catholic Truth Society, London, 1985), p. 4; D. Bartolini, *Decree (of the Congregation of Sacred Rites) confirming the Honour given to the Blessed Martyrs John Cardinal Fisher, Thomas More, and others, Put to Death for the Faith from the Year 1535–1583* (Rome, 1886). I am grateful to Father Ian Dickie, archivist of the Westminster Diocesan Archives, for this information.

45 Pye, *The Life of Cardinal Reginald Pole*, pp. 155–6.

46 PRO, SP11/11, no. 41. I am grateful to Dr Charles Knighton for providing me with this reference.

47 *CSP*, Venetian, 1557–1558, no. 1287.

48 Catherine Pole, countess of Huntingdon received Stokenham, Yealmpton and the hundred of Coleridge in Devon, Newton Montague in Dorset, Ringwood and Christchurch in Hampshire, Ware in Hertford and Yarlington, Congresbury, Somerton and Donyatt Park in Somerset on 22 June, 1554. Lady Winifred Hastings, married to the earl of Huntingdon's younger brother, Sir Thomas, received Aston Clinton, Aston Chevery and the fee farm and rent of Aylesbury in Buckinghamshire, Clavering in Essex, Bushey in Hertford, Brixton and Swainstone on the Isle of Wight, Caister with all the fisheries in North Kelsey and yearly rents called 'Boyes rente' in South Kelsey in Lincoln, Llanfair and Llangyfiw in Monmouth, Aldbrough, Catterick, Cottingham and Hangwest Frendles in Yorkshire and Earlstoke in Wiltshire, also on 22 June 1554. *CPR*, 1553–1554, pp. 147–8, 186–7.

49 PRO, SP11/1, no. 17. Once again I am grateful to Dr Charles Knighton for kindly providing me with this reference.

50 A. H. Anderson, 'Henry, Lord Stafford (1501–1563) in local and central government', *EHR*, 78 (1963), 226.

51 Anderson, 'Henry Lord Stafford (1501–63) and the lordship of Caus', p. 14.

52 *HMC*, 78 Hastings, vol. 2, pp. 3, 4.

53 PRO, WARD 7/13. Ursula's Inquisition Post Mortem is dated 27 October 1570. Lord Stafford died in 1563.

54 Cross, *The Puritan Earl*, pp. xvii, 84–5.

55 *L&P*, XVII, no. 880, f. 43b.

56 *CSP*, Spain, 1538–1542, no. 167.

57 *L&P*, XIV (i), no. 191 (3).

58 He was involved in the muster of March 1539, in May 1540 he delivered letters from the king ordering a sessions to be held in Sussex and in December 1545 he was licensed to export 1,000 dicker of leather. Ibid., no. 652; ibid., XV, no. 681; ibid., XX (ii), no. 1068 (31).

59 Ibid., XIV (i), no. 1127.

60 Ibid., XIV (ii), no. 782.

61 Ibid., XVI, no. 19.

62 Ibid., no. 32; *APC*, vol. 7, p. 32.

63 *L&P*, XVI, nos. 74, 75.

64 Ibid., no. 708.

65 Ibid., nos. 721, 747.

66 Ibid., XVIII (i), no. 623 (92); ibid., XIX (i), no. 610 (116).

67 Hume, *Chronicle of King Henry VIII*, pp. 133–4. The imperial ambassadors

in England in 1553 also testified to Geoffrey's presence at Liège. *CSP*, Spain, 1553, p. 241.

[68] HMC, *Calendar of the Manuscripts of the Most Honourable the Marquis of Salisbury, K.G. &c. &c. &c. preserved at Hatfield House, Hertfordshire*, part 1 (London, 1883).

[69] *CSP*, Spain, 1553, pp. 241–2.

[70] *CPR*, 1554–1555, p. 351.

[71] Arthur, Geoffrey's eldest son, and his younger brother Edmund were arrested for treason in 1562. Arthur was incensed that the Protestants intended to advance the earl of Huntingdon, Lord Montague's grandson, as a claimant to the throne, and decided to press his own claim. However, he agreed to forgo his claim and support Mary, Queen of Scots providing he was created duke of Clarence. Both he and Edmund remained in the Tower until their deaths, commonly felt to be by 1570, for in that year their mother died and Arthur and Edmund were excluded from her will, which describes Thomas as her eldest son. Both brothers carved inscriptions at the Tower: the Salt Tower contains their names while in the Beauchamp Tower the following three inscriptions can be found: 'Edmond Poole', 'Deo Servire/Penitentiam Inire/Fato Obedire/Regnare Est/ A Poole/1564/IHS' (To be subject to God, to enter upon penance, to be obedient to fate, is to reign, A Poole, 1564, Jesus), 'Dio Semin in Lachrinis/in Exaltatiane Meter/Ae 21 E Poole/1562' (They that sow in tears, shall reap in joy, age 21 E Poole, 1562). A further inscription recorded by the Royal Commission on Historical Monuments in the 1930s is as follows: 'IHS/a passage perillus maketh a port pleasant/ Ao 1568, Arthur Poole, Ao sue 37' (the latter part of this is translated as 'The year 1568, Arthur Poole, His 37th year'). I am grateful to Jeremy Ashbee at the Tower of London for information about Arthur's and Edmund's inscriptions. *CSP*, Spain, vol. 1, item 188, p. 262; *CSP*, Foreign, 1562, item 1098; PRO, Prob. 11/52 (28 Lyon). Also, see my article on Arthur in *New Dictionary of National Biography* (Oxford, forthcoming).

[72] A letter from Geoffrey's eldest son, Arthur, possibly to William Cecil in 1559 in which he offers his services to Elizabeth, claims that this was not so and that Reginald 'would never see him and left him nothing in his will'. *CSP*, Domestic, 1547–1580, p. 145.

[73] Dodds and Dodds, *The Pilgrimage of Grace*, vol. 2, p. 286.

[74] *CSP*, Venetian, 1557–1558, no. 1287.

Appendix III

[1] Apart from those manors which were repossessed by Henry VIII, this list of Margaret's estates is based upon the minister's accounts, PRO, SC6/Hen VIII/6874 and 6875, unless otherwise stated.

[2] *L&P*, XIX (i), no. 1035 (18).

[3] Portland MS DDP 59/2, Nottingham Record Office. Information courtesy of Derbyshire Record Office and *L&P*, XIV (ii), no. 293.

[4] *L&P*, XVIII (ii), no. 327 (11).

[5] Ibid., XIX (i), no. 812 (94).

[6] For the following four manors, ibid., XVIII (i), no. 623 (92).

[7] PRO, SC12/11/34; *L&P*, XVI, no. 947 (31).

[8] Sold to William Bower in 1538. PRO, E40/1362.

9 PRO, CP25/2/43/299, f. 27.
10 D. A. Crowley (ed.), *VCH, Wiltshire*, vol. 13 (Oxford, 1987), p. 188.
11 I am grateful to David Grummitt for this information.
12 *L&P*, XIX (i), no. 442 (26).
13 Ibid., V, no. 909 (21).
14 PRO, CP25/2/37/245, f. 66.
15 *Lists and Indexes*, vol. 34, p. 81.
16 PRO, CP25/2/43/299, f. 27.
17 *Lists and Indexes*, vol. 34, pp. 185, 190.
18 PRO, SP1/102, f. 129; *Lists and Indexes*, vol. 34, p. 190.

Bibliography

ᕦᖶ

Primary Sources

Manuscripts

The British Library, London

Additional Charters	159, 160, 54005
Additional MSS	6113, 7099, 16673, 21480, 36918, 37146, 38133, 38174, 39404 A, 46354, 48976, 59899
Arundel MSS	97
Cotton MSS	Cleopatra, E. VI Julius B. XII Titus B. I Vespasian, F. XIII Vitellius B. XVIII Appendix L
Egerton MSS	985, 2219, 2642
Harleian MSS	283/142, 807/18, 1074, 1408/34, 2194, 3881, 4780, 6807, 6215, 6220/1, 6233
Harleian Charters	43
Landsdowne MSS	216
Roy Roll Charters	14B XXXIX
Royal MSS	7C XVI
Sloane MSS	S/6674
Stowe MSS	554, 1047

Public Record Office, Kew

Chancery Series	C.142/154	91
	C.1.401	11
	C.1.761	28

Early Chancery Proceedings	E.504	2
	E.111	131
Patent Rolls	C.66	561, 573, 579, 620, 689, 748
Exchequer Records	C.82	653
Feet of Fines	CP25/2/37	245
	CP25/2/43	30, 299
	CP25/1/22	127
	CP25/2/43	299
Exchequer Various Accounts	E.36	120, 143, 155, 159, 210, 214, 215, 216, 217, 219, 222, 225, 247, 248
	E.40	1362
	E.101/61	19
	E.101/72	3, 4
	E.101/328	7
	E.101/329	2
	E.101/412	10, 15, 16, 18, 19, 20
	E.101/413	1, 2, 4, 5, 6
	E.101/414	7
	E.101/415	14, 15
	E.101/416	1, 2, 3
	E.101/419	16
	E.101/420	4, 15, 10
	E.101/421	10
	E.101/490	12
	E.101/515	10
	E.101/516	14, 19
	E.101/517	1, 2, 3
	E.101/518	42, 46
	E.150	928
	E.163/9	20
	E.179/69	2, 16, 26
	E.210	9238
	E.312/8	5
	E.314	79
	E.317	Essex 12
	E.403	850
	E.405	68
	E.515	10

Court of Wards	WARD 7/13	35
	C.60	287
Warrants for Issues		
15 Henry VI–23 Henry VII	E.404	53–86
King's Bench	KB8/11	1, 2
Lord Chamberlain's Department		
	LC9	50
	LC2	1
Court of Requests	Req. 2/2	182
Chancery and Exchequer		
Ancient Correspondence	SC1	58
Ministers' Accounts	SC6/Hen VII	1492, 1493, 1494, 1550, 1551, 1552, 1553, 1554, 1555
	SC6/Hen VII–VIII	6928, 7019
	SC6/Hen VIII	219, 220, 221, 222, 223, 1503, 1504, 1505, 1506, 6874, 6875
Chamberlains' Accounts:		
Of Chester	SC6/Hen VII	1492, 1493, 1494, 1495, 1496, 1498, 1499, 1592, 1593, 1594, 1552, 1553
	SC6/Hen VIII	337
Of North Wales	SC6/HenVII	1591, 1592, 1593, 1594, 1595, 1857
	SC12/11/34	3, 4
State Papers	SP1	7, 18, 26, 29, 46, 50, 57, 59, 75, 78, 88, 102, 105, 106, 136, 138, 139, 140, 142, 144, 175
	SP2	CASEN
	SP3	6/50
Star Chamber	Stac 2/18	167

	Stac 2/22	248, 377
	Stac 2/25	260
	Stac 2/29	112, 171
	Stac 2/19	306, 315, 334, 337
	Stac 2/25	224, 260

PCC, Wills	Prob. 11/32 (8 Populwell)	John Babham
	Prob. 11/40 (1 Noodes)	Gertrude Courtenay, marchioness of Exeter
	Prob. 11/18 (2 Holder)	Sir Richard Delabere
	Prob. 11/19 (26 Aylofte)	Sir Thomas Delabere
	Prob. 11/34 (26 Bucke)	Oliver Frankelyn
	Prob. 11/29 (18 Spert)	Sir Roger Lewknor
	Prob. 11/25 (35 Hogen)	George Neville, Lord Bergavenny
	Prob. 11/22 (36 Porch)	Sir Edmund Pakenham
	Prob. 11/6 (35 Wattys)	Geoffrey Pole esq.
	Prob. 11/52 (28 Lyon)	Constance Pole

Gwynedd Archives Service, Caernarfon
Tanybwlch Collection   Z D V/1

Hertfordshire County Record Office
Hertford CO Records,   no. 6454   Bond between the Countess of
Salisbury and Ralph Buckberd
concerning the payment of Quit
Rent by the manor of Bournehall
to the manor of Bushey

Portsmouth Record Office
PCRO/906A   Survey carried out on the manor of Warblington
in 1632, by William Luffe, general surveyor to
Richard Cotton esq., lord of the manor

Westminster Abbey Muniments
WAM   5479, A, B, C, D, E, G, H, I, J, K, L, M, N, O, P, Q, R, S, T, U, V.
12241, 2324, 2331, 2332, 17757, 22824, 22826, 32364, 32365,
32377, 32380, 32407

Printed Primary Sources

The place of publication is London unless otherwise indicated.

Calendars

Calendar of the Close Rolls, 1399–1509 (18 vols, 1927–63).

Calendar of the Fine Rolls, 1399–1509 (11 vols, 1931–62).
Calendar of Inquisitions Post Mortem, 1485–1509 (3 vols, 1898–1955).
Calendar of Papal Registers, 1417–1513 (12 vols, 1906–89).
Calendar of the Patent Rolls, 1399–1558 (25 vols, 1897–1939).
Calendar of State Papers Domestic Series, 1547–1580, ed. R. Lemon (1856).
State Papers King Henry VIII, 1509–1547 (11 vols, 1830–52).
Calendar of State Papers, Domestic, Edward VI, 1547–1533, ed. C. S. Knighton (1992).
Calendar of State Papers, Foreign, Elizabeth, 1558–65, ed. J. Stevenson (1863–70).
Calendar of State Papers, Spanish, 1547–1603, ed. G. A. Bergenroth, P. De Gayangos, G. Mattingly, M. A. S. Hume and R. Tyler (20 vols, 1866–1954).
Calendar of State Papers, Venetian, 1202–1603, ed. R. Brown, G. C. Bentinck and H. F. Brown (11 vols, 1864–97).
Catalogue of Ancient Deeds (6 vols, 1890–1915).
Journals of the House of Lords, vol. 1: 1509–1577 (1846).
Letters and Papers Illustrative of the Reigns of Richard III and Henry VII, ed. J. Gairdner (2 vols, 1861–3).
Letters and Papers, Foreign and Domestic, of the Reign of Henry VIII, 1509–47, ed. J. S. Brewer, J. Gairdner and R. H. Brodie. (21 vols, 1862–1910).

Society of Antiquaries
Collection of Ordinances and Regulations for the Government of the Royal Household, printed by J. Nichols, (London, 1790).

Buckingham Record Society
A Calendar of Deeds and Other Records Preserved in the Muniment Room at the Museum, Aylesbury (1941).
Chibnal, A. C. and Woodman, A. Vere (eds), *Subsidy Roll for the County of Buckingham anno 1524* (Aylesbury?, 1950).
Chibnal, A. C., *The Certificate of Musters for Buckinghamshire in 1522*, vol. 17 (HMSO, 1973).

The Camden Society
Bruce, J. (ed.), *Letters and Papers of the Verney Family to 1639*, old series, 61 (1853).
Collier, J. P., *The Trevelyan Papers prior to AD 1558*, old series, 67 (3 vols, 1857).
Davies, J. S. (ed.), *An English Chronicle of the Reigns of Richard II, Henry IV, Henry V, and Henry VI*, old series, 64 (1856).
Hamilton, W. D. (ed.), *Chronicle of England during the Reigns of the Tudors* by Charles Wriothesley, Windsor Herald, new series, 20 (2 vols, 1877).

Hay, D. (ed. and trans.), *The Anglica Historia of Polydore Vergil A.D. 1485–1537*, third series, 74 (1950).

Jerdan, W., *The Rutland Papers*, old series, 21 (1842).

Kingsford, C. L. (ed.), *Two London Chronicles from the Collections of John Stowe*, third series, 12 (1910).

Kingsford, C. L. (ed.), *The Stonor Letters and Papers 1290–1483*, third series, 29, 30 (2 vols, 1919).

Nichols, J. G. (ed.), *The Chronicle of Calais*, old series, 35 (1846).

Nichols, J. G. and Bruce, J. (eds), *Wills from Doctors Commons, 1495–1695*, old series, 83 (1863).

Powell, E., *The Travels and Life of Sir Thomas Hoby, Kt., of Bisham Abbey, Written by Himself, 1547–1564*, Camden Miscellany, third series, 4 (1902).

Sneyd, C. A. (trans.), *A Relation or Rather a True Account of the Island of England*, old series, 37 (1847).

Stapleton, T. (ed.), *Plumpton Correspondence*, old series, 4 (1839).

Catholic Truth Society
The Catholic Martyrs of England and Wales (1985).

Dugdale Society
Hilton, R. H. (ed.), *Ministers Accounts of the Warwickshire Estates of the Duke of Clarence 1479–80*, vol. 21 (Oxford, 1952).

Early English Text Society
Hanham, A. (ed.), *The Cely Letters 1472–1488* (Oxford, 1975).

Harleian Society
W. B. Bannerman (ed.), *The Visitations of the County of Sussex, Made and Taken in the Years 1530. By Thomas Benolte, Clarenceux King of Arms; and 1633–44 by John Philpot, Somerset Herald, and George Owen, York Herald for Sir John Burroughs, Garter and Sir Richard St. George Clarenceux*, vol. 53 (1905).

Selden Society
Bayne, C. G. (ed.), completed by W. H. Dunham (jnr), *Select Cases in the Council of Henry VII* (1958).

Leadam, S. (ed.), *Court of Requests, Select Cases, 1497–1569*, vol. 12 (1898).

Surtees Society
R. B. Dobson (ed.), *York City Chamberlains Account Rolls 1396–1500* (1980).

Sussex Archaeological Collections
'Inventories of Goods of the Smaller Monasteries and Friaries in Sussex', vol. 44 (1901).

Sussex Record Society
Attree, F. W. T. (trans.), *Sussex Inquisitions Post Mortem, 1485–1649*, vol. 14 (Lewes, 1912).

Yorkshire Archaeological Society
Raine, A. (ed.), *York Civic Records* (1), vol. 98 (Leeds, 1938).

Other Primary Sources
Allen, H. M. and Allen, P. S. (eds), *Letters of Richard Fox, 1486–1527* (Oxford, 1929).
Anstis, J. (ed.), *The Register of the Most Noble Order of the Garter* (2 vols, 1724).
Armstrong, C. A. J. (trans.), *The Usurpation of Richard III* by Dominic Mancini (Gloucester, 1989).
Bartollini, D., *Decree (of the Congregation of Sacred Rites) confirming the Honour given to the Blessed Martyrs, John Cardinal Fisher, Thomas More, and Others, Put to Death for the Faith from the Year 1535–1583* (Rome, 1886).
Bentley, S. (ed.), *Excerpta Historica or, Illustrations of English History* (London, 1831).
Bickley, F. (ed.), *HMC, Reports 78, Hastings* (2 vols, 1930).
Bohn, J., *The Chronicles of the White Rose of York* (Gloucester, 1974).
Brown, R. (trans.), *Four Years at the Court of Henry VIII* by Sebastian Giustinian (2 vols, 1854).
Byrne, M. S. C. (ed.), *The Lisle Letters* (6 vols, 1981).
Clive, R. H., *Documents Connected with the History of Ludlow and the Lords Marchers* (1841).
Cokayne, G. E., *Complete Peerage of England, Scotland, Ireland and Great Britain* (12 vols, 1910–59).
Crump, C. G. and Cunningham, W. R. (eds), *Calendar of the Charter Rolls*, vol. 6 (1927).
Dasent, J. R. (ed.), *Acts of the Privy Council of England 1550–52*, vol. 3 (1891).
Davies, R., *Extracts from the Municipal Records of the City of York during the Reigns of Edward IV, Edward V and Richard III* (1843).
Ellis, H. (ed.), *Hall's Chronicle* (1809).
Ellis, H. (ed.), *The Concordance of History: The New Chronicles of England and France* by Robert Fabyan, 1516 (1811).
Foster, J., *Register of Admissions to Gray's Inn 1521–1889* (1889).
Gairdner, J. (ed.), *Memorials of King Henry the Seventh* (1858).
Gairdner, J. (ed.) (intro., R. Virgoe), *The Paston Letters*, (Gloucester, 1983).
Hammond, P. W. and Horrox, R. (eds), *British Harleian Manuscript 433* (4 vols, Gloucester, 1983).

Hearne, T. (ed.), *Joannis Lelandi Antiquarii de Rebus Britannicis Collectanea* (1770).

Holinshed, Raphael, *Chronicles of England, Scotland and Ireland*, vol. 2 (6 vols, 1586; reprinted London, 1896).

Hume, M. A. S., *Chronicle of King Henry VIII of England* (1889).

Index of Inquisitions Preserved in the Public Record Office, Henry VIII–Philip and Mary, vol. 23 (New York, 1963).

Kingsford, C. L. (ed.), *Chronicles of London* (Dursley, 1977).

List of Original Ministers' Accounts Preserved in the Public Record Office, vol. 34 (ii), *Lists and Indexes* (Dublin, 1910).

Luders, A. et al., *Statutes of the Realm* (11 vols, 1810–28).

Madden, F., *The Privy Purse Expenses of Princess Mary* (1831).

Merriman, R. B., *Life and Letters of Thomas Cromwell* (2 vols, Oxford, 1968).

Morisyne, R., *An Invective ayenste the Grest and Detestable Vice, Treason, wherein the Secrete Practises, and Traiterous Workinges of theym, that Suffrid of late are Disclosed* (1539; reprinted New York, 1972).

Muller, J. A. (ed.), *The Letters of Stephen Gardiner* (Westport, CT, 1970).

Nichols, J. G. (ed.), *Collectanea Topographica et Genealogica* (3 vols, London, 1834–7).

Nicolas, H., *Proceedings and Ordinances of the Privy Council of England*, vol. 7: 32–3 Henry VIII (1837).

Nicolas, N. H., *Testamenta Vetusta* (1826).

Nicolas, N. H. (ed.), *Privy Purse Expences of Elizabeth of York: Wardrobe Accounts of Edward the Fourth* (London, 1830).

Plaisted, A. H., *The Manor and Parish Records of Medmenham Buckinghamshire* (1925).

Pollard, A. F., *The Reign of Henry VII from Contemporary Sources* (3 vols, London, 1913).

Pronay, N. and Cox, J. (eds), *The Crowland Chronicle Continuations: 1459–1486* (Gloucester, 1986).

Pye, B. (trans.), *The Life of Cardinal Reginald Pole* by Lodovico Beccatelli, Archbishop of Ragusa (1766).

Records of the Honourable Society of Lincoln's Inn, vol. 1: *Admissions 1420–1799* (1896).

Register of Admissions to the Honourable Society of the Middle Temple, 15th C–1944, vol. 1 (1944).

Riley, H. T. (trans.), *Ingulph's Chronicle of the Abbey of Croyland* with the continuations of Peter of Blois and anonymous writers (1854).

Ross, C. (intro.), *The Rous Roll* by John Rous (Gloucester, 1980).

Stephen, L. and Lee, S. (eds.), *Dictionary of National Biography* (63 vols, 1885–1900).

Strachey, J. et al. (eds), *Rotuli Parliamentorum, 1278–1504* (6 vols, 1767–83).

Sylvester, R. S. (ed.), *St. Thomas More: The History of King Richard III and Selections from the English and Latin Poems* (1976).

The Third Report of the Deputy Keeper of the Public Records Office (1842).

The 37th Annual Report of the Deputy Keeper of the Public Records Office, pt. 2 (1876).

Thomas, A. H. and Thornley, I. D. (eds), *The Great Chronicle of London* (1938).

Valor Ecclesiasticus (6 vols, 1810–34).

The Victoria History of the Counties of England (The University of London Institute of Historical Research).

Wallis Chapman, A. B. (trans. and intro.), *The Black Book of Southampton, 1497–1620*, vol. 3 (Southampton, 1915).

Wheatley, H. B. (intro.), *Stowe's Survey of London* (1956).

Williamson, J. B. (ed.), *The Middle Temple Bench Book* (1937).

Wood, M. A. E., *Letters of Royal and Illustrious Ladies*, vol. 1 (London, 1846).

Yates, J. B. (ed.), *Chetham Miscellanies*, vol. 2 (London, 1856).

Secondary Sources

Allington-Smith, R., 'Not Yorkist but anti Lancastrian: Henry Despenser, bishop of Norwich, 1370–1406', *The Ricardian*, 10 (124) (1994), 16–18.

Anderson, A. H., 'Henry Lord Stafford (1501–1563) in local and central government', *EHR*, 78 (1963), 225–42.

Anderson, A. H., 'Henry, Lord Stafford (1501–63) and the lordship of Caus', *WHR*, 6, 1 (1972), 1–15.

Anglo, S., 'The court festivals of Henry VII: a study based upon the account books of John Heron, treasurer of the chamber', *Bulletin of the John Rylands Library*, 43, 1 (1960), 12–45.

Archbold, W. A. J., 'Sir William Stanley and Perkin Warbeck', *EHR*, 14 (1899), 529–34.

Archer, R. E., 'Rich old ladies: the problem of late medieval dowagers', in A. J. Pollard (ed.), *Property and Politics: Essays in Later Medieval English History* (Gloucester, 1984), pp. 15–35.

Archer, R. A., ' "How ladies . . . who live on their manors ought to manage their households and estates": women as landowners and administrators in the later Middle Ages', in P. P. J. Goldberg (ed.), *Woman is a Worthy Wight: Women in English Society c. 1200–1500* (Gloucester, 1992), pp. 149–81.

Arthurson, I., *The Perkin Warbeck Conspiracy 1491–1499* (Stroud, 1994).

Ashelford, J., *A Visual History of Costume: The Sixteenth Century* (London, 1993).

Attreed, L. C., 'From Pearl maiden to Tower princes: towards a new history of medieval childhood', *Journal of Family History*, 9 (1983), 43–58.

Baker, C. H., 'Margaret Plantagenet, countess of Salisbury', *Burlington Magazine*, 62 (1933), 212–17.

Ballard, G., *Memoirs of Learned Ladies* (London, 1775).

Barron, C. M., 'Centres of conspicuous consumption: the aristocratic townhouse in London, 1200–1550', *London Journal*, 20 (1995), 1–16.

Bean, J. M. W., *The Decline of English Feudalism 1215–1540* (Manchester, 1968).

Beer, B. L., *Rebellion and Riot: Popular Disorder in England during the Reign of Edward VI* (Kent, OH, 1982).

Beeston, D., A *Strange Accident of State: Henry VII and the Lambert Simnel Conspiracy* (Derby, 1987).

Bell, D. C., *Notices of the Historic Persons Buried in the Chapel of St. Peter ad Vincula in the Tower of London* (London, 1877).

Bellamy, J., *The Tudor Law of Treason* (London, 1979).

Beltz, G. F., *Memorials of the Most Noble Order of the Garter* (London, 1841).

Bennett, M., *Lambert Simnel and the Battle of Stoke* (Gloucester, 1987).

Bernard, G. W., 'The rise of Sir William Compton, early Tudor courtier', *EHR*, 96 (1981), 754–77.

Bernard, G. W., *The Power of the Early Tudor Nobility: A Study of the Fourth and Fifth Earls of Shrewsbury* (Sussex, 1985).

Bernard, G. W. (ed.), *The Tudor Nobility* (Manchester, 1992).

Bindoff, S. T., *Tudor England* (Harmondsworth, 1966).

Bindoff, S. T., *The History of Parliament: The House of Commons 1509–1558*, vol. 3 (3 vols, London, 1982).

Block, J. S., *Factional Politics and the English Reformation* (Woodbridge, 1993).

Bloom, J. Harvey, *The Register of the Gild of Holy Cross, The Blessed Mary and St John the Baptist of Stratford-upon-Avon* (London, 1907).

Boase, C. W. (ed.), *Register of the University of Oxford, 1449–63, 1505–71*, vol. 1 (Oxford, 1885).

Boase, G. C., *Collectanea Cornubensia: A Collection of Biographical and Topographical Notes relating to the County of Cornwall* (Truro, 1890).

Brandi, K. (trans. C. V. Wedgewood), *The Emperor Charles V* (London, 1954).

Brewer, J., *The Reign of Henry VIII*, ed. J. Gairdner (London, 1884).

Brigden, S., 'Popular disturbance and the fall of Thomas Cromwell and the reformers, 1539–1540', *Historical Journal*, 24 (1981), 257–78.

Brodie, D. M., 'Edmund Dudley: minister of Henry VII', *TRHS* (fourth series, 15, 1932), 133–61.

Buck, A. R., 'The politics of land law in Tudor England, 1529–1540', *Journal of Legal History*, 11 (1990), 200–17.

Budgen, W., 'The divorce of Sir William Barentyne, 1540', *Sussex Notes and Queries*, 9 (1942–3), 168–70.

Bush, M. L., 'The Tudors and the royal race', *History*, 55 (1970), 37–48.

Bush, M. L., 'The problem of the far North: a study of the crisis of 1537 and its consequences', *Northern History*, 6 (1971), 40–63.

Camm, B., *Forgotten Shrines* (London, 1910).

Campbell, W. (ed.), *Materials for a History of the Reign of Henry VII* (2 vols, 1873–7).

Carlton, C., 'The widow's tale: male myths and female reality in 16th and 17th century England', *Albion*, 10, 2 (1978), 118–29.

Carpenter, C., 'The duke of Clarence and the Midlands: a study in the interplay of local and national politics', *Midland History*, 2 (1986), 23–48.

Casey, K., 'Women in Norman and Plantagenet England 1066–1399', in B. Kanner (ed.), *The Women of England from Anglo Saxon Times to the Present: Interpretive Bibliographical Essays* (London, 1980), pp. 83–123.

Chambers, E. K., *Sir Thomas Wyatt and Some Collected Studies* (London, 1933).

Chambers, R. W., *Thomas More* (London, 1935).

Chrimes, S. B., *Lancastrians, Yorkists and Henry VII* (London, 1964).

Chrimes, S. B., *Henry VII* (London, 1972).

Clifford, A. G. C., *Iadis by a Descendant* (Venice, 1988).

Cobby, E. A., *The Lewknors of Sussex* (Cranleigh, 1991).

Colvin, H. M. et al., *The History of the King's Works* (6 vols, London, 1963–82).

Comber, J., *Sussex Genealogies: Barentyne and Dedisham and Lewknor of Sussex* (Horsham Centre, 1931 and Lewes Centre, 1933).

Compton, W. B., *History of the Comptons of Compton Wynyates* (London, 1930).

Condon, M. M., 'Ruling elites in the reign of Henry VII', in C. Ross (ed.), *Patronage, Pedigree and Power in Late Medieval England* (Gloucester, 1979), pp. 109–42.

Conway, A., *Henry VII's Relations with Scotland and Ireland 1485–1498* (Cambridge, 1932).

Cooper, C. H., *Memoir of Margaret Countess of Richmond and Derby* (Cambridge, 1874).

Cooper, W. D., 'Pedigree of the Lewknor family', *SAC*, 3 (1850), 89–102.

Cornwall, J., *Revolt of the Peasantry 1549* (London, 1977).

Cornwall, J. C. K., 'Sussex wealth and society in the reign of Henry VIII', *SAC*, 114 (1976), 1–26.

Cornwall, J. C. K., *Wealth and Society in Early Sixteenth Century England* (London, 1988).

Cross, C., *The Puritan Earl: A Life of Henry Hastings Third Earl of Huntingdon 1536–1595* (London, 1966).

Cross, C., *Church and People 1450–1660* (London, 1976).

Crossley, F. H. and Ridgway, M. H., 'Screens, lofts, and stalls situated in Wales and Monmouthshire', *Archaeologia Cambrensis*, 110–11 (1961–2), 59–102.

Crowley, D. A., *Victoria County History, Wiltshire*, vol. 13 (Oxford, 1987).

Cruickshank, C., *Henry VIII and the Invasion of France* (Stroud, 1990).

Davies, C. S. L., *Peace, Print and Protestantism* (St Albans, 1977).

Davies, C. S. L., 'The Pilgrimage of Grace reconsidered', in P. Slack (ed.), *Rebellion, Popular Protest and the Social Order in Early Modern England* (Cambridge, 1984), pp. 16–38.

Davies, C. S. L., 'Bishop John Morton, the Holy See, and the accession of Henry VII', *EHR*, 102 (1987), 2–30.

Denton Cheney, A., 'The Holy Maid of Kent', *TRHS*, new series, 18 (1904), 107–30.

Dickens, A. G., 'Sedition and conspiracy in Yorkshire during the later years of Henry VIII', *Yorkshire Archaeological Journal*, 34 (1939), 379–98.

Dodds, M. H. and Dodds, R., *The Pilgrimage of Grace 1536–1537 and the Exeter Conspiracy 1538* (2 vols, London, 1971).

Doran, S., *England and Europe, 1485–1603* (London, 1986).

Dowling, M., *Humanism in the Age of Henry VIII* (London, 1986).

Duffy, E., *The Stripping of the Altars: Traditional Religion in England c.1400–c.1580* (London, 1993).

Dugdale, W., *The Baronage of England* (London, 1675).

Dugdale, W., *A Perfect Copy of the Nobility to the Great Councils and Parliaments of the Realm* (London, 1685).

Dugdale, W., *The Antiquities of Warwickshire* (London, 1730).

Dugdale, W., *Monasticon Anglicanum* (London, 1846).

Dyer, C., *Standards of Living in the Middle Ages* (Cambridge, 1989).

Edwards, R., *The Itinerary of King Richard III 1483–1485* (London, 1983).

Ellis, T. E., *Banners, Standards and Badges from a Tudor MS* (London, 1904).

Elton, G. R., 'The law of treason in the early Reformation', *Historical Journal*, 11 (1968), 211–36.

Elton, G. R., *The Tudor Constitution: Documents and Commentary* (Cambridge, 1968).

Elton, G. R., *England under the Tudors* (London, 1971).

Elton, G. R., 'Tudor government: the points of contact II. The council', *TRHS*, fifth series, 25 (1975), 195–211.

Elton, G. R., *Reform and Reformation* (London, 1977).

Elton, G. R., 'Politics and the Pilgrimage of Grace', in B. C. Malament (ed.), *After the Reformation: Essays in Honour of J. H. Hexter* (Manchester, 1980), pp. 25–56.

Elton, G. R., *Policy and Police: The Enforcement of the Reformation in the Age of Thomas Cromwell* (Cambridge, 1985).

Emerson, K. L., *Wives and Daughters: The Women of Sixteenth Century England* (New York, 1964).

Emerton, E., *Desiderius Erasmus of Rotterdam* (London, 1899).

Erickson, A. L., 'Women's property relations in early modern England' (unpublished Ph.D. thesis, University of Cambridge, 1986).

Evans, H. T., *Wales and the Wars of the Roses* (Cambridge, 1915).

Fenlon, D., *Heresy and Obedience in Tridentine Italy: Cardinal Pole and the Counter Reformation* (Cambridge, 1972).

FitzGerald, B., *The Geraldines: An Experiment in Irish Government 1169–1601* (London, 1951).

Fletcher, A., *Tudor Rebellions* (London, 1990).

Fox, A. and Guy, J., *Reassessing the Henrician Age: Humanism, Politics and Reform 1500–1550* (Oxford, 1986).

Fritze, R. H., 'Faith and faction: religious changes, national politics, and the development of local factionalism in Hampshire, 1485–1570' (unpublished Ph.D. thesis, University of Cambridge, 1981).

Froide, A. M., 'Marital status as a category of difference: singlewomen and widows in early modern England', in J. M. Bennett and A. M. Froide (eds), *Singlewomen in the European Past, 1250–1800* (Philadelphia, 1999), pp. 236–69.

Fryde, E. B., Greenway, D. E., Porter, S. and Roy, I. (eds), *Handbook of British Chronology* (London, 1986).

Gairdner, J., *History of the Life and Reign of Richard the Third* (Cambridge, 1898).

Gaskell, G. A., *Dictionary of Scripture and Myth* (New York, 1988).

Gasquet, F. A., *Cardinal Pole and his Early Friends* (London, 1927).

Gee, J. A., *The Life and Works of Thomas Lupset* (Oxford, 1928).

Goldberg, P. J. P. (ed.), *Woman is a Worthy Wight. Women in English Society c. 1200–1500* (Stroud, 1992).

Goodman, A. and Mackay, A., 'A Castillian report on English affairs, 1486', *EHR*, 88 (1973), 92–9.

Goody, J., 'Inheritance, property and women: some comparative considerations', in J. Goody, J. Thirsk and E. P. Thompson (eds), *Family and Inheritance: Rural Society in Western Europe 1200–1800* (Cambridge, 1976), pp. 10–36.

Gray, M., 'The dispersal of Crown property in Monmouthshire 1500–1603' (unpublished Ph.D. thesis, University of Wales, Cardiff, 1984).

Grazebrook, R. M., *A Short History of Stourton Castle and the Royal Forest of Kinver* (London, 1919).

Griffiths, R. A., *The Principality of Wales in the Later Middle Ages: The Structure and Personnel of Government*, vol. 1: *South Wales, 1277–1536* (Cardiff, 1972).

Griffiths, R. A., 'Richard duke of York and the royal household in Wales, 1449–1450', *WHR*, 8 (1976), 14–25.

Griffiths, R. A. (ed.), *Boroughs of Medieval Wales* (Cardiff, 1978).

Griffiths, R. A., 'Public and private bureaucracies in England and Wales in the fifteenth century', *TRHS*, fifth series, 30 (1980), 109–30.

Griffiths, R. A., *The Reign of King Henry VI: The Exercise of Royal Authority, 1422–1461* (London, 1981).

Griffiths, R. A., *The Making of the Tudor Dynasty* (Gloucester, 1985).

Griffiths, R. A., *King and Country: England and Wales in the Fifteenth Century* (London, 1991).

Griffiths, R. A., *Sir Rhys ap Thomas and his Family* (Cardiff, 1993).

Grummitt, D. I., 'The economic and social history of Calais and the Pale under English rule between 1485 and 1558' (unpublished Ph.D. thesis, London University, 1977).

Gunn, S. J., *Charles Brandon, Duke of Suffolk c. 1484–1545* (Oxford, 1988).

Gunn, S. J., 'Peers, commons and gentry in the Lincolnshire revolt 1536', *Past and Present*, 123 (1989), 52–79.

Gunn, S. J., 'Tournaments and early Tudor chivalry', *History Today*, 41, 6 (1991), 15–21.

Gunn, S. J., *Early Tudor Government 1485–1558* (London, 1995).

Guy, J., *Tudor England* (Oxford, 1990).

Guy, J. (ed.), *The Tudor Monarchy* (London, 1997).

Gwyn, P., *The King's Cardinal* (London, 1990).

Halsted, C. A., *Life of Margaret Beaufort Countess of Richmond and Derby* (London, 1845).

Hammond, P. W., 'The coronation of Elizabeth of York', *The Ricardian*, 6, 83 (1983). 270–2.

Hammond, P. W., 'The illegitimate children of Richard III', in J. Petre (ed.), *Richard III Crown and People* (London, 1985), pp. 18–23.

W. E., Hampton, 'The White Rose under the first Tudors, part 1', *The Ricardian*, 7, 97 (1987), 414–20.

Hanham, A., 'Richard III, Lord Hastings and the historians', *EHR*, 72 (1972), 233–48.

Hanham, A., *Richard III and his Early Historians 1483–1535* (Oxford, 1975).

Hanham, A., 'Edmond de la Pole and the spies 1449–1506', in S. M. Jack (ed.), *Rulers, Religion and Rhetoric in Early Modern England: A Festchrift for Geoffrey Elton from his Australasian Friends* (Parergon, 1988), pp. 103–20.

Harris, B. J., 'Marriage sixteenth century style: Elizabeth Stafford and the third duke of Norfolk', *Journal of Social History*, 15 (1982), 371–82.

Harris, B. J., *Edward Stafford, Third Duke of Buckingham, 1478–1521* (Stanford, CA, 1986).

Harris, B. J., 'Power, profit, and passion: Mary Tudor, Charles Brandon, and the arranged marriage in early Tudor England', *Feminist Studies*, 15 (1989), 59–88.

Harris, B. J., 'Property, power and personal relations: elite mothers and sons in Yorkist and early Tudor England', *Signs*, 15 (1990), 606–32.

Harris, B. J., 'Women and politics in early Tudor England', *Historical Journal*, 33 (1990), 259–81.

Harris, B. J., 'Aristocratic women and the state in early Tudor England', in C. Carlton, R. L. Woods, M. L. Robertson and J. S. Bloch (eds), *State*,

Sovereigns and Society in Early Modern England: Essays in Honour of A. J. Slavin (Stroud, 1998), pp. 3–24.

Harris, B. J., 'The view from my lady's chamber: new perspectives on the early Tudor monarchy', *Huntington Library Quarterly*, 60, 3 (1998), 215–47.

Harvey, N. L., *Elizabeth of York, Tudor Queen* (New York, 1973).

Hasted, E., *History of Kent* (Canterbury, 1797–1801).

Heal, F., *Hospitality in Early Modern England* (Oxford, 1990).

Herlihy, D., *Medieval Households* (London, 1985).

Hicks, M., 'Descent, partition and extinction: the Warwick inheritance', in M. Hicks (ed.), *Richard III and his Rivals: Magnates and their Motives in the Wars of the Roses* (London, 1991), pp. 323–35.

Hicks, M., 'The Neville earldom of Salisbury, 1429–71', in M. Hicks (ed.), *Richard III and His Rivals: Magnates and their Motives in the Wars of the Roses* (London, 1991), 353–63.

Hicks, M., *Richard III and his Rivals: Magnates and their Motives in the Wars of the Roses* (London, 1991).

Hicks, M., *False, Fleeting, Perjur'd Clarence* (Bangor, 1992).

Hogrefe, P., 'Legal rights of Tudor women and their circumvention by men and women', *Sixteenth Century Journal*, 3, 1 (1972), 97–105.

Hogrefe, P., *Tudor Women, Commoners and Queens* (Ames, 1975).

Hogrefe, P., *Women of Action in Tudor England* (Ames, 1977).

Holderness, B. A., 'Widows in pre-industrial society: an essay upon their economic functions', in R. M. Smith (ed.), *Land, Kinship and Life-Cycle* (Cambridge, 1985), pp. 423–42.

Höllger, C., 'Reginald Pole and the legations of 1537 and 1539: diplomatic and polemical responses to the break with Rome' (unpublished D.Phil. thesis, University of Oxford, 1989).

Horrox, R., *Richard III: A Study of Service* (Cambridge, 1991).

Horrox, R. (ed.), *Fifteenth Century Attitudes: Perceptions of Society in Late Medieval England* (Cambridge, 1994).

Horsfield, T. W., *The History, Antiquities and Topography of the County of Sussex* (2 vols, Dorking, 1974).

Houlbrooke, R. A., *The English Family 1450–1700* (New York, 1984).

Howard, M., *The Early Tudor Country House: Architecture and Politics 1490–1550* (London, 1987).

Howard, M., 'Power and the early Tudor courtier's house', *History Today*, 37, 5 (1987), 44–5.

Howarth, R. W., *Some Notes on the Castle at Sheriff Hutton* (Bangor, 1993).

Hoyle, R. W., 'Henry Percy earl of Northumberland, and the fall of the House of Percy, 1527–1537', in G. W. Bernard (ed.), *The Tudor Nobility* (Manchester, 1992), pp. 180–211.

Hurstfield, J., *Freedom, Corruption and Government in Elizabethan England* (London, 1973).

Hutchins, J., *The History and Antiquities of the County of Dorset*, edited by W. Shipp and J. Hodson (Wakefield, 1973).

Hutchinson, J., *Herefordshire Biographies* (London, 1890).

Hutchinson, J., *A Catalogue of Notable Middle Templars* (London, 1902).

Ives, E., 'Faction at the court of Henry VIII: the fall of Anne Boleyn', *History*, 57 (1972), 169–88.

Ives, E., *The Common Lawyers of Pre-Reformation England* (Cambridge, 1983).

Ives, E., *Anne Boleyn* (Oxford, 1988).

Ives, E., *Faction in Tudor England* (London, 1989).

Ives, E., Knecht, R. J. and Scarisbrick, J. J. (eds), *Wealth and Power in Tudor England; Essays Presented to S. T. Bindoff* (London, 1978).

James, M. E., 'Obedience and dissent in Henrician England: the Lincolnshire Rebellion 1536', *Past and Present*, 48 (1970), 3–78.

Jansen, S. L., *Political Protest and Prophecy under Henry VIII* (Woodbridge, 1991).

Jones, M. K. and Underwood, M. G., *The King's Mother* (Cambridge, 1992).

Kendall, P. M., *Warwick the Kingmaker* (London, 1972).

Klapisch-Zuber, C. (ed.), *A History of Women in the West*, vol. 2: *Silences of the Middle Ages* (London, 1994).

Knecht, R. J., *Francis I* (Cambridge, 1988).

Knowles, D., *The Religious Orders in England*, vol. 3: *The Tudor Age* (Cambridge, 1959).

Lander, J. R. (ed.), *Crown and Nobility 1450–1509* (London, 1976).

Lander, J. R., 'The treason and death of the duke of Clarence', in J. R. Lander (ed.), *Crown and Nobility 1450–1509* (London, 1976), pp. 242–66.

Lander, J. R., *Government and Community: England 1450–1509* (London, 1988).

Lehmberg, S. E., 'Parliamentary attainder in the reign of Henry VIII', *The Historical Journal*, 18 (1975), 675–702.

Levine, M., 'Richard III: usurper or lawful king?', *Speculum*, 34 (1959), 391–401.

Levine, M., *Tudor Dynastic Problems 1460–1571* (London, 1973).

Levine, M., 'The place of women in Tudor government', in D. J. Guth and J. W. McKenna (eds), *Tudor Rule and Revolution: Essays for G. R. Elton from his American Friends* (Cambridge, 1982), pp. 109–23.

Lewis, D., 'The court of the president and Council of Wales and the Marches from 1478–1575', *Y Cymmrodor*, 12 (1897), 1–64.

Lleufer Thomas, D., 'Further notes on the Court of the Marches with original documents', *Y Cymmrodor*, 13 (1900), 97–163.

Loades, D. M., *Politics and the Nation 1450–1660* (London, 1988).

Loades, D. M., *Mary Tudor: A Life* (Oxford, 1989).

Loades, D. M., *The Tudor Court* (Bangor, 1992).

Loades, D. M., *The Politics of Marriage* (Stroud, 1994).

Lobel, M. D. (ed.), *The City of London from Prehistoric Times to c. 1520*, vol. 3 (Oxford, 1989).

Lockyer, R. (ed. and intro.), *The History of the Reign of King Henry the Seventh* by Francis Bacon (London, 1971).

Lockyer, R., *Tudor and Stuart Britain 1471–1714* (London, 1971).

Lockyer, R., *Henry VII* (New York, 1983).

Long, C. E., 'Wild Darell, of Littlecote', *Wiltshire Archaeological Magazine*, 4 (1857), 209–32.

Long, W. H. (ed.), *The Oglander Memoirs 1595–1648* (London, 1888).

Lower, M. A., *A Compendious History of Sussex, Topographical, Archaeological and Anecdotal* (2 vols, London, 1870).

Loyd, L. C. and Stenton, D. M. (eds), *Sir Christopher Hatton's Book of Seals Presented to F. M. Stenton* (Oxford, 1950).

Lyster Denny, H. L., *Memorials of an Ancient House: A History of the Family of Lister or Lyster* (Edinburgh, 1913).

MacFarlane, A., *Marriage and Love in England: Modes of Reproduction 1300–1840* (Oxford, 1986).

MacGibbon, D., *Elizabeth Woodville 1437–1492* (London, 1938).

MacNalty, A. S., *Henry VIII: A Difficult Patient* (London, 1952).

Maitland, F. W., *The Constitutional History of England* (Cambridge, 1931).

Malden, H. E., *A History of Surrey* (London, 1905).

Malfatti, C. V. (ed. and trans.), *Two Italian Accounts of Tudor England* (Barcelona, 1953).

Marmion, J. P., 'Cardinal Pole in recent studies', *Recusant History*, 13 (1973), 56–61.

Mattingly, G., 'A humanist ambassador', *Journal of Modern History*, 4 (1932), 175–85.

Mattingly, G., *Catherine of Aragon* (London, 1944).

Mayer, T. F., 'A diet for Henry VIII: the failure of Reginald Pole's 1537 legation', *Journal of British Studies*, 26 (1987), 305–31.

Mayer, T. F., 'A fate worse than death: Reginald Pole and the Parisian theologians', *EHR*, 102 (1988), 870–91.

Mayer, T. F., 'If martyrs are to be exchanged with martyrs: the kidnappings of William Tyndale and Reginald Pole', *Archiv fur Reformationsgeschichte*, 81 (1990), 286–307.

Mayer, T. F., *Reginald Pole Prince and Prophet* (Cambridge, 2000).

McFarlane, K. B., *The Nobility of Later Medieval England* (Oxford, 1973).

Mertes, K., *The English Noble Household 1250–1600* (Oxford, 1988).

Miller, H., *Henry VIII and the English Nobility* (Oxford, 1989).

Morgan, R. R. and Morgan, S., 'Warblington Castle', *Portsmouth City Records Office, Newsletter,* 7 (1990).

Morgan, R. R. and Morgan, S., 'Warblington Castle', *Hampshire Field Club and Archaeological Society,* section newsletters, new series, 15 (1991).

Muir, K., *Life and Letters of Sir Thomas Wyatt* (Liverpool, 1963).

Murphy, B. A., *Bastard Prince: Henry VIII's Lost Son* (Stroud, 2001).

Myers, A. R., *The Household of Edward IV* (Manchester, 1959).

Neame, A., *The Holy Maid of Kent* (London, 1971).

Nash, M. L., 'Quarr and the mystery of Princess Cecilia', *Hampshire County Magazine* (1974), 57–9.

O'Day, R., *Education and Society 1500–1800* (New York, 1982).

Orme, N., *From Childhood to Chivalry: The Education of English Kings and Aristocracy 1066–1530* (London, 1984).

Outhwaite, R. B., *Inflation in Tudor and Early Stuart England* (London, 1969).

Owen, H. and Blakeway, J. B., *A History of Shrewsbury* (2 vols, London, 1825).

Page, W. (ed.), *Victoria County History (VCH), Hampshire and the Isle of Wight*, vol. 3 (London, 1908).

Page, W. (ed.), *VCH, Hampshire and the Isle of Wight*, vol. 5 (London, 1912).

Page, W. (ed.), *VCH, Buckinghamshire*, vol. 2 (London, 1969).

Page, W. and Ditchfield, P. H. (ed.), *VCH, Berkshire*, vol. 3 (reprinted, London, 1972).

Parks, G. B., 'The Parma letters and the dangers to Cardinal Pole', *Catholic Historical Review*, 46 (1960), 299–317.

Paul, J. E., *Catherine of Aragon and her Friends* (London, 1966).

Payne, A., 'The Salisbury Roll of Arms, c. 1463', in D. Williams (ed.), *England in the Fifteenth Century* (Woodbridge, 1987), pp. 187–98.

Pennant, T., *Some Account of London* (London, 1790).

Petre, J. (ed.), *Richard III: Crown and People* (Gloucester, 1985).

Pickthorn, K., *Early Tudor Government: Henry VII and Henry VIII* (2 vols, Cambridge, 1934).

Pierce, H., 'The life, career and political significance of Margaret Pole, countess of Salisbury, 1473–1541' (unpublished Ph.D. thesis, University of Wales, Bangor, 1997).

Pierce, H., 'The king's cousin: the life, career and Welsh connection of Sir Richard Pole, 1458–1504', *WHR*, 19, 2 (1998), 187–225.

Pollock, L., *Forgotten Children: Parent–Child Relations from 1500–1900* (Cambridge, 1983).

Pollock, L., 'Teach her to live under obedience: the making of women in the upper ranks of early modern England', *Continuity and Change*, 4 (1989), 231–58.

Pollock, L., 'Younger sons in Tudor and Stuart England', *History Today*, 39, 6 (1989), 23–9.

Pollock, F. and Maitland, F. M. (eds), *The History of English Law before the Time of Edward I*, ed. S. F. C. Milsom, 2 vols (Cambridge, 1968).

Potter, D., 'Foreign policy', in D. MacCulloch (ed.), *The Reign of Henry VIII: Politics, Policy and Piety* (London, 1995), pp. 101–33.

Potter, H. P., *An Historical Introduction to English Law and its Institutions* (London, 1932).

Powell, K. and Cook, C., *English Historical Facts 1485–1603* (London, 1977).

Prior, M., *Women in English Society 1500–1800* (London, 1985).

Quail, S., *Spirit of Portsmouth* (Portsmouth, 1989).

Randell, K., *Henry VIII and the Government of England* (London, 1991).

Randell, K., *Henry VIII and the Reformation in England* (London, 1993).

Rawcliffe, C., *The Staffords, Earls of Stafford and Dukes of Buckingham 1394–1521* (Cambridge, 1978).

Rees, D., *Sir Rhys ap Thomas* (Llandysul, 1992).

Richardson, W. C., *Tudor Chamber Administration 1485–1547* (Baton Rouge, 1952).

Richardson, W. C., *The White Queen* (London, 1970).

Rigby, S. H., *English Society in the Later Middle Ages: Class, Status and Gender* (London, 1995).

Robinson, C. J., *A History of the Castles of Herefordshire* (London, 1869).

Robinson, W. R. B., 'Princess Mary's itinerary in the Marches of Wales 1525–1527: a provincial record', *Historical Research*, 71, 175 (1998), 233–52.

Rose-Troup, F., *The Western Rebellion of 1549* (London, 1913).

Rosenthal, J. T. (ed.), 'Aristocratic widows in fifteenth-century England', in B. J. Harris and J. K. McNamara (eds), *Women and the Structure of Society* (Durham, NC, 1984), pp. 36–47.

Rosenthal, J. T., 'Aristocratic marriage and the English peerage 1350–1500: social institution and personal bond', *Journal of Medieval History*, 10 (1984), 181–94.

Rosenthal, J. T. (ed.), *Medieval Women and the Sources of Medieval History* (Athens, GA, 1990).

Ross, C., *Richard III* (London, 1990).

Ross, C., *Edward IV* (London, 1991).

Routh, E. M. G., *Sir Thomas More and his Friends* (London, 1934).

Rowland, B. (trans. and intro.), *Medieval Woman's Guide to Health: The First English Gynaecological Handbook* (Kent, OH, 1981).

Rowse, A. L., *Bosworth Field and the Wars of the Roses* (London, 1971).

Roxburgh, R. F., 'Lincolns Inns of the 14th Century', *Law Quarterly Review*, 94 (1978).

Russell, C., *The Crisis of Parliaments 1509–1660* (Oxford, 1985).

Saltzman, L. F. (ed.), *VCH, Sussex*, vol. 4 (London, 1973).

Scarisbrick, J. J., *Henry VIII* (London, 1988).

Schenk, W., 'The student days of Cardinal Pole', *History*, 33 (1948), 211–25.

Schenk, W., *Reginald Pole Cardinal of England* (London, 1950).

Scofield, C. L., *The Life and Reign of Edward the Fourth* (2 vols, London, 1967).

Shahar, S., *The Fourth Estate: A History of Women in the Middle Ages*, trans. C. Galai (London, 1991).

Shahar, S., *Childhood in the Middle Ages*, trans. C. Galai (London, 1992).

Shaw, W. A., *The Knights of England* (London, 1906).

Sheehan, M. M., 'The influence of canon law on the property rights of married women in England', *Mediaeval Studies*, 25 (1963), 109–24.

Simmonds, S. N., *Warblington Church* (Havant, 1979).

Skeel, C. A. J., *The Council in the Marches of Wales* (London, 1904).

Skeel, C. A. J., 'Wales under Henry VII', in R. W. Seton-Watson (ed.), *Tudor Studies Presented to A. F. Pollard* (London, 1924), pp. 1–25.

Slavin, A. J., 'Cromwell, Cranmer and Lord Lisle: a study in the politics of reform', *Albion*, 9 (1977), 316–36.

Smith, J. B., 'Crown and community in the principality of north Wales in the reign of Henry Tudor', *WHR*, 3, 2 (1966), 145–71.

Smith, L. B., *Treason in Tudor England* (London, 1986).

Smith, R. B., *Land and Politics in the England of Henry VIII* (Oxford, 1970).

Stacy, W. R., 'Richard Roose and the use of parliamentary attainder in the reign of Henry VIII', *Historical Journal*, 29 (1986), 1–15.

Starkey, D. R., 'The development of the Privy Chamber 1485–1547' (unpublished Ph.D. thesis, University of Cambridge, 1973).

Starkey, D. R., 'From feud to faction', *History Today*, 32, 11 (1982), 16–22.

Starkey, D. R. (ed.), *Rivals in Power* (London, 1990).

Starkey, D. R., *The Reign of Henry VIII: Personalities and Politics* (London, 1991).

Starkey, D. R. (ed.), *Henry VIII: A European Court in England* (London, 1991).

Starkey, D. R. and Coleman, C. (eds), *Revolution Reassessed: Revisions in the History of Tudor Government and Administration* (Oxford, 1986).

Starkey, D. R., Morgan, D. A. L., Murphy, J., Wright, P., Cuddy, N. and Sharpe, K., *The English Court: From the Wars of the Roses to the Civil War* (London, 1992).

Stone, R., 'Bonds, patronage and the gentry in the reign of Henry VII (1485–1509): the evidence of the Close, Patent and Fine Rolls' (unpublished MA thesis, University of Lancaster, 1988).

Storey, R. L., *The End of the House of Lancaster* (London, 1966).

Storey, R. L., *The Reign of Henry VII* (London, 1968).

Strickland, A., *Lives of the Queens of England* (8 vols, London, 1854).

Strong, R., *Tudor and Jacobean Portraits* (London, 1969).

Sutton, A. F. and Hammond, P. W., 'The problems of dating and the dangers of redating: the acts of court of the Mercers' Company of London 1453–1527', *Journal of the Society of Archivists*, 6, 2 (1978), 87–91.

Thomas, H., *A History of Wales 1485–1660* (Cardiff, 1972).

Thomas, R. S., 'The political career, estates and connection of Jasper Tudor earl of Pembroke and duke of Bedford (d.1495)' (unpublished Ph.D. thesis, University of Wales, Swansea, 1971).

Thomas, R. S., 'Geoffrey Pole: a Lancastrian servant in Wales', *National Library of Wales Journal*, 17 (1971–2), 277–86.

Thomas, W. S. K., *Tudor Wales 1485–1603* (Llandysul, 1983).

Thomson, P., *Sir Thomas Wyatt and his Background* (London, 1964).

Thornley, I. D., 'The treason legislation of Henry VIII', *TRHS*, third series, 11 (1917), 87–123.

Thorp, J. D., 'The history of the manor of Coates', *Transactions of the Bristol and Gloucestershire Archaeological Society*, 50 (1928).

Todd, B. J., 'The remarrying widow: a stereotype reconsidered', in M. Prior (ed.), *Women in English Society 1500–1800* (London, 1985).

Tucker, M. J., *The Life of Thomas Howard Earl of Surrey and Second Duke of Norfolk 1443–1524* (London, 1964), pp. 54–92.

Tucker, M. J., 'Life at Henry VII's court', *History Today*, 19, 5 (1969), 325–31.

Underwood, M. G., 'Politics and piety in the household of Lady Margaret Beaufort', *Journal of Ecclesiastical History*, 38 (1987), 39–52.

Vernon Harcourt, L. W., *His Grace the Steward and the Trial of Peers* (London, 1907).

Vodden, D. F., 'Correspondence of William Fitzwilliam earl of Southampton' (unpublished M.Phil. thesis, University of London, 1977).

Wake, J., *The Brudenells of Deene* (London, 1954).

Walker, D., *Medieval Wales* (Cambridge, 1990).

Walker, G., 'The "expulsion of the minions" of 1519 reconsidered', *Historical Journal*, 32 (1989), 1–16.

Walker, S. S., 'The marrying of feudal wards in medieval England', *Studies in Medieval Culture*, 4, 2 (1974), 209–24.

Walker, S. S., 'Widow and ward: the feudal law of child custody in medieval England', in S. Mosher Stuard (ed.), *Women in Medieval Society* (Pennsylvania, 1976), pp. 159–72.

Ward, F., 'The divorce of William Barentyne', *SAC*, 68 (1927), 279–81.

Ward, J. C., *English Noblewomen in the Later Middle Ages* (London, 1992).

Ward, J. C., 'The English noblewoman and her family in the later Middle Ages', in C. E. Meek and M. K. Simms (eds), *'The Fragility of her Sex'? Medieval Irishwomen in their European Context* (Dublin, 1996), pp. 119–35.

Ward, J. C., 'English noblewomen and the local community in the later Middle Ages', in D. Watt (ed.), *Medieval Women in their Communities* (Cardiff, 1997), pp. 186–203.

Warnick, R., *Women of the English Renaissance and Reformation* (London, 1983).

Warnick, R., 'The Lady Margaret, countess of Richmond; a noble woman of independent wealth and status', *Fifteenth Century Studies*, 9 (1984).

Watson, F. (ed.), *Vives and the Renascence Education of Women* (London, 1912).

Wedgwood, J. C., *History of Parliament: Biographies of the Members of the Commons House 1439–1509* (London, 1936).

Weightman, C., *Margaret of York, Duchess of Burgundy 1446–1503* (Gloucester, 1989).

Whitlock, R. A., *Calendar of Country Customs* (London, 1978).

Williams, B., 'Elizabeth of York's last journey', *The Ricardian*, 8, 100 (1988, 18–19.

Williams, D., 'The family of Henry VII', *History Today*, 4, 2 (1954), 77–84.

Williams, M. N. and Echols, A., *Between Pit and Pendulum: Women in the Middle Ages* (Princeton, NJ, 1994).

Williams, P., *The Council in the Marches of Wales under Elizabeth I* (Cardiff, 1958).

Williams, P., 'Government and politics in Ludlow, 1590–1642', *Transactions of the Shropshire Archaeological Society*, 56 (1961), 282–94.

Williams, P., 'English politics after Bosworth', *History Today*, 35, 9 (1985), 30–6.

Williams, P., *The Tudor Regime* (Oxford, 1991).

Williamson, J. A., *The Tudor Age* (New York, 1982).

Wolffe, B. P., 'The management of the English royal estates under the Yorkist kings', *EHR*, 61 (1956), 1–27.

Worthington, P., 'Royal government in the Counties Palatine of Lancashire and Chester 1450–1509' (unpublished Ph.D. thesis, University of Wales, Swansea, 1991).

Wright, T., *The History and Topography of the County of Essex* (London, 1831).

Wright, T., *History of Ludlow* (London, 1841–3).

Xavier, M. F., *Blessed Margaret Pole and her Family* (Chichester, 1983).

Youings, J. A., 'The Council of the West', *TRHS*, fifth series, 10 (1960).

Young, A., *Tudor and Jacobean Tournaments* (London, 1987).

Zeeveld, W. G., *Foundations of Tudor Policy* (London, 1948).

Index

Elizabeth Plantagenet, queen of England, wife of Henry VII 11, 47
chronology: coronation of 12, 13, 16–17; attended by MP 18 illegitimacy declared and significance of 12, 152, 163
Elizabeth Tudor, queen of England, daughter of Henry VIII 101, 102, 152
Elizabeth Woodvyll, queen of England, wife of Edward IV 2, 5, 7
Ellesborough, Buckinghamshire, manor of 14, 15, 18, 36
Elmer, Mistress Frances 99–100
Elton, G. R. 129, 144, 149
Erasmus, Desiderius 44
Erneley, Dorothy, in MP's household, possibly connected to Sir John Erneley or William Erneley 60–1
Erneley, Sir John 60–1
Erneley, William 61, 168
Essex, earl of *see* Bourchier
Eston, Northampton, manor of 81
Étaples, treaty of 22
Evans, John, bailiff of Medmenham and Ellesborough 29
Exeter, marquess of *see* Courtenay

Faenza, bishop of 106, 156
Farleigh Castle 1
Ferdinand, king of Aragon 11, 25
Fetherstone, Dr Richard 101
Field of the Cloth of Gold 49, 86
Fifield, Oxford, manor of 18
Finneux, chief justice 146
Fisher, John 103
Fitzalan, Henry, Lord Maltravers (1533–44), son of William 111
Fitzalan, Thomas, earl of Arundel (1487–1524) 67, 68, 89
Fitzalan, William, earl of Arundel (1524–44) 67, 126, 149
Fitzroy, Henry, duke of Richmond and Somerset, illegitimate son of Henry VIII 95, 96
FitzWalter, Robert Lord, earl of Sussex 71, 111, 141
Fitzwilliam, Sir William, earl of Southampton (1537–42) 87, 115, 154, 167, 169

chronology: investigates gossip about the Pole family (1538) 126–7, 154, 155; interrogates MP (1538) 137–9; unhappy about her incarceration at his residence 172–3; appointed chief steward of MP's lands in England, Wales and the marches (1539) 165; granted the manor of Warblington (1539) 165; tries to help Sir Geoffrey Pole (1540) 129, 155, 181–2
dislike of MP 155, 172–3
Flamank, John 30
Fortescue, Henry, deputy steward of MP 76
Fortescue, Lewis, member of MP's council 79
Fowell, John 123
Fowler, Sir Simon 168
Francis I, king of France 87, 98, 107, 123, 132, 133, 142, 156, 159, 169, 172, 173
Frankelyn, Johanne, in MP's household, wife of Oliver Frankelyn 60, 83
Frankelyn, Oliver, receiver-general and comptroller of MP's household 84
career in service of MP 79–80, 83
chronology: tried to protect MP (1538) 83, 137; receives the manor of Clyst St Mary, Devon (1545) 165
evidence of (1538) 121, 137
French campaign (1513) 34
Friend, William, schoolmaster of Chichester prebendal school 112
evidence against (1538) 128, 167
fortunate to survive the fall of the Poles 167
Fritze, R. H. 158
Frye, Margaret, reeve of MP 82

Gairdner, James 23
Gardiner, Dr Stephen, bishop of Winchester 105, 118
Gaunt, John of 152
Geoffrey, Thomas, reeve of MP 83
Gifford, James 73
Glanville, Bertha, wife of Ranulf 58
Glanville, Ranulf 58
Goddard, Dr William 5
Goodrich, Thomas, bishop of Ely interrogates MP (1538) 115, 137–9